CW00506307

A Short Political History of Britain from the Glorious Revolution to Brexit

Mark Skinner

Text Copyright © 2017 Mark Skinner

All Rights Reserved

Table of Contents

INTRODUCTION

I should begin this short political history of Britain by laying my cards on the table. I am neither a professional historian nor political scientist - indeed until recently my knowledge of the British political system and its colourful history was sketchy at best. I had attempted righteous indignation at the Blair government's flagrant disregard for international law in invading Iraq in 2003 and shaken my head wryly at the Liberal Democrat climb-down on student fees during the coalition years. But, beyond a knee-jerk, right-on reaction to hypocrisy and greed, I had never really engaged with the business of domestic politics at all.

Yet during the 2015 general election campaign I started to become aware of a greater intensity of feeling in the country than I had experienced hitherto. Perhaps it was partly due to the fact that the result was regarded as such a close run thing and a second successive hung Parliament considered inevitable - somewhat laughably as we now know - but the anodyne wonk-speak and tit-for-tat macho point scoring of the political class suddenly seemed to have some actual relevance to the day to day life of 21st century Britain. The nation became obsessed by deals and putative coalitions between just about every party going, to the point where at least one political commentator seriously broached the possibility of a Conservative/Labour union. This kind of wild talk made a mockery of the usual staid clichés of 'bellwether constituencies' and 'three way marginals'. Nothing less than a delirious upheaval in the very fabric of British political existence felt like it was being proposed.

We all now know that the threatened internecine deal brokering never materialised. Yet despite one party managing to form a majority government after all, the British electorate still provided a wealth of soap-opera shocks - the ignominious collapse of the Liberal Democrats, the unexpectedly well-founded grievances of UKIP regarding the injustice of the first-past-the-post electoral system and the stunning coup perpetrated by the Scottish National Party north of the border. The concomitant near-obliteration of Labour in Scotland was merely the most depressing occurrence for the party on a night full of them. The subsequent soul searching that went on during the party's leadership contest in turn produced a result both staggeringly unexpected and entirely predictable. In short, British politics was exciting again.

But that just made me suspect that, actually, it probably always had been. Ashamed of my own ignorance I found that I wanted to know more of what had gone before. I had always instinctively positioned myself to the left on the political spectrum but I realised that, beyond a vague awareness that that was what decent, creative, hipster-ish people were supposed to do, I hadn't done my research at all. The Conservatives - or pejoratively Tories, after the initial incarnation of the party pre-Robert Peel - were all inherently evil and had never passed a single piece of legislation that hadn't resulted in the tragic death of an impoverished child. Squaring this pantomime grotesque with the fact that they had been the dominant party of government for the past 200 years was difficult. Were that many millions of voters really that stupid or venal? Or, just possibly, was the truth a little more complex? I felt I needed to know more.

But, frustratingly, I couldn't seem to find the kind of book that I wanted to read on the subject. There were either general volumes on the entirety of British history, others covering the political, social and cultural history of a particular timeframe or more academic works of political science that, likewise, covered distinct eras. I was looking for a general, introductory history of the politics of the British Isles which culminated in the present day and started in... well, I wasn't sure really.

When should a short political history of Britain begin? With the Magna Carta of 800 years ago and the flexing of baronial muscles over levying taxes? With Simon de Montfort's 13th century 'speaking place,' the first Parliament not to be summoned by the ruling monarch and whose fundamental composition was later adopted by Henry III? With the 'people power' of the 1381 Peasants' Revolt or the Putney Debates of 1647 which attempted to formulate a fresh constitution for the nation after the overthrow of the monarchy? What these keystone historic events all have in common is a direct opposition to the idea of the divine right of kings and a sense that it takes more than one person – more than one social class in some cases – to govern the nation. The abandonment of an absolutist monarchy for Cromwell's puritanical republic could have signalled the beginning of the modern political system. But by 1660 the Stuart dynasty was back on the British throne with precious few lessons learnt from the preceding Civil Wars. The narcissism and unfettered autocracy of an absolutist monarch stifled any attempt to govern in a reasoned manner beneficial to the nation's subjects - or at least those subjects who were deemed to possess a stake in the country.

The Glorious Revolution of 1688 was the moment when the concept of the people affirming their rights in tandem with, if not necessarily over, their monarch caught fire. William and Mary were certainly no mere puppet leaders and royal interference in Parliamentary business would continue at least until the reign of William IV (1830-1837). But they were also bound by conventions and laws that prevented a repeat of Stuart autocracy and paved the way - although it was a long, long time in coming - for eventual democracy. For this reason and the fact that it saw the emergence of the standard two-party political system – very much factions rather than distinct organisations at that stage - the Glorious Revolution, and the background to it, is the jumping off point for this narrative.

I started writing this book primarily to cement certain facts and sequences of events in my mind but the more I read the more I realised that, yes, the history of British politics *is* uniquely fascinating. The nobles of the nation conspiring to depose their monarch, the derring-do of empire building, the dramatic loss of the American colonies, the spectre of bloody revolution, the irresistible march of electoral reform, the jingoistic era of gunboat diplomacy, a titanic Prime Ministerial personality clash and a ruthless rush for African territory. And that's all before the onset of the 20th century.

And whilst I would still regard myself as left of centre politically the fluctuations in ideology, motives and reputation of the main parties - Tories/Conservatives, Liberals, Labour - make any attempt to pigeonhole them impossible. There have been right wing Labour Prime Ministers - Callaghan, Blair - and Conservative Prime Ministers who were firmly ensconced on the left by the end of their tenure, even if they may have started out with more right wing views - Disraeli, Heath.

The thing that becomes most apparent after the most cursory observation of political parties past is how little there was to choose between them ideologically. Arguably the Tories never had much of an ideology, seeing themselves merely as the natural, aristocratic party of power. But it is interesting how the Whigs, although nominally more reform minded, were just as elitist and condescending towards any class below the landed gentry. Robert Peel's skilful rebranding of the Tories as the – slightly - more caring, sharing Conservatives was little more than a Regency PR exercise although the burgeoning importance of Capitalism to his rebooted party was of course fundamental. The emerging Liberals, with their supposedly radical emphasis on libertarian self-help, actually retained a good deal of the titled gentlemen intellectuals of their Whig forerunners. Gladstone and Disraeli constantly tried to outdo each other in terms of reform but the key point is that they were essentially in agreement over what needed to be reformed. The pre-First World War Liberal government headed initially by Asquith and then Lloyd George was a truly revolutionary administration born of incredible times - their welfare reforms, unprecedented financial attack on the wealthy and iconoclastic treatment of the House of Lords make them a particular favourite of mine. Yet after the high drama of World War One the hero-of-the-hour Lloyd George sunk into lethargy, corruption and disgrace, paving the way for the most blandly consensual series of governments imaginable in the inter-war years. After the waging of total war gave Socialism the ultimate fillip, post-war austerity harpooned the noble aspirations of Attlee and his fellow travellers. From then until Thatcher British Prime Ministers tended to be more concerned with holding their parties together than changing the fabric of society. The desperate measures of both Conservative and Labour governments in the 1970s were largely interchangeable and led to the decisive break with consensus politics that had reigned supreme for the previous three decades. This is why the politics of the 1980s still feels so vibrant, dynamic and passionate in the 21st century - for almost the first time the two main parties in the British political system were spouting wildly differing doctrine whilst utterly and completely loathing each other and everything that their rivals stood for. Ordinary citizens frequently got caught in the crossfire. Yet under Major the Conservatives ceased to intimidate, bulldoze and terrify, instead limping distastefully towards near-oblivion in the wake of Tony Blair's messianic reshaping of Labour. A large part of New Labour's success lay in pulling the right-wing rug from under the beleaguered Conservatives' feet, condemning them to abject pointlessness for the best part of a decade. The subsequent saturation of the political class in the 2010s hardly needs stating here, whereas the vitriolic EU referendum campaign has divided British political parties internally – Conservative ranks split nearly 50/50 and an already dysfunctional Labour railing against the ineffectiveness of their new leader. The big ideological haemorrhage is now taking place in general society rather than Westminster and it is one based more on class, age and demographics than plain old left and right.

This tradition of consensus is amusingly at odds with the testosterone fuelled adversarial nature of Westminster debate. Maybe the closer the main parties are in their thinking the more vehemently they feel they must lambast each other. The extremity of the adversarial side of British politics is one of two things that make it stand out from other Western democracies. The other is the brutal simplicity of a system where the governing party can do pretty much whatever they like. In marked contrast to the convoluted checks and balances of the American system the British Constitution - whatever exactly is comprised in that mythologised phrase - provides the leader of the party that won the latest general election with almost untrammelled power. The fabled separation of powers between the executive (the Prime Minister and their cabinet), legislature (Parliament) and judiciary was intended to limit the power of any of its component parts. This scarcely holds in the British system, where the executive is also a fundamental part of the legislature. The overwhelming bureaucracy introduced into government since the dawn of New Labour may have diluted this power slightly but the fact remains that, domestically at least, the British Prime Minister can do things to his country that other Western leaders could only dream of doing to theirs. Whether or not this is a good thing is well beyond the scope of this little book.

It is rather fitting that this book both begins and ends with the issue of sovereignty. Back in the late 17th century the political discourse was all about removing that privilege from the literal sovereign and placing it in the hands of the people via elected representatives. True, the 'people' constituted 5% of the total population of Britain and the means of election were thoroughly corrupt, but the symbolism of the shift was undeniable. In 2016 52% of the British people – now a full franchise – voted to leave the European Union that Britain had been a member of since 1973. On one level or another almost all those who championed Brexit had a problem with the amount of British sovereignty perceived to have been lost to a faceless institution in Brussels. Arguably the grand narrative of British political history has been the will to make the people truly sovereign – from the 19th century battle to expand the electorate to the early 20th century clamour for universal suffrage to the passionate debate about whether or not the EU infringes our democracy. Rightly or wrongly the British have always held their political system in high regard, even when they have not extended the same respect to their politicians. What remains to be seen is whether, in a post-Brexit United Kingdom, sovereignty has become an outdated concept and matters little in the context of the pragmatic pressures of a globalised society.

What you hold in your hands is a very superficial narrative history of British politics from the Glorious Revolution to Brexit, penned by an enthusiastic amateur for other enthusiastic amateurs. Those with political science qualifications or years of active party membership will no doubt be appalled by its brevity, lack of depth and – generally - non-partisan approach. I can only hope they will like the writing.

A brief note on semantics before we begin. As alluded to earlier we all know that the term Tory is a modern day synonym for Conservative. However, as the Tory party was the official forerunner of the Conservative party and therefore a distinct incarnation of that organisation I have refrained from using it in its pejorative sense. Tory in the context of this book refers solely to the Tory party, the dominant party of government before its transformation into the Conservative party in 1834.

1

THE COURT, THE COUNTRY AND THE KING

In November 1688 England experienced its first foreign invasion since William of Normandy's troops landed at Pevensey over 600 years previously. The invading general was a ruthless Dutch war hero bent on usurping the incumbent monarch at any cost and his fleet, at 463 ships containing over 40,000 highly trained soldiers, was three times the size of the Spanish Armada.

And yet this potentially crushing conquest ended up being virtually bloodless, for the nascent subjugation was not all that it seemed. To start with the conqueror, William of Orange, King of the Netherlands, had been explicitly invited to invade by a committee of seven nobles at the heart of government. For another the reigning monarch James II capitulated almost instantly, fleeing to France in the wake of his wife, Mary of Modena, and infant son, also named James.

The mood of the nation was more one of jubilation, or at least relief, than fear and trembling. His recently acquired subjects quite willingly wore orange ribbons in tribute as William processed through London, crowds lining the streets to welcome him warmly. Some of James' most respected generals, such as John Churchill - who a few years previously had fought against the Dutch and would later be lionised as the maverick victor of Blenheim - were similarly accommodating to their new master. Even the humiliated Stuart King himself contributed to the smooth transition of power. By ostentatiously throwing the Great Seal of England into the Thames during his panicked flight from the capital James effectively legitimised his abdication. When William and his wife Mary, James' daughter and the ostensible reason for the faux-invasion in the first place, were crowned joint monarchs of England the following April the outrageous, highly treasonable Glorious Revolution had been achieved with barely a hitch.

It could have been very different. Despite James II's deep unpopularity with both court and public at large, he was still the rightful King thanks to the centuries old law of succession. There were still many people who regarded that law as sacrosanct. Over the next 60 years there would be numerous attempts by members of James' line to regain control of the British throne and, although they came to nought, the threat of Jacobitism - the movement taking its name from the Renaissance Latin form of James – was a constant source of anxiety and paranoia to the nation's ruling elite.

But just why did the Glorious Revolution come about? For a cabal of some of the country's leading noblemen to collude in the invasion of a foreign power, ultimately benevolent or not, evinces the level of national crisis that had been reached during the reign of James II. Just under 40 years earlier England had executed its monarch in a stunning rejection of the 'divine right of Kings' and the concomitant absolutism that that doctrine engendered. How had things come to a point where another English King required urgent removal from the throne?

Although the English people may have tired of the joyless repression and unstinting puritanism of the Commonwealth it was with a mixture of fatalism and trepidation that many accepted the 1660 Restoration of the Stuart dynasty. The most bloody and divisive civil war in the nation's history had been fought over the issue of the King's divine appointment by God and whether he had the right to rule in absolute autocracy. Oliver Cromwell's republican experiment may have ultimately failed but few wished to see the kind of entitled arrogance and flagrant abuse of power of Charles I reinstated by his son Charles II. The killing of a King is not something the English take lightly and to continue as though nothing had happened in the 18 years since 1642 would have been wholly unacceptable.

But despite this fact the formal parliamentary declaration that 'the government is, and ought to be, by King, Lords and Commons' was a criminally vague and non-committal statement backed up by remarkably few concrete pieces of legislation. All it fundamentally came down to was that Charles was prohibited from raising taxes without permission from Parliament. The King retained a number of pre-war prerogatives and there was no specific codification of the rights of Parliament either over or in conjunction with the sovereign.

All of which was rather dangerous when dealing with an extravagant, high living playboy King like Charles II. Notorious for his string of mistresses and lavish, debauched court Charles II's accession to the throne ushered in an era of excess and hedonism that Parliament soon discovered they were supposed to foot the bill for. Yet even more concerning than Charles' expensive peccadillos was his distinctly ambiguous religiosity. The Puritans and non-conformists seen as responsible for the most heinous atrocities of the Commonwealth were purged by the heavily Anglican 'Cavalier' Parliament. But Catholicism was viewed as even more suspect - the 17th century equivalent of fundamentalist doctrines like Communism, Fascism and extremist Islamism.

The murderous reign of Queen Mary (1553-1558) had stemmed from her Catholic fanaticism, with the revival of the centuries-old Heresy Acts returning the country to oppressive Roman rule. Whilst numerous high profile Protestants were executed those rich enough escaped into exile. It was one of these emigres who most perpetuated anti-Catholic feeling upon his return to Britain during the reign of Elizabeth I. John Foxe's Actes and Monuments - more commonly known as Foxe's Book of Martyrs - was published in 1563 and caused a sensation. With its didactic accounts of the Marian persecutions of Protestants Foxe's book cemented the idea of Catholic inhumanity in the culture of the time. The notorious Gunpowder Plot of 1605 which saw a motley group of Catholics attempt to blow up the Houses of Parliament further stoked the idea that Catholics venerated a foreign demagogue above the authority of the sovereign and Parliament. Charles I's perceived sympathy for the Catholic cause was a key factor in the anti-Stuart movement that resulted in the English Civil Wars and his own eventual execution in 1649.

It wasn't long after the Restoration that Charles II's behaviour began to arouse suspicion. In 1662 he married the Catholic Catherine of Braganza - which had obvious ramifications for the succession - whilst his ill-concealed Francophile affections stoked rumours of an alliance with one of the greatest Catholic powerhouses in Europe. The fact that he concealed the existence of a treaty committing England to join France in an attack on Dutch traders confirms that fears over his duplicitous nature were well founded. Add to this heady brew the issue of his brother James' highly *un*ambiguous Catholicism and it was no wonder that Parliament was wary.

Their worst fears appeared realised in 1672 when Charles unilaterally passed the Declaration of Indulgence. This inflammatory bill attacked two of Parliament's most sacred cows - the inviolability of its right to make laws and the suppression of religious dissenters. The sovereign now claimed that he had the ability to suspend laws and that Catholic and Protestant dissenters were able to worship freely. Parliament flexed its muscle when it met again the following year, forcing the King to withdraw the act. But the damage to Charles' character had been done. He may not have been as unbending as his brother but England clearly had a monarch with a sense of his own divine entitlement and a Catholic sympathiser to boot.

Charles' act of arrogant folly forced Parliament to clamp down even harder on perceived papists by introducing two Test Acts that severely limited the freedoms and opportunities for the country's Catholics. The first made the positions of all government officials and military officers dependent on the conditions of taking Holy Communion in the Church of England and renouncing the doctrine of transubstantiation. The second - instituted in 1678 after the hysteria generated by the dissenter Titus Oates' fabricated 'Popish Plot'- prevented any non-Anglican from sitting in Parliament. The King's brother James, Duke of York had been forced to resign as Lord High Admiral as a result of the first act and had only retained his seat in the House of Lords after an amendment to the second act passed by only two votes.

Oates' fallacious report of a Jesuit conspiracy to murder Charles and restore full blooded Catholicism to the country was a game changer in the nation's perception of the papist threat. Edmund Berry Godfrey, the magistrate who first heard the case, was later murdered and alleged conspirators were executed in an orgy of paranoid repression. The threat of a shadowy group of Jesuits enforcing Catholicism on the English nation may have been entirely untrue but, now that it was clear that Catherine of Braganza would produce no royal heirs, there was an increasing terror of James claiming the throne for the Catholic faith instead.

Suddenly it was not enough to try to prevent James from sitting in Parliament - he had to be excised from the royal succession. For the first time two distinct factions or parties sprang up within Parliament – the royalist and traditionalist 'Court Party' and the more radical, reforming 'Country Party.' They are known more commonly to history by the equally disparaging nicknames of Tory – an Irish cattle thief – and Whig – from the Scottish Whiggamore, an abusive term for a Presbyterian.

For now the Tories nominally had the upper hand thanks to Charles' ability to select his own ministers. He had replaced the more moderate 'Cabal Government' with Thomas Osborne, Lord Danby, one strong royalist acting as Lord High Treasurer. Whilst Danby was unashamedly reactionary and authoritarian he was also an intelligent and highly organised politician who whipped the royal finances into shape and established a proto- civil service to manage and control many aspects of Parliamentary business. He also persuaded his sovereign that, in the light of the Oates crisis, his views on religious toleration were adding fuel to the fire being stoked by a coalition of Whigs and Protestant dissenters. Realising that his open regard for the Catholic faith may be jeopardising his brother's chances of succeeding him Charles ordered James into exile, first to Brussels and then Edinburgh.

It was a wise move. The mood of the country was becoming increasingly febrile with the Whig cause, led by Anthony Ashley Cooper, 1st Earl of Shaftesbury, gaining rapid support across the country. Shaftesbury - a former member of the 'Cabal Government' that had been toppled by Danby - was virulently anti-Rome and fought tirelessly for ways of curbing the Duke of York's flagrant Catholicism. During the 1679 Parliament he introduced the Exclusion Bill which sought to pass James' barring from the Crown into law. As the bill looked set to win in the Commons Charles simply used his royal prerogative to dissolve Parliament, which he also did the following two years when the bill resurfaced.

As one of the leading lights of the notorious Green Ribbon Club Shaftesbury was certainly not above manufacturing scare-mongering rumour and seditious intrigue to further the Country Party's ends. Operating out of the Kings Head Tavern at Chancery Lane End the club was named after the badge of the radical Levellers and was arguably the first political club extant in Britain. Its members may have had a hand in the machinations of the Rye House Plot of 1683 - a conspiracy to assassinate both the King and the Duke of York - and the future Monmouth Rebellion, amongst other outrages. Shaftesbury himself was forced to flee England in 1681 having been narrowly acquitted for treason. He never saw the effects of the Glorious Revolution, dying two years later in Amsterdam.

Events were now moving on apace and the King was understandably scared for his life. Danby - always unpopular with all but his most loyal supporters - had fallen from grace, the victim of a cunning ruse to link him with the now near-mythical Popish Plot and the associated murder of Godfrey. Fearful of recalling a Whig dominated Parliament Charles refused to allow fresh elections in blatant contravention of the Triennial Act, which required elections every three years. Then suddenly, in the wake of the Rye House Plot, the pendulum of public opinion seemed to swing back to the Royalist position. The English nation may have been deeply uncomfortable about an avowedly Catholic heir to the throne but would only accept so many fabricated conspiracies and so much open treachery. By 1684 Charles felt that the immediate danger had subsided sufficiently to recall the Duke of York from his Scottish exile. The following year Charles II died of mercury poisoning and, with no other credible alternative, his brother James ascended to the throne of England.

For all of Charles II's Machiavellian duplicity and arrogant displays of power he was a shrewd enough political operator to keep his options open. His assent to the marriage of his niece Mary to the fiercely Protestant William of Orange was a cleverly pragmatic move, although he could scarcely have predicted how devastating the union would be for his brother's reign. Charles' image of the fun loving, womanising charmer also proved attractive to an English populace who remembered all too clearly the brutality and pious intolerance of Cromwell's Commonwealth.

If James II had possessed an iota of his brother's charisma and astuteness he may well have been able to weather the storm wrought by his unfortunate choice of religion. Unfortunately he was cast more in the mould of his intractable father - charmless, brittle and unable to understand anybody else's point of view. No sooner had he been crowned than the Duke of Monmouth - Charles' eldest illegitimate son and thoroughgoing Protestant - invaded the West Country from Holland. He declared himself King on June 18th 1685 but a month later the Churchill-led Kings' army decimated the rebels in the last pitched battle in England, at Sedgemoor. The vicious retribution of the 'Bloody Assizes' was designed to demonstrate the power and loyalty that the Catholic monarch commanded. However, it would not be long before that loyalty was severely tested.

James used the Monmouth Rebellion as an excuse to create a huge standing army liberally sprinkled with Catholic officers, a decision that required the immediate suspension of the Test Act that he himself had fallen foul of nearly a decade earlier. By extension James believed that this now gave him the right to suspend whatever laws he wanted. History was repeating itself and once again Parliament stood firm. Therefore James dissolved it and hoped for a more sympathetic lot next time.

Contemporaneously James went to war with the Anglican church who had up until now - and perhaps surprisingly - been remarkably supportive of their new King. Indignant at the anti-Catholic sermons that resounded from the majority of the nation's pulpits he set up a commission into the issue that resulted in a raft of arbitrary sackings and decisively fractured his relationship with the Church of England.

James' determination to force Catholicism down English throats exceeded the wildest fears of those who had sought to exclude him from the throne. There appeared to be no depths to which he wouldn't stoop to place Catholics in positions of influence or find ways to repeal anti-Catholic legislation. He manipulated elections -although he never seemed to get the result he wanted -, forcibly inserted Catholics into senior University positions and cosied up to Protestant dissenters by issuing a Declaration of Indulgence in 1687 in the hope that this would turn them against the Church of England. If anything the crushing unsubtlety of the ruse only brought Anglicans and dissenters closer together.

And yet James could even have survived all of this. After all, a large number of his demands were merely replications of his late brother's decrees and, with no Catholic heir to succeed him, there was an argument for riding out the storm until his death. After his demise his two Protestant daughters would then vanquish popery from the royal line forever. This argument was blown out of the water in June 1688 when James' wife Mary of Modena sensationally gave birth to a baby boy. Attempts to cast the offspring as a 'changeling' carried into the royal bedchamber in a warming pan cut little ice - this Catholic child now superseded his half-sisters in ascending the throne.

Events came to a head when the King insisted on the Declaration of Indulgence being read out in every church in the land. Seven bishops petitioned him against acting on this provision and a fulminating James had them imprisoned. The entire affair was a humiliating disaster for the monarch as the bishops were acquitted and the vast majority of the clergy refused to read the Declaration anyway. By now even his most trusted associates, such as Churchill, recognised that James II had to go.

But if James were to be usurped who would Parliament put on the throne in his place? It had to be a non-Catholic with a connection to the royal line and so the only realistic option was James' Protestant daughter Mary whom Charles II had married off to William of Orange. The evening after the bishops had been acquitted, therefore, seven leading politicians - including the vengeful Lord Danby - composed a letter to the Dutch King politely requesting that he invade the country and depose the ruling monarch.

William couldn't get underway quick enough. It was not merely noble altruism or spousal loyalty that led to his enthusiastic agreement to the incredible plot. Uniting the Protestant English and Dutch nations gave him a formidable counter to the Catholic alliance that Louis XIV would forge with James as well as providing the inveterate warmonger with more men and resources for other military campaigns. Whilst it was his wife who continued the royal Stuart bloodline William was definitive that he would be no consort. They would reign jointly, although in actuality he would call the shots.

After landing at Torbay in Devon William was content to play a waiting game, speculating on whether James' own troops would turn on him independently. As the invading force marched ponderously towards the capital the doomed King declined French support for fear of further antagonising his subjects. Although the outright mutiny that William had hoped for never quite transpired it soon became clear that James' soldiers were far from keen to engage in battle and skirmishes at Wincanton and Reading proved easy victories for the Dutch invader. The high profile defection of Churchill to the Dutch side was a mortal blow for the Stuart monarch whilst James' cause became so hopeless that his other daughter Anne switched sides to her sister and brother-in-law's camp soon afterwards. With even his own progeny deserting him James' only remaining option was to flee. Yet, plagued by nosebleeds, even the humiliated King's flight was riddled with farce. Upon reaching Faversham he was spotted by a group of fishermen, promptly arrested and returned to London. It was left to his usurper to engineer an 'escape' across the channel for him.

*

The lessons of 1660 would be learnt 28 years later. In place of the vagaries surrounding the relationship between sovereign and subjects Parliament drafted a Bill of Rights that codified the supremacy of the people and paved the way for constitutional monarchy. In practical terms it denied the Crown the rights to suspend laws, raise a standing army, raise taxes without the consent of Parliament and meddle in legal process. Ideologically it stood the divine right of Kings on its head. The sovereign was no longer appointed by God but by the people on the understanding that the sovereign ruled justly and fairly. Consequently, the people - via Parliament - had the right to remove them if they failed to do so. Less far-sightedly, although unsurprisingly, the bill also stipulated that no Catholic could ascend the throne and nor could any existing monarch marry one.

Although a seismic change in the constitution of the nation this wasn't quite the resounding victory for Parliament that history sometimes casts it as. William had accepted the crown upon invitation and should he choose to abdicate England faced the very real possibility of James II's return. James did in fact attempt an invasion of his own in 1690 but was once again defeated by the Dutchman at the Battle of the Boyne. Therefore the sovereign retained significant powers - he could still choose his own ministers and control the length of parliamentary sessions. Also, as mentioned earlier, William fully expected Parliament to finance his military escapades. It would take the establishment of another royal foreigner on the British throne to truly put Parliament in the ascendancy.

2

COCK ROBIN AND THE HOUSE OF HANOVER

When George I, Elector of Hanover, arrived in London in September 1714 he did not require an ostentatious army or fleet of warships to ensure the Crown. By the 1701 Act of Settlement he was rightful ruler of the nation, although there were certainly others whose claims were stronger. Childlessness had been the great curse of the later Stuarts - Mary had died without producing an heir and her sister Anne who succeeded her suffered the infant deaths of her 14 children. With the Jacobites still bent on returning James to the throne it was imperative that Parliament plan for a smooth Protestant succession no matter how diluted the royal blood might be.

George was the great grandson of the first Stuart king James I. He was pompous, diffident, spoke next to no English and regarded his new acquisition with a mixture of bafflement and contempt. But he was not a Catholic and that, frankly, was all that mattered. Besides, the new-fangled constitutional monarchy experiment had proved a qualified success under both William and Mary and later Anne. Having a ruler who was more interested in playing cards with his coterie of foreign courtiers and amusing himself with his two mistresses, the Elephant and the Maypole - named for their strikingly dissimilar body shapes - was arguably exactly what the body politic needed.

Not that George was entirely aloof from the political business of the nation. He had no interest in domestic affairs but, like William before him, he had agreed to accept the Crown as a means of consolidating his empire and so made sure to look out for his best interests in foreign policy. But he regarded Britain merely as an impressive adjunct to his absolutist monarchy in Hanover and so proved distinctly less inclined to interfere than his Stuart predecessors.

George's reign thus marks the beginning of the domination of the political system in Britain. The monarch was still the figurehead of the nation and was regarded with deference and respect. They could - and did - still interfere in political business and the creation of ministries but increasingly it was Parliament and a succession of talented - and not so talented- individuals who would oversee the running of the country. Things would never be the same again.

The divisions within Parliament that had sprung up during the Exclusion Crisis remained in place after William and Mary had restored Protestant rule. It is important to remember, however, that the Tories and Whigs were, at this time, separate factions within a Parliamentary whole rather than two distinct official parties. Numbers of each ebbed and flowed as MPs frequently switched sides on different issues, often according to reasons of patronage or upon the receipt of a particularly healthy bribe.

Due to their closeness to Charles II the Tories were regarded with suspicion as closet Jacobites scheming with the deposed King, whilst the Whigs rode the wave of support and good feeling engendered by their decisiveness in the Glorious Revolution. Unsurprisingly William and Mary relied heavily on Whig-based ministries although their reluctant support for the King's costly foreign wars provided ammunition for the Tories to carp from the sidelines. The Nine Years War - fought predictably against Louis XIV's France - proved so expensive that the Whigs were forced to come up with some ingenious measures to finance it, including the establishment of the Bank of England in 1694 to raise loans for the conflict and manage the national debt.

Politically, the two key issues of the latter Stuart period were religious dissent and the Union of England with Scotland. Based on the policy of 'mine enemy's enemy is my friend' Anglicans had joined forces with Protestant dissenters and other Non-Conformists to block the Catholic threat to the Crown. There was now a growing call for these dissenters to be rewarded for their part in denying James II.

In 1689 Parliament passed the Toleration Act which permitted Protestant dissenters freedom of worship as long as they recognised the divinity of Christ. This did not please much of the Anglican clergy, who refused to make the necessary liturgical amendments, and nor did it play well with the religiously conservative Tories. Fearful of the Church of England losing its identity if too many dissenters were allowed to be subsumed within it they bided their time until Anne became Queen and then sought to nullify the effects of the act. Alongside this they also campaigned fervently for the closing of a key loophole that many dissenters had exploited in the infamous Test Act. The Act had barred those who had not taken Holy Communion in the Church of England from public office – but the problem was that dissenters could still take Communion in this way, thus fulfilling the requirements of the Test Act and allowing them access to office. Yet if the Tories had hoped that Anne would be sympathetic to their petitioning they were to be sorely disappointed. Whig bishops in the House of Lords were always going to block any attempt to outlaw occasional conformity and the new Queen did not feel inclined to overrule them.

One area where Anne *did* utilise her right of royal veto was during the unedifying and bad-tempered negotiations to combine England with Scotland into the United Kingdom. She had been unhappy with early versions of the Act of Union and finally asserted her constitutional power by brushing aside a proposed militia bill. The veto has never been used since.

The whole process of unification was carried through somewhat grudgingly, with England using bully boy tactics to squeeze the Scots into submission. It had become diplomatically necessary to combine the old neighbours due to the problem of Scottish sympathy with James II's son the 'Old Pretender'- James himself having died in 1701 - and given the dangerously close proximity of the two countries. Add to this nagging worry the historical friendship between Scotland and France as well as various ugly trading disagreements and it was clear why heavy handed politicians in London were keen to neutralise the danger north of the border.

The trigger for unification came in 1705 when the Scottish Estates insisted on a separate law of succession to the throne of Scotland. Determined to put the uppity Celts in their place Parliament ceased trade with Scotland and threatened to seize all assets held in England unless she consented to Union. The Scots had little choice and the Act of Union was forced through in 1707. Nevertheless they fared tolerably well from the deal - probably due to Anne's Scottish heritage - retaining a strong sense of identity and autonomy on issues of law, education and religion.

Yet the majority of Scots had never wanted the Union and the crass, arrogant manner in which the English had imposed it bred ill-feeling which festers - and is highly politically relevant - to this day. They felt woefully under-represented in the House of Commons with a paltry 45 MPs who were either ignored or mocked, whilst their equally desultory clutch of peers were soon compromised by the decision to exclude those who also held British peerages. Given this derisory treatment it is small wonder that Jacobitism continued to both flourish and intensify in Scotland.

After three failed uprisings between 1708 and 1719 the Jacobites came closest to reinstating Catholic Stuart rule in 1745, when the Old Pretender's son Charles - variously known as the Young Pretender or Bonnie Prince Charlie - led a Scottish army to victory at Prestonpans and then occupied Edinburgh. Soon they had moved into England, getting as far as Derby before they were checked. After retreating back to Scotland they were massacred by the Duke of Cumberland's troops at Culloden, a hideous mismatch where the Scottish sword bearers were slaughtered by British canon. Culloden effectively spelled the end of Jacobitism in Scotland.

The remaining few years of Anne's reign was dominated once more by concerns over the succession. In theory the appropriate provisions had been made thanks to the Act of Settlement that named the House of Hanover as the legitimate branch of the royal line. But there were many in the government, the church and society in general who found the brazen illegality of the Glorious Revolution hard to stomach and still viewed the Young Pretender as the legitimate heir.

Jacobite sentiment had been stirred up again by the High Church priest Henry Sacheverell whose attack on the toleration of dissent had explicitly called into question the foundations on which William and Mary's and - by extension - Anne's rule was based. Whilst Sacheverell was successfully impeached his punishment was trifling and he was able to tour the country whipping up dangerously seditious feeling that played right into the hands of the gleeful Tories. They duly won a landslide in the 1710 election by portraying the Whigs - not unreasonably - as abandoning the Church of England, and were finally able to outlaw occasional conformity and suppress dissenters' schools in the Schism Act.

Yet more far-reaching and troubling than the immediate victory of the Tories was the fear that when Anne died and the time came for the House of Hanover to take up its regal post there would either be a rebellion in favour of the Young Pretender or that the distant, pampered Protestants would simply decline the offer. In the event neither happened. There was isolated talk of a Tory stand to bring back the Catholic Stuarts but the majority of the party recognised that such a move was far too much of a risk and, in any case, Anne had ensured that the leading figures in her final government were avowedly pro-Hanover. Nonetheless George, Elector of Hanover, stalled for a month on the off-chance of a Jacobite rebellion. But finally the new monarch was safely installed in London in the Autumn of 1714 and Parliament breathed a collective sigh of relief.

In 1701 a self-possessed, eminently clubbable Norfolk country squire called Robert Walpole entered Parliament as MP for Castle Rising. His gift for conciliating between opposing factions was identified when he smoothed over a dispute between the Whig government and the rest of the party in 1705 and by 1708 he had been appointed Secretary at War followed by Treasurer of the Navy two years later.

A strong marker for his future career was laid down in 1712 when he was impeached and imprisoned in the Tower of London on charges of corruption due to his dealings with forage contracts for Scotland. His incarceration lasted six months and he was expelled from Parliament. Although he would never be jailed again his tenure as the longest serving British Prime Minister in history has become emblematic of a peculiarly eighteenth century era of widespread corruption, outright bribery, political manipulation and self-serving patronage. Walpole was the ultimate political fixer - undoubtedly with his fingers in many unethical pies but always smart enough to cover his own back and protect those whose support he relied upon. This latter ability earned him the enigmatic nickname of 'The Screen'. In the 21st century he would have been vilified. In the 18th he was, and is, viewed as a kind of maverick hero.

With the accession of George I the incumbent Tory government was thrown out and the Whigs commenced their 50 year domination of the political landscape. Walpole the bluff, genial country gent rose through the ranks with a speed and confidence that made eventual leadership seem inevitable. He joined the government as Paymaster of the Forces and the following year was appointed First Lord of the Treasury and Chancellor of the Exchequer, where he introduced the sinking fund to set aside revenue in times of surplus to repay future national debt. After an uncharacteristic fit of principle forced him to resign in 1717 he returned as Paymaster two years later, just in time for the defining moment of his burgeoning career.

The South Sea Company had been founded in 1711 as a rival interest to the Bank of England in assuming the national debt. Drunk on the promise of untold riches from foreign trade in cloth and slaves affluent investors started to pour money into the project. The trouble was there was never the remotest possibility of the company turning a profit and its directors - in collusion with many high profile politicians and even the King himself - were forced to keep up the charade by paying out huge dividends from the original investments. This forced the share price up to a spectacular degree - by summer 1720 shares had risen by over 1000% and eventually the more savvy investors began to realise that something was up. The following rush to cash in shares sent the price plummeting, resulting in the financial ruin of all those investors who were still dreaming of limitless wealth from across the seas.

Among those who had made the most of their insider knowledge to sell his shares at hugely inflated prices was Robert Walpole. Yet it was the same Robert Walpole who took the subsequent investigation by the scruff of the neck and brilliantly defended both his government and King - and, of course, himself - from wrongdoing, pinning the majority of the blame on the rapidly fleeing company officials. It was a statesmanlike performance which did not go unnoticed.

By April the following year all potential rivals to Walpole had either died or resigned and - in an unprecedented move – he became First Lord of the Treasury, Chancellor of the Exchequer and Leader of the Commons – a triumvirate of positions that posterity has decreed makes him the first British Prime Minister. For all his numerous faults and moral lapses, he was an exceptional statesman for the lion's share of his incredible 20 year term and it is largely because of his astute governing of the nation that the role of Prime Minister became an established part of the British political fabric.

Walpole was the first in a long line of British political figures, from Baldwin to Macmillan to Boris Johnson, who carefully cultivate an affable public image that belies their genuine razor sharp personality. He played the country squire to perfection, fully aware that Parliamentary power stemmed from the landed gentry, emphasising his prodigious alcohol consumption and love of the land. In reality he was naturally at home in the City, an early adopter of the new science of statistics and highly skilled in the finer points of high finance.

Walpole built his ministry on the dual policies of sustained peace and low taxes, and, thanks in no small part to the efforts of his de-facto foreign minister Lord Townsend in achieving alliances with Prussia and Russia, he managed to successfully steer Britain clear of military conflict until 1739. It would be naïve, however, to imagine that it was solely the wisdom and popularity of his policies that kept him in office for so long. Walpole used every means at his disposal to block Tory ministers from positions of power as well as bribing countless MPs and appropriating illegal funds to fight election campaigns. His exploitation of the Civil List and shameless ingratiation with Queen Caroline ensured that he remained in office when the time came for her husband, George II, to take the Crown. His warm, gregarious nature also made him adept at managing disparate interests within Parliament.

Yet, as Enoch Powell famously stated, 'all political careers end in failure' and there is a certain irony that it was not the relentless corruption and palm greasing that Walpole indulged in that led to his downfall but a combination of the two problems he thought he had solved: entanglement in European warfare and the assertion of the royal prerogative.

Niggling disagreements and wounded pride concerning the rights of British merchants to trade with Spain's American colonies escalated into petty evasions of Spanish customs payments by British ships. The result was their impounding by the Spanish authorities. Despite Walpole's best efforts to negotiate a settlement war between Britain and Spain subsequently broke out in 1739. Known as the War of Jenkins' Ear due to the report of Captain Robert Jenkins that he had had the eponymous organ lopped off by a Spanish soldier it was exactly the kind of pointless squabble that Walpole had worked so hard to keep Britain detached from. It achieved nothing save the renewal of hostilities between Spain and France and the tarnishing of the Prime Minister's reputation as a statesman of peace.

The war was depressing but would not on its own have justified Walpole's departure from office. It was the conflict of interest between himself and George II over the prestige and security of Hanover that really did for him. When Maria Theresa became ruler of the Holy Roman Empire in 1740

Prussia, France, Spain and Bavaria all saw it as a green light to stake their claims to the empire. In accordance with established diplomatic alliances Walpole sided with Maria Theresa only to be overruled by his monarch who, in order to shield Hanover from the predatory might of Prussia, rushed through a neutrality agreement in 1741 and supported the French claim. Prussia then invaded and kick-started the War of the Austrian Succession, a grinding pan-European conflict that lasted nine years.

His authority fatally undermined Walpole's ministry started to fall apart. In 1742 a by-election defeat in Chippenham saw the government lose their majority and the first and longest serving Prime Minister of the United Kingdom was forced to resign. Robert Walpole had presided over a golden age for Georgian Britain, keeping her free from costly military campaigns- both in the financial and humanitarian senses - for nearly twenty years. He had also expertly balanced the interests of the Crown with that of the people, at least until the threat to Hanover became too great for George II to ignore. He bestrode the era like a colossus, the first 'personality politician' of the Parliamentary age.

There is a curious postscript to Walpole's career as well. In 1744 - two years after his fall from grace and one year before his death - a nursery rhyme appeared in 'Tommy Thumb's Pretty Song Book' called 'Who Killed Cock Robin?' The rhyme recounts the death of the titular bird and the involvement of various other animals in either its demise or burial. It has been suggested that Cock Robin is none other than Walpole - Robin being the diminutive form of Robert and his ministry being previously referred to by its critics as a 'Robinocracy' - and that the rhyme is an allegory for the fall of the government. If true, it is a suitably bizarre tribute to a larger than life figure who has passed into British history.

3

THE VAGARIES OF EMPIRE

The reason that Robert Walpole was able to sell the idea of sustained peace to the British people was that, just before he assumed his positions in George II's first government, the outgoing Tory ministry had signed a treaty which turned the United Kingdom into a global power. The 1713 Treaty of Utrecht concluded Britain's part in the War of the Spanish Succession which had been raging for 12 years and bequeathed her St. Kitts, Hudson Bay, Newfoundland, Nova Scotia, Gibraltar and Minorca. It also, crucially, permitted access to trade with Spain's South American colonies.

Up until this point Britain's colonial possessions had been piecemeal, ad-hoc acquisitions rather than a solid foundation for the world's largest empire. Walpole's peace had allowed the nation to breathe and led to a flourishing in the arts, architecture and philosophy but by the time of his downfall the mood music had become more bellicose - there were few things European countries in the 18th century liked more than a good war.

Unfortunately Walpole was succeeded as Prime Minister by a parade of weak, unworldly non-entities entirely unsuited to propagating successful military campaigns. The one statesman who truly understood aggressive foreign policy was also the most loathed at the royal court. Yet despite the best efforts of both George II and his grandson George III to block his ambition this exceptionally perceptive and astute individual eventually rose to prominence, transforming the fortunes and prestige of Great Britain along the way.

*

Aloof, combative and single-minded William Pitt was about as different from Robert Walpole as it was possible to be. So it is no surprise that upon entering Parliament in 1735 he sided with a faction of rebel Whigs called the Patriots against Walpole's perceived passivity in foreign affairs. This decision revealed a streak of cussedness in Pitt that would threaten to scupper a glittering career at every turn. From the start he voiced opinions and forged alliances that courted controversy and attracted opprobrium from the ruling elite.

Cultivating the friendship of your sovereign's son and heir may at first glance appear a sensible political strategy but the Hanoverians put little store by filial love or loyalty. George II loathed his son Frederick, Prince of Wales and the feeling was mutual, the antipathy between them possibly due to George I's reputed favouritism towards his grandson. Pitt joined a number of MPs in an unofficial opposition to both Walpole and George, presided over by the Prince of Wales.

And, as time went on, he made sure of his King's contempt by becoming known as an outspoken critic of George's European adventures on behalf of the House of Hanover. As we will see Pitt was no pacifist but he regarded the direct benefits to Britain as the only measure of a worthwhile military campaign. The Hanoverians had never made any secret of their preference for their native empire.

It was the War of Jenkins' Ear that brought Pitt to the attention of many in Parliament, his advocacy of a belligerent, hard-line response to the Spanish standing in marked contrast to Walpole's weary acceptance of the conflict. Typically, Pitt was enraged by what he saw as a deeply flawed campaign. He highlighted numerous examples of strategic incompetence from the government, such as failing to press home British advantage before France entered the conflict and fundamental misjudgements about attacking in adverse weather conditions. Bitterly disappointed at the inconsequential conclusion to the conflict Pitt believed that Spanish colonies had been there for the taking if only Britain had pushed harder.

By 1746 Pitt's natural brilliance could be ignored no longer. Recognising that such an unbending attitude towards the King was frustrating his chances of high office he reluctantly backtracked on his criticisms of the subsidies handed out to further Hanoverian interests. George, for his part, finally relented and appointed him Paymaster of the Forces in Henry Pelham's ministry - a post that would give him a perfect opportunity to demonstrate the honesty and integrity that would become his hallmark qualities. Previous paymasters had taken advantage of the interest accruing on payments to line their own pockets but Pitt very publically refused to do this. Whether or not this stand was just carefully managed PR such a selfless action won him the admiration of both the people and, somewhat grudgingly, the King.

Even in such a relatively minor role Pitt was one of the dominant voices driving policy, usually advocating increased efforts in aggressive foreign diplomacy. When the War of the Austrian Succession - which had subsumed the War of Jenkins' Ear and various other smaller conflicts - ended in 1748 Pitt again felt frustrated at the timidity of British negotiations and comparative lack of territorial gains. He was finally to have his chance to change the direction of Britain's military ideology when the cast of the War of the Austrian Succession reconvened in 1756 for its similarly punishing sequel, the Seven Years War.

The Seven Years War was an incredibly wide ranging conflict, with theatres across the globe drawing every major power into the brutal fighting. Britain started badly with a string of defeats, the most infamous of which was the loss of Minorca to the French. There were accusations of governmental complicity in the fall of the island which fatally damaged the standing of the Prime Minister, the Duke of Newcastle. The new ministry was nominally headed by the Duke of Devonshire but Pitt was the de-facto leader, determined to reverse the losses that Britain had incurred.

To achieve this Pitt hit upon a strategy of sheer genius. Realising that the war raging in Europe was one of grinding attrition he bankrolled the formidable Prussian forces to keep France at bay there and then utilised the dominance and expertise of the Royal Navy to take on French forces around the globe. This technique paid off spectacularly in 1759 - 'the Year of the Three Victories' that established Britain as the greatest colonial power in the world.

During the War of the Austrian Succession the French had taken the city of Madras from the hands of the British East India Company, leading to a sustained assault on company interests in southern India. In 1756 French belligerence went too far. Although it was an Indian nawab who suffocated 123 Europeans in the 'Black Hole of Calcutta' the atrocity was committed with full French collusion. Retribution was swift. The following year the daring young colonel Robert Clive led 3,200 British troops to a resounding victory over 40,000 Indian soldiers at Plassey. From this impressive base the British took Bombay and then in 1759 repelled the French at Madras to secure a fledgling Indian empire for the Crown.

The French were also a serious threat to British interests in North America. After cutting their lines in the Ohio Valley the previous year, General James Wolfe commanded a lightning attack on Quebec which secured for the British the area of Canada known as New France. Personally appointed by Pitt to lead the assault on Quebec Wolfe's command had faltered initially with a three month long siege of Quebec City eventually resulting in a dispiriting defeat. But, in one of those against-the-odds gambles later celebrated in Victorian history books, the undeterred general ordered a speculative ascent of the supposedly unscalable cliffs west of the city. On the Plains of Abraham the British forces surprised the French under the command of the Marquis de Montcalm and routed them within a quarter of an hour. As befits such a stirring tale of derring-do Wolfe was killed heroically in battle and his demise commemorated in a suitably grandiose painting 11 years later. Montcalm died the following day of his injuries. The French were almost entirely driven from Canada, with only Montreal clinging on until the following year.

Added to the capture of Guadeloupe in the West Indies this was a remarkable series of successes which not only reversed the earlier setbacks but far outstripped them. Pitt's popularity with the public was at an all-time high but Parliament was only too aware of the escalating cost of waging global military conflict. Pitt was desperate to prolong the war by attacking Spain but he faced a significant problem in the form of the new King, George III. Unlike his predecessors this monarch viewed himself as a home grown Englishman and was much more prone to interfering in the process of government. He was not quite Charles I or James II but for a large amount of his 60 year reign Parliament did not enjoy quite the same freedoms it had done under the early Hanoverians.

George dismissed Devonshire and installed the staunch Tory Earl of Bute as Prime Minister in order to obtain a swift conclusion to the war. When the Treaty of Paris was signed in 1763 Britain gained Canadian New France, all land to the east of the Mississippi and Florida. She also, as a point of pride, reclaimed Minorca. It was hardly a bad return but Pitt, once more fuming at the lost opportunities, tendered his resignation. Nonetheless, the success of Pitt's military and political strategy during the Seven Years War cannot be overstated. Without it there may have been no British Raj in India and Britain's overseas trading capacity would have been drastically reduced.

For nobody understood the crucial importance of global trade as clearly as Pitt. The developed world was on the cusp of rapid industrialisation and Pitt could see which way the wind was blowing. Britain may take the lead but it would not take long for the likes of France, Prussia and Spain to catch up. If Britain made the most of her head start she could ensure her economic dominance through the exploitation of raw materials from her collection of colonies, trading to ever expanding markets. In this, as in so much else, William Pitt was proved absolutely right.

Something else that Pitt was right about was the growing unrest in Britain's 13 North American colonies, although he must accept some of the blame - however indirectly - for the revolution that stunned a complacent United Kingdom the following decade. For it was because of the crippling national debt incurred by fighting the Seven Years War that a series of taxes was imposed upon these colonies in 1764 and 1765.

The events leading up to the American War of Independence were a catalogue of over-reactions, misunderstandings and plain poor decisions that ultimately cost Britain one of her most prized possessions. The taxes that then Prime Minister Lord Grenville imposed upon imports of sugar, molasses and printed matter - the so-called Stamp Tax - were entirely reasonable under the circumstances. The British navy and army had protected the North American colonies from French conquest and they were not the only British possessions to have to pay these taxes. But the colonists refused to stump up and began to boycott British goods.

A change of government and a typically eloquent speech from Benjamin Franklin saw the repeal of the taxes and a lifting of the boycott. But part of the problem within Parliament was that George III was attempting to assert his control by hiring and firing ministers seemingly at will. Consequently there was no consistency in government and no clear line taken on how to deal with the increasingly self-possessed colonists. Pitt recognised early on that attempts to coerce or suppress them were doomed to fail but, even though George reluctantly appointed him Prime Minister in 1766 with the honorific of Earl of Chatham, his influence was limited. He was powerless to prevent the hated Townsend Act - named after the Chancellor of the Exchequer Charles Townsend whose brainwave it was - in 1767 which taxed imports of paper, glass and tea. The boycott resumed and by the following year Pitt's illustrious career was over.

An atmosphere of mutual distrust and suspicion simmered until 1773 when Lord North's government made the fateful decision to allow the British East India Company to sell cheap Indian tea - subject of course to the tax - in the American colonies. In a scene worthy of the later fiction of James Fennimore Cooper a band of outraged tea merchants and smugglers donned Native American disguises and boarded three British ships docked in Boston harbour. The tea that they threw overboard in the dead of night totalled £10,000.

From the Boston Tea Party onwards the conflict ceased to be about injurious import duties and became an ideological battle for freedom. The American colonies had always enjoyed a certain amount of autonomy and now they were shouting for liberty. Britain responded foolishly once again by passing the Five Coercive Acts which - amongst other things - closed Boston harbour until the cost of the sunken tea had been repaid, allowed Parliament to control who ran the Massachusetts government and permitted trials of royal officials to take place in Britain if it was perceived they would not get a fair trial in North America.

Militant assemblies sprang up all over the colonies and collective breaths were held on both sides of the Atlantic. The tension broke in April 1775 when the British governor of Massachusetts attempted to confiscate a stockpile of arms belonging to the rebels at Lexington and Concord, incurring casualties of a thousand men. Britain had sleepwalked into a disastrous war.

Against a background of skirmishes along the eastern seaboard the Declaration of Independence was drafted on 4th July 1776. It was largely the work of future president Thomas Jefferson and, alongside a tract called 'Common Sense' by the British-born agitator Thomas Paine, became the cornerstone of the nascent American constitution. Its passionate appeal to equality, liberty and human rights bolstered the self-belief and determination of the rebels and confused, hapless Britannia had no effective answer.

The problem with recently accruing a considerable empire at the expense of other great European powers is that those aggrieved nation-states will constantly be on the lookout for signs of vulnerability. After an American victory at Saratoga in 1777 left Britain looking utterly directionless the French and Spanish rubbed their hands and sent their fleets and armies to support the rebels. The war had already been slipping away from Britain and now she was vastly outnumbered with two of the best equipped fighting forces in the world both gunning for her. Humiliating surrender duly took place at Yorktown in 1781. Two years later another Treaty of

Paris made the inevitable official - Great Britain had lost her American colonies and become a little less great in the process.

*

Yet as devastating a blow as the loss of America was it needs to be seen within the context of a British empire that was constantly expanding and enriching both the culture and economy of the Mother Country through remorseless trade. In addition to military entanglements Britain prided herself on her tradition of exploration, with intrepid voyagers such as James Cook staking his King's claim to Botany Bay, the Sandwich Islands and large swathes of the Pacific coastline.

This rapidly moving nature of global affairs required a state that was leaner, more efficient and considerably more centralised. The many headed bureaucratic beast that is so often railed against in modern society has its roots in the sudden swelling of the civil service in the mid to late 18th century. Britain's novel use of credit to finance overseas enterprises made an army of bureaucrats essential and the concomitant rise of the Industrial Revolution required that the income raised be spent on the construction of ever more state of the art ships and weaponry. This in turn fuelled upswings in local economies where a particular industry or trade was prevalent. The 'workshop of the world' was open for business.

But there were dark storm-clouds as well as clear blue sky. One of Britain's - and the world's - most profitable trades was in human beings. The trafficking of slaves did not start in the eighteenth century but it grew spectacularly during that period as methods of traversing the globe improved and demand for labour massively increased. Traders made the bulk of their money from the Triangular Route involving the exchange of slaves, rum and sugar between Africa, the Americas and either Europe or the United States. It is a bitter fact that the new home comforts and luxuries that the British people were enjoying as the spoils of conquest were built on the appalling treatment and exploitation of enslaved Africans.

The voices of dissent were growing. In 1750 Horace Walpole denounced the trade in the House of Commons and various Christian denominations also campaigned for abolition. 1772 saw the formal outlawing of slavery in England and the emergence of a young Tory called William Wilberforce who would make it his life's work to eradicate the evil practice throughout the empire. But amongst all the boys-own yarns of imperial conquest and exotic exploration it is worth remembering that there was also a more shameful and sinister side to Great Britain's frenzied empire building.

4

REVOLUTIONARY RIVALS

In 1763 the firebrand journalist and MP for Aylesbury John Wilkes was arrested under a general warrant and imprisoned in the Tower of London. His crime may not seem especially heinous to modern sensibilities but in an eighteenth century Britain ruled by a self-important and prickly monarch the article which appeared in his radical journal the 'North Briton' was considered borderline treason. In it Wilkes stated that George III's praise of the Treaty of Paris that concluded the Seven Years War was false and insincere. Small beer one may think considering the vitriol that had been reserved for previous sovereigns such as Charles I or James II. Yet the very fact that George had overreacted so dramatically to the slur highlighted that the same archaic system of royal prerogative and privilege was just as securely in place as it had been a century before.

Wilkes was released after claiming immunity as a Member of Parliament but anybody who thought the matter would end there was reckoning without his inexhaustible supplies of establishment-baiting zeal. He was arrested again for publishing an obscene parody of Alexander Pope's poem 'Essay on Man' and forced to flee the country. Upon his return in 1768 he was elected MP for Middlesex despite being rearrested and sentenced to two years in prison. When the Commons refused to recognise him all hell broke loose. Wilkes had always championed Parliamentary reform and whatever one may have thought of his behaviour there was no denying that the system, built on patronage, bribery and corruption, stank to high heaven. He was now seen by mobs of radical activists as a martyr to the cause and outbreaks of violence accompanied by the scrawled graffiti 'Wilkes and Liberty' became commonplace. When his jail sentence was read out there was rioting outside the court and seven people were killed in the ensuing crackdown.

Wilkes had the support of many of his fellow politicians, including a young, charismatic Whig by the name of Charles James Fox. The impassioned speech that Fox made in defence of Wilkes, delivered to the House of Commons in 1769, was just one of many in a long career founded equally on heartfelt radicalism and barefaced opportunism. From the closing years of the eighteenth century till well into the 19th he would be joined by many other courageous politicians who had decided they had had enough of the rotten, insular world of Parliament and the continued authority of the Crown. Events in America and in Europe would chime with the revolutionary spirit of the times in Great Britain, creating a palpable sense of danger and excitement not experienced since the days of the Glorious Revolution. In such a cauldron of emotion and ideological conflict heated rivalries were bound to emerge. There would be none more vicious and protracted than that between Fox and a brilliant political prodigy with a singular Parliamentary heritage.

When William Pitt the Younger entered Parliament in 1781 at the tender age of 21 the comparative veteran Fox, who was a decade older, welcomed him warmly. As the acknowledged oratorical master of the Commons he could afford to do so and for a considerable time his attitude towards the precocious youngster was one of patrician condescension. The trouble was that everyone apart from Fox could see that Pitt was a rare talent who potentially outstripped the more experienced man. The previous titans in our tale – Walpole and Pitt the Elder – had had no equals with whom to collaborate or against whom to compete. Now, for the first time, there were two Parliamentary giants of the same generation and the political and personal possibilities were highly exciting.

They did not disappoint. Cracks started to appear in their relationship the following year when Fox, Foreign Secretary in all but name, opposed a bill to curb bribes during elections. Pitt, unsurprisingly given the moral rectitude of his father, supported it. If one was looking for a convenient

43

example of the two MPs' contrasting characters then this Bill was it. Fox himself was not massively corrupt - certainly not when compared to Walpole at any rate - but he was a hard-living, larger-than-life figure who believed rules were made to be broken. He also, somewhat ironically, continued the tradition embraced by the elder Pitt of cosying up to the Prince Regent. This antagonised the King no end as - naturally being a Hanoverian - he couldn't stand the sight of his own son. Fox viewed bribery as no bad thing if it enhanced the engagement of both voter and politician. Pitt was his polar opposite - just as aloof as his father but possibly even chillier and more clinical in demeanour. For him bribery equalled corruption and corruption was plain wrong - there was no grey area. During the course of the next 20 years Fox's poetic flights of polemical fancy and appeals to common sentiment would be trumped time and again by Pitt's unerring intelligence and rational argument.

Within a few months Pitt was the youngest ever Chancellor of the Exchequer and Fox was on the opposition benches having intemperately resigned from government. But for all of Fox's dissolute behaviour he was ferociously ambitious and had decided, in a brazen bid to seize power, on an astonishing volte face. For the last six years he had remorselessly pilloried the former Prime Minister Lord North for his mishandling of the American Revolution - Fox having been an avowed supporter of the rebels. Suddenly he made explicit overtures to North to form a coalition to bring down the ministry of Lord Shelburne, who Fox arguably loathed even more.

It was a breathtakingly cynical marriage of convenience and it worked, if only in the short term. Pitt was the only other option available to an infuriated George III and the Chancellor wisely elected to bide his time and wait for an opportunity to sabotage the Fox-North coalition himself. He found it in Fox's proposed India Act which sought to take regulation of the rapacious East India Company out of the company's own hands and give it to a central commission accountable to Parliament. In reductive terms it was an embryonic dispute between Capitalism and Socialism but unfortunately for Fox money was king in the booming business of world trade. His morally ambiguous persona led many to suspect that he wanted to be a part of the commission himself the better to purloin a share of the company's profits.

Nonetheless Fox still had a fervent following in both Parliamentary houses and, having sailed through the Commons, the bill looked set to squeak through the Lords. That was until the King decided to intervene yet again, making it known that any peers who backed the bill would cease to be friends of the Crown. Fox's India Act was sunk and so too was Fox. Pitt now accepted the offer to form a government and George delightedly dismissed Fox, North and the Duke of Portland, the ministry's puppet leader.

Pitt may have won the ultimate prize but hardly anybody took him seriously. He was just 24 years old and wildly inexperienced whilst Fox's continued popularity meant that Pitt was in charge of a similarly green minority government. Fox took bets on whether the ministry would last a week. It survived for nearly 18 years.

With staggering confidence in one so young Pitt rode out the initial storm and slowly but surely won round enough Members of Parliament and enough of the voting public to first command a majority and then ensure total dominance. He was able to skilfully balance the good of the country with the desires of his monarch and demonstrated admirable diplomatic abilities in his dealings with the United States and Canada.

Yet it was in his handling of the economy that he truly excelled, exposing the grumbling Fox for the old fashioned mercantilist that he was. Pitt was an avid admirer of the Scottish Enlightenment economist Adam Smith whose revolutionary 'Wealth of Nations' had been published in 1776. Rather than the standard mercantile economy based on high exports and low - or no - imports Smith espoused the idea of free trade, correctly arguing that the intrinsic value of money is based on supply and demand and the amount of labour that goes into producing it. A mercantile system in effect just hoarded money, flooding the economy and resulting in inflation. What free trade did was encourage competition by identifying the natural value of a commodity due to the level of demand. It is not for nothing that Smith has been called the father of Capitalism.

All of this confirmed Pitt as the thrusting pioneer of a new, commerce-led Britain and made Fox look like yesterday's man. Yet when the King succumbed to his first bout of 'madness' in 1787 - probably brought on by porphyria - there was a real possibility of the Prince Regent taking over and appointing his beloved Fox Prime Minister. Pitt played for time desperately, searching for royal precedents and tinkering with legislation, whilst Fox frantically lobbied for his patron's right to power. The crude battle for political power forced both men into hypocritical positions - Pitt the ardent royalist questioning the sacred rule of primogeniture and Fox the radical iconoclast insisting upon the same rule's sanctity. In the end the King recovered and Fox was frustrated once again. But the wunderkind of British politics was about to face his toughest challenge yet.

On the 14th of July 1789 a mob of Parisian rioters stormed the old prison of the Bastille, asserting the primacy of the French people and calling on Louis XVI to recognise the need for a constitutional rather than absolute monarchy. There were obvious parallels for most Britons with both the Civil War and the Glorious Revolution and, almost to a man, the sentiment in the country was one of rejoicing that another nation had thrown off the shackles of despotism and embraced liberty. The recent American Revolution, which had been positively welcomed by a number of radical British MPs, had shown what could be accomplished by the will of the people and - for a while - it appeared as though a glorious new world order really was dawning.

Pitt, a reformer at heart, was gratified at the news in his usual detached, analytical way. Fox was a rabid Francophile and self-proclaimed man of the people who regarded it ecstatically as the greatest event in the history of the world. The most heavyweight voice of negativity belonged to an old friend of Fox who had supported the rebels in the American War of Independence and had an impeccable radical pedigree.

Edmund Burke was the Member of Parliament for Malton but is known to history primarily as an influential political theorist and philosopher. His belief in the steady evolution of civilization, with politics the catalyst for gradual adaptation, typified the reform-minded ideology of Whiggism as opposed to the dogmatic defence of tradition that defined the Tories. He viewed the American Revolution as a prime example of such shifting strands in the progression of history and welcomed the self-government that it engendered. But he saw something very different in the wholesale iconoclasm of the French Revolution. Burke's Whiggism was all about flexibility and adapting the existing institutions to improve the lot of society. The French revolutionaries, by contrast, seemed to him to be hell-bent on destroying every existing institution and then improvising new ones. His 'Reflections on the Revolution in France' - published the year after the storming of the Bastille - predicted with uncanny accuracy the violence, bloodlust and anarchy that would befall revolutionary France. Yet at the time his views were regarded as reactionary and ignorant.

His fiercest critic was the most celebrated radical pamphleteer of the day, Thomas Paine. Building on the anti-establishment rhetoric of 'Common Sense' Paine unleashed 'The Rights of Man' in 1791, a savagely eloquent and persuasive riposte to Burke's respect for the preservation of institutions. These institutions, argued Paine, were founded centuries ago by the despotism of monarchs. They favoured the ruling elite at the expense of the common man and were full of empty pomp and ceremony. According to Paine the only institutions that were worth anything were those that sprang from the rights of man and furthered the good of all society.

Altruistic as Paine's sentiments may have been it was Burke who was ultimately proved correct. By 1793 Louis XVI had been guillotined, the brutal regime of the Terror was underway and revolutionary France had added Great Britain to the list of European states that she was waging war with. Pitt, who was now firmly on the side of Burkean opinion, responded in a measured fashion by limiting the scope of Britain's war aims against the French Republic - he ruled out restoring the Bourbon royal line - and cutting dead any attempts at home grown reform for fear they could be manipulated for revolutionary ends. Fox - admirably true to his radical principles if hopelessly out of step with the rest of the nation - continued to condemn both Pitt and British hostilities as an affront to liberty.

By late 1794 he had something more concrete to accuse his nemesis of. The continued existence of various pro-revolution societies such as the Friends of the People and the London Corresponding Society coupled with the very plausible threat of French invasion stiffened Pitt's resolve. He began a sustained period of implementing draconian legislation aimed at the total nullification of revolutionary activity. His first act was the suspension of Habeas Corpus, allowing any persons suspected of sedition to be incarcerated indefinitely without trial. This was followed a year later by the Treasonable Practices Act, which extended the definition of treason to include words as well as deeds, and the Seditious Meetings Act, which made any unlicensed gathering of more than 50 people illegal.

This was not only a key moment in the British reaction to the French Revolution but also in the political career and legacy of William Pitt the Younger. He had entered Parliament as a reformer but the palpable danger presented by the uprising across the Channel had forced him into cracking down on exactly the kind of free speech and Parliamentary reform that he would have welcomed - in moderation - in peacetime. It is from this period that the image of the hard-line, right-wing - itself a term coined in revolutionary France – high Tory Pitt comes into existence.

Such restrictive measures had the predictable result on Charles James Fox. In his eyes the British campaign was no longer about defeating France but crushing all liberties and human rights no matter how self-evident or harmless they may be. This was Charles I, James II and George III all rolled into one. Britain would be returned to pre-Civil War days, forever under the yoke of an absolute monarch with a deluded 'divine right' to rule. The fact that few people were actually prosecuted under these laws was irrelevant to Fox and his ever-decreasing rump of supporters in the Commons. This was an affront to the Glorious Revolution of 1688 and everything that it stood for.

By the summer of 1799 the Directory ruling France had almost bankrupted the nation and was struggling to coordinate the military campaign. Briefly it seemed as though hostilities may be coming to an end. But a brilliant young general called Napoleon Bonaparte had other ideas, staging a coup against the Directory and installing himself as French First Consul in November. Faced with this fresh development Pitt was forced to make economic as well as social changes. Walpole's Sinking Fund was extended and income tax introduced, whilst further harsh legislation was pushed through outlawing trade unions and collective bargaining. This was largely due to naval mutinies at Spithead and Nore which threatened to destabilise the war effort.

The seemingly interminable conflict was taking its toll on the Prime Minister whose moniker of 'the Younger' now looked like a cruel joke. A heavy drinker by nature he was 40 going on 70 and utterly exhausted by his long and eventful time in office. He had worked tirelessly to eliminate the conditions conducive to home-grown revolution, even if his methods had appeared excessive at times. As the 18th century dissolved into the 19th Pitt was looking for a way out. A golden opportunity presented itself in 1801.

Ireland's union with Britain echoed that of Scotland's nearly a century earlier. Much as Scotland had been seen as a back door for Jacobitism Ireland was viewed as the equivalent for French Jacobinism, especially after a series of thwarted invasions in the late 1790s. This Union was accomplished with a similar sense of simmering anger and injustice and Irish MPs in the new combined Parliament were just as hard done to as their Scottish counterparts. Yet there was one crucial facet of the negotiations which was not followed through and it was this that provided Pitt with his get-out clause. With a spark of his old reforming zeal he had been keen to secure a level of emancipation for the much-maligned Irish

Catholics but George III would not hear of it. So Pitt stunned the nation by resigning.

But the ponderous ministry of Henry Addington only served to highlight how indispensable Pitt had become and just over three years later he was back. However, the various petty squabbles - generally with Fox - and factions within Parliament made it almost impossible to govern with any security. Therefore little was achieved in the great man's second term, save the forging of an alliance with Russia, Sweden and Austria and the resounding naval victory of Nelson at Trafalgar. Crippled by ill health and intolerable levels of stress the statesman that had held Britain together at one of her darkest hours died on 23rd January 1806.

Fox - who from either mean spiritedness or high moral principle refused to pay tribute to Pitt - now took his place in a laughably termed 'Ministry of All the Talents' headed by William Grenville and Henry Addington. Amongst these non-entities only Fox could truly be said to have displayed any talent in his career although by now he too was on his last legs, terminally ill and robbed of his righteous fury since the death of his great rival.

Predictably the government was listless and indecisive and certainly no match for Napoleon who was still marauding around Europe at whim. Even the one historic piece of legislation that the ministry passed was something of an anti-climax. The clamour for abolition of the slave trade had reached such a pitch that it was clear that the practice would have to be outlawed. Yet, in a nation collectively exhausted by perpetual war, the bill passed practically unnoticed. Campaigners would have to wait until 1834's abolition of slavery throughout the empire to really celebrate the extinction of such a colossal evil.

By September 1806 Fox too was dead and an era of almost soap-opera proportions passed into history. British politics was returned to a period of forgettable, unstable ministries and interchangeable Prime Ministers. The 'Ministry of All the Talents' dissolved with barely a whimper the following year and a similarly ineffective government under the leadership of the Duke of Portland replaced it. It was not until Spencer Perceval took charge in 1809 that the country had a leader with a degree of ability, but he was still no match for the great Pitt or even the mercurial, self-destructive Fox.

There would be numerous captivating duels - literally, on one occasion - between politicians down the centuries but the Pitt-Fox feud was where the thrill of adversarial British politics caught fire. Many later contests would be pale imitations of the eloquent barbs that the two pioneers traded in, yet for all Westminster's unedifying spectacles great public figures locking horns over the state of the nation is an important part of what makes the British political system unique.

5

KEEPING THE PEACE

On 11th May 1812 Spencer Perceval, the capable Prime Minister of Great Britain for the past three years, entered the House of Commons to attend an inquiry into the global trade crisis caused by the naval blockade imposed upon Napoleon's France. He would not leave the building alive. His death at the hands of John Bellingham, an aggrieved ex-employee of the East India Company, remains – mercifully - the sole assassination of a serving British Prime Minister. But such a shocking and unexpected act, coming at a time when the nation had been at war for nearly two solid decades , prompted a lot of worried talk about whether the whole system of British government was on the verge of collapse.

Ten years later the Foreign Secretary Robert Stewart, known commonly as Viscount Castlereagh, slit his throat with a pen-knife having suffered for months from public vilification and dreadful overwork. Once again the country was deeply shocked, in this case that such a high profile political figure would choose to end their life because of the emotional repercussions of serving in government.

Both men had played their part in an astonishing narrative of backbiting and betrayal worthy of a Jacobean drama. George Canning, the other chief protagonist and last man standing, took over Castlereagh's job at the Foreign Office. After five years there he finally attained the position of Prime Minister, the role he had always considered himself destined for and for which he had bullied, bluffed and blustered ever since he entered Parliament. Just 119 days after accepting the premiership he too would be dead, having achieved nothing in the top job except a footnote in the history books as the British Prime Minister with the shortest tenure.

The period between Pitt the Younger's death in 1806 and the return of the Whigs to power in 1830 was filled with darkness, strife and threat both at home and abroad. The war with France looked to have been won in 1814 only for the seemingly indestructible Napoleon to escape from exile and reform his army. Such a long and punitive conflict was having a greater and greater effect on discontent at home with the clamour for change becoming ever more militant. Even when the dazzling Corsican general had been irrefutably defeated at Waterloo the dire state of the British economy pushed a lot of her struggling subjects to breaking point. And in the midst of the biggest national crisis since the Civil War the dominant figures in the government were sniping at each other and fighting farcical duels. These were strange times indeed.

*

Pitt's death left a huge hole in Parliament that no other politician of the day could have hoped to fill. He had proved himself a decisive statesman, a shrewd economist and a wily operator in the bear-pit of the Commons. Nobody held the former Prime Minister in higher regard than George Canning, an acolyte who had served in the latter half of his first government and then, when Pitt was out of office, campaigned tirelessly for his reinstatement. Upon Pitt's return Canning, fully expecting to secure the post of Foreign Secretary, was fobbed off with Treasurer of the Navy - although this doesn't seem to have dimmed his fervent admiration of his hero's political genius. Yet the fact that Canning was later snubbed again for his preferred position does strongly indicate that however highly Canning may have rated Pitt the feeling was not necessarily reciprocated.

In Pitt's defence he was not the only one to have had issues with George Canning. For one thing Canning came from the working classes at a time when Parliament was overwhelmingly dominated by the aristocracy and landed gentry. Henry Addington – the PM between Pitt's two terms – had been the son of a physician and this alone had been enough to effectively stymie his administration from the off. The fact that Canning's parents had been a drunk and an actress made political success an extremely tall order, even before his disagreeable personality had been factored in to the equation. Canning was obnoxious, astonishingly arrogant and utterly tactless, regarding himself as superior to any other politician of the age except Pitt, whose natural successor as Prime Minister he considered himself to be.

Nevertheless, after a spell in opposition during the debacle of the 'Ministry of all the Talents' Canning finally got his hands on the Foreign Office in a new ministry under the - once again nominal - leadership of the Duke of Portland. But Canning always had his eye on the next rung of the governmental ladder and had identified Viscount Castlereagh, installed in the War Office, as his closest rival. After some inadvisable decisions by Castlereagh led to a series of military reverses Canning swiftly stuck in the knife and told Portland he would resign unless the War Secretary was sacked. Given Canning's unpopularity within Parliament this might have seemed like an empty threat but, at a time when the war against Napoleon was going from bad to worse, the Foreign Secretary was the only member of the government with any kind of dynamism or energy, and Portland knew that it would play badly with the country if the common little upstart were got rid of.

So Portland dithered and procrastinated until another error of judgement by Castlereagh convinced him to accede to Canning's demand. Before he could carry it through, however, Portland fell ill and decided to retire. With the top job now up for grabs Canning could hear destiny calling but - unfortunately for him - Castlereagh now discovered the truth about his rival's duplicity and sensationally challenged him to a duel.

At 6am on 21st September 1809 ramblers on Putney Heath would have been faced with the bizarre sight of two leading cabinet ministers firing pistols at one another. It goes someway to illustrating the animosity between Canning and Castlereagh that, rather than accepting convention and shooting to miss, they appear to have genuinely tried to kill - or at least maim - each other. Canning allegedly shot a button off Castlereagh's coat whilst Castlereagh in turn hit Canning in the thigh. It goes without saying that both men subsequently resigned. Canning's hubris and petulance had led to his removal from government at precisely the time when he could realistically have claimed the leadership.

The lucky recipient of the whole fiasco was Spencer Perceval, a more level-headed, equable fellow, who became the country's first half-decent Prime Minister since Pitt the Younger. He had a lot to contend with - the failings of the Peninsular War, George III's descent into permanent madness which led to the accession of the Prince Regent and an outbreak of workers' unrest which highlighted the humanitarian cost of the Industrial Revolution.

The importance of maintaining the fight against Napoleon required industrial production to scale new heights in efficiency and speed. More machines in the hands of unskilled workers necessarily meant that specialist artisans became expendable. From 1811 a loosely organised group of textile workers known as Luddites - named after the anti-industrialist folk hero Ned Ludd - began expressing their anger and frustration at this loss of work by smashing machines such as stocking frames and power looms around the industrial Northern heartland. Their actions did not stop at crude vandalism however, with death threats sent to magistrates and food merchants and battle joined with the army in Lancashire.

Perceval responded to these upheavals with the measured authority that betrayed his former occupation as a barrister. He even attempted to reunite the feuding duellers after the dust from the scandal had been allowed to settle. Castlereagh eventually consented to rejoin the government but Canning would not even consider an alliance with the man who had shot him in the leg. Thus when Perceval was tragically murdered in 1812 Canning had once again managed to rule himself out of a snap leadership election.

Desperate for some kind of stability the Prince Regent opted for the steady, pedestrian Lord Liverpool as his next Prime Minister and it proved a sage decision. Although no inspiring statesman Liverpool was - like Clement Attlee over a century later - a highly effective administrator and man-manager. He would remain in office for the next 15 years, a testament to his quiet authority and conscientious leadership. Meanwhile Castlereagh benefitted from Canning's intractability and made his chequered reputation as Foreign Secretary.

*

Viscount Castlereagh is one of the most misunderstood figures in British political history. Perceived as plodding, negative and humourless at home he became one of the world's leading statesmen to overseas observers. Reactionary in domestic matters, in foreign affairs he pursued a policy out of step with the narrow nationalism that coursed through early 19th century Britain. Castlereagh favoured the balance of the great European powers when his countrymen were clamouring for imperial gain. In so doing he played his part in preserving the peace of post-Napoleonic Europe until the Crimean War forty years later. Whilst his hard-line view on domestic reform was a product of the age his mature, intelligent understanding of foreign affairs mark him out in retrospect as a political heavyweight. Sadly, in his own lifetime he was either hated or disregarded by his countrymen.

When the Napoleonic Wars finally came to a well overdue conclusion in 1815 the task of settlement looked supremely daunting. From the start Castlereagh – alongside the legendarily icy Austrian diplomat Metternich - recognised that punitive retribution towards France would only serve to foster further revolutionary sentiment. There must of course be punishment but there should also be conciliation. So, whilst he called for the restoration of the Bourbon monarchy and the strengthening of France's neighbours, he also backed the withdrawal of the army of occupation and a lowering of the financial indemnity imposed.

Unsurprisingly such concessions to the perpetrators of the bloodiest, most protracted conflict in living memory were greeted with outraged indignation. But the second plank of Castlereagh's settlement strategy aroused even more anger and disbelief. Where Pitt the Elder would have pushed for every last inch of territory for the Crown Castlereagh consciously sacrificed imperial gains in exchange for a fair and equal sharing of power between the great nation-states of Europe. The most contentious 'one that got away' was the restoration of the Dutch East Indies, which was seen by many a British observer as of considerable potential benefit to the economy.

There was also much grumbling about the extent to which the maintenance of a fair balance of power would needlessly involve Britain in affairs that did not concern her. It is an interesting echo of the heated debates of the following century about the United Kingdom's relationship with Europe and her associated bodies and institutions - an echo made all the louder by Castlereagh's commitment to a Congress system whereby the major nations would convene to thrash out any differences of opinion that had emerged.

With the benefit of hindsight it is clear that these were laudable aims. The problem was that Castlereagh was the only person who really wanted them to succeed. After nearly 20 years of war the prospect of a lasting peace was undoubtedly enticing but the desire for conquest and empire was too deeply ingrained in the fabric of the times for it to do anything other than lay dormant. The considered division of possessions that Castlereagh was sure would create harmonious balance ended up simply creating new power blocs and military alliances, whilst the much trumpeted Congress system was dead in the water after 1822's gathering at Verona. The most farsighted Foreign Secretary that Britain had thus far produced became a symbol of derision and disgust. The scorn and the pressure proved too much and Castlereagh killed himself the same year, allowing his deadliest rival to take his place and dismantle everything that he had attempted to achieve.

Canning's path back to the heart of government had been predictably stormy. He had seemingly turned over a new leaf by accepting a junior post in 1816 but was then forced to resign four years later following his unwillingness to aid in the prosecution of his old friend Queen Caroline - wife of the freshly crowned George IV - for adultery. Yet brash and opinionated as he was, there were always some people who wanted him back and, fortunately for him, one of them happened to be the Prime Minister. Liverpool admired his vigour and oratory even if he didn't care for him much personally and so, after Castlereagh's tragic demise, Canning found himself at the Foreign Office once again.

Canning's vision of diplomacy fitted much more snugly with that of the rest of the country. Out went the careful equilibrium of European interests and the ill-fated Congress system - not least because Metternich would have nothing to do with him - to be replaced by bombastic patriotism tempered by a more liberal approach to the freedoms of former colonies. A key example of this standpoint was Canning's recognition of the independence of Mexico, Buenos Aires and Colombia – formerly Spanish possessions which the Congress system would have restored to Spanish and Portuguese rule. These colonies were seen as being lucrative new markets for British goods and therefore his decisive intervention on the issue was applauded in the industrial heartland of the United Kingdom. He employed similarly aggressive tactics in his dealings with the United States, again undoing the hard work of his predecessor. Only in the muddy and convoluted drama of Greek independence could he ill afford to see things in black and white, hedging his bets before reluctantly joining expansionist Russia in liberating the Greeks from Turkish rule.

Canning's style was certainly more in keeping with Britain's sense of herself as the world's premier superpower and it is no surprise that he enjoyed vastly more popularity than Castlereagh. Yet he was able to throw his weight around the European stage precisely because Castlereagh had made the continent that much more harmonious. Canning simply never had to prove himself in a truly do-or-die scenario and thus the adulation he received for his antagonistic posturing came relatively cheaply. Castlereagh not only had the far harder task but ended up paying a far higher price too.

*

Away from the cut and thrust of European realignment there were turbulent times at home. Winning a war, especially a long drawn out and attritional one, hardly ever feels like a victory. The supreme irony of waging war against revolution is that revolution is far more likely when the military battle is won.

Liverpool's administration consisted of two very different periods. From 1815 to 1822 growing discontent and unrest in the country was met with the kind of suppression and severity that Pitt the Younger had favoured at the height of the French Revolution. The reasons for the unrest were largely economic. The cost of fighting Napoleon had deepened the national debt by a colossal amount and this figure was exacerbated by a number of crop failures and a drop in the value of gold. The lifting of the prohibition on imported corn forced the government to pass the notorious 1815 Corn Law – of which much more later – which protected British produce but at very high prices for the consumer. By 1819, in a desperate bid to hold back rapidly escalating inflation, Liverpool had been reduced to returning to the gold standard. The consequent deflation that this move caused only added to the crippling depression.

The people that these measures hit hardest were the same people who had risked their lives and worked their hearts out for the cause. Thousands of demobbed soldiers returned home to find that there was no work for them, whilst those workers in the industries vital for the war effort lost their jobs now there was no need of such scale of production. In addition, those soldiers who had remained in the army of occupation needed to be paid for as well. As combating poverty was not yet viewed as the responsibility of the government the parishes became clogged with the penniless and destitute and poor relief spiralled out of all control to

£18 million. In this atmosphere of helplessness and suffering it is no wonder that opposition was mounted and rebellion proposed.

Whilst the Luddites continued their machine wrecking, the North of England also saw both peaceful demonstrations such as the March of the Blanketeers in 1816 and more militant action like the Pentrich Uprising of the following year. There was also unrest in the capital with 1816's Spa Field Riots, intended originally to be a peaceful protest but hijacked by revolutionaries with stolen arms.

Disturbances like this were far more prevalent during the years directly after the Napoleonic Wars than they ever had been at the conflict's height. Yet whilst there was undoubtedly the momentum for revolution it was never really matched by a strong enough inclination. Many of the leading figures of the movement, such as 'Orator' Hunt, were advocates of peaceful protest and the radical fringes never made enough headway into the mainstream.

But Liverpool's ministry - like Pitt the Younger's before it - was taking no chances. The most infamous demonstration that took place in this period was the 1819 rally at St. Peter's Fields in Manchester, organised by the vociferous Parliamentary reformer Henry 'Orator' Hunt. He was midway into a speech concerning the absurdity of a large, industrial powerhouse such as Manchester remaining unrepresented in Parliament, when the meeting was suddenly and violently broken up by the local militia. These were not the highly skilled and organised troops that had battled Napoleon and within minutes they had bulldozed through the crowd killing 11 and wounding a further 400.

Yet far from decrying this appallingly disproportionate military intervention - which has gone down in history as the Peterloo Massacre - the government took it as its cue to stamp down hard on any kind of public disorder, no matter how peaceful or innocuous. Liverpool had already suspended Habeas Corpus in the wake of the Pentrich Uprising and now his Home Secretary Lord Sidmouth -aka the former Prime Minister Henry Addington - passed the incredibly repressive Six Acts.

These forbade all unpermitted public meetings, gave local magistrates almost limitless powers, restricted bail conditions and criminalized firearms. The acts were also aimed squarely at printed matter as well as public actions. There was an increase in the penalties for authors of agitating pamphlets and a tax on newspapers to discourage any publications that did not toe the government line.

But Liverpool was no Pitt the Younger and he and his government had badly misjudged the mood of the time. The unveiling of the Six Acts inspired the Cato Street Conspiracy of the following year, and although this plot to assassinate the Prime Minister and his cabinet was foiled it was evident that there would be more attempted executions should the government continue down such a repressive road. By ham-fisted clampdowns Liverpool had only intensified the disaffection and anger in the country and it was clear that something would have to give. The stage was set for a crusade to reform not only Parliament but the entire moral fabric of the country.

6

THE FIGHT FOR REFORM

By 1822 the voting franchise, division of constituencies and electoral process of Great Britain was not fit for purpose. The Industrial Revolution had ushered in a new epoch in human civilization and drastically transformed the geopolitics of the nation. In the space of a few decades Britain had gone from a predominantly rural country dependent on agricultural produce to the greatest industrialised society in the world. Urban metropolises like Manchester, Leeds and Birmingham were at the forefront of the kind of mass production unheard of 50 years earlier.

Yet Parliament had stood still, stubbornly refusing to acknowledge the rise of urbanised areas and clinging to an anachronistic golden age of country squires and landed gentry. Most of the new municipal powerhouses had no Parliamentary representation whatsoever whilst in a 'pocket borough' like Old Sarum in Salisbury – former seat of none other than Pitt the Elder – wealthy landowners would install friends and family to ensure the desired parliamentary candidate was returned. The preponderance of these 'rotten boroughs' – often areas of uninhabited marshland or medieval ruins – not only grossly distorted the spread of the population throughout the country, they also facilitated a culture of corruption and privilege which stifled any attempt at reform from within Parliament. Politicians who lost their seat in one constituency could easily have another one 'found' for them by a vested interest, which is how so many desperately bad MPs managed to hang around for so long.

Hand in hand with this geographical inequality went a convoluted and multifarious voting franchise. There were both county and borough elections and the qualifications to be able to vote in each were completely different. To form part of the county electorate you only had to be a landowner whose land brought in a rent of 40 shillings per annum, whereas borough qualifications varied depending on which borough you happened to be in. Thus in some all freemen could vote and in others membership of the borough corporation was required. But regardless of which archaic process was implemented in which constituency the fact remained that only a fraction of the population was allowed to vote.

Essentially, only men with significant property were considered to have a stake in the running of the nation. This figure was roughly 500,000 out of a population of nearly 20 million. Those who worked every hour in the day to earn enough to survive on clearly didn't merit a vote and, even if they did, their innate ignorance and philistinism would undoubtedly mean that they would make the wrong decision.

And even those who were enfranchised were required to publically announce their vote as they were casting it, thus adding to the culture of patronage, bribery and intimidation. Electoral corruption had been widespread since Walpole's day but the country had changed out of all recognition since then. There was growing bitterness that the majority of society had no say in who their leaders would be.

As we have seen, the dire economic situation after 1815 brought many of these grievances out into the open. The suppression so callously enacted by Lord Liverpool's Tory government reinforced the sense that the masses were a troublesome irrelevance to the ruling elite and therefore the only way for them to get their voices heard was wholesale reform of the Parliamentary system. But whether they had a realistic chance of getting what they wanted was an entirely different matter.

1822 was the year that Lord Liverpool and his cabinet suddenly embarked on a different course. The accepted wisdom is that the suicide of Castlereagh and the departure of Lord Sidmouth removed the two most reactionary Tories from the cabinet, allowing a younger generation of more liberal, reform-minded ministers to assert their authority.

There may be some truth in this. Sidmouth's replacement at the Home Office was the intellectually brilliant Robert Peel who, alongside the other liberal newcomers William Huskisson and Frederick Robinson, wasted no time in implementing a number of progressive policies. In short order they drafted a general reduction on import tariffs, the easing of the Navigation Acts which limited foreign trade within the empire and the amendment of the Corn Law by introducing a more flexible sliding scale of duties. All these policies were designed to stimulate free trade which had fallen from favour due to the siege mentality fostered by the Napoleonic wars. Peel was just as big a cheerleader for free trade as Pitt the Younger had been, although he would later face a battle against the mercantile tradition within his own party that would come to destroy his career. In addition to the above measures the Combination Acts outlawing trade unions were repealed and the prison system underwent a moderate level of reform. The high profile of George Canning at the Foreign Office also contributed to a more muscular liberalism within the Tory high command.

But such a dramatic U-turn in government policy cannot simply be accounted for by a moderate change of personnel. The deceptively shrewd Liverpool had finally recognised that fighting against reform was a battle he could never hope to win. The calls for change were coming from too many sections of society and areas of the country to continue to be quashed by draconian legislation. Despite the tax legions of newspapers were being launched, all agitating for reform, whilst the number of high profile campaigners such as William Cobbett and Leigh Hunt was growing by the day.

Yet Liverpool's ministry stopped short of actual Parliamentary reform. A concrete change to the franchise or the existing electoral map was anathema to what was still a strongly traditional Tory government at heart. The gradual amelioration of various social problems and a move to more enlightened economic policy was as far as they were prepared to go.

All of this started to unravel with the loss of Liverpool to a stroke in 1827. His underrated ability to manage a cabinet of large egos with differing opinions was sorely missed as the government yo-yoed between the autocratic hectoring of Canning and the lily-livered cluelessness of Robinson - now Viscount Goderich. Within two years they were on to their third choice of leader, the legendary hero of Waterloo Arthur Wellesley, Duke of Wellington.

However, the assumption that a leader of military genius would also be a leader of political genius was soon disproved. Pivotal things were accomplished during his administration – Peel's creation of the Metropolitan Police in 1829 and Wellington's own insistence on a measure of Catholic emancipation for Ireland – but subtle party diplomacy was alien to the Iron Duke and he stretched the existing rifts within the Tories to breaking point. In fairness to Wellington Catholic emancipation was a surprisingly enlightened and brave step to take but it infuriated the 'ultra' right-wing of the party. The Prime Minister's attempts to win them round backfired spectacularly and, whilst he officially resigned over a separate, comparatively trivial matter, it was clear that it had been the Irish issue that had sealed his ministry's fate. When the virulently anti-Whig George IV died in 1830 the effective prohibition on non-Tory governments was lifted, inaugurating a Whig hegemony.

The Whig governments that dominated the 1830s are commonly seen as a beacon of progressive light, embracing reform wholeheartedly in a manner that the Tories - perpetually terrified of any change to the existing order - never could. Yet we should be cautious in attributing too much radical zeal to the ministry of Earl Grey in particular. The admittedly impressive slew of legislation passed by the Whigs was a combination of three distinct factors - the paternalistic notion of a cadre of aristocrats bestowing benevolence and generosity to those less fortunate than themselves, the opportunistic enfranchising of the kinds of people who would be likely to vote for their party and the pragmatic necessity to forestall full-blown democracy by granting a number of carefully formulated concessions.

The touchstone Reform Act of 1832 is a case in point. In 1830 the resumption of home grown unrest in the form of the Swing Riots, a rebellion of Southern farm workers, reinforced the sense that Britain was a powder keg with an ever-shortening fuse. Unlike Lord Liverpool, however, the new Prime Minister Earl Grey realised that only through Parliamentary reform would the kind of revolutionary activity that was currently rampaging throughout Europe be averted in the United Kingdom.

What this expressly did *not* mean was the kind of democracy adopted by the blossoming United States of America. The idea of all men being created equal - unless you happened to be a slave of course - was repellent even to the more Foxite members of the government. The Whigs may not have despised the working classes as thoroughly as the Tories did but they certainly did not think they should be trusted with any degree of power. The raison d'etre of Parliamentary reform as far as the Whigs were concerned was to enfranchise the rapidly expanding middle class, partly because they had a genuine respect for their abilities but primarily because they would probably cast their newly won votes for the Whigs. The same was true of the branch of the Act that dealt with redistribution of constituencies. It made perfect political sense for the Whigs to want the big Northern cities – packed with self-made businessmen and industrialists - represented at the expense of minute pocket boroughs that were entirely controlled by the landed classes.

The Great Reform Act was chiefly the handiwork not of Grey but the younger Liberal - with a capital L - pioneer Lord John Russell. He had originally proposed a reform bill as early as 1822 which had been met with predictable horror from Liverpool's government. Much of his time in frustrated opposition had been spent redrafting another proposal and, despite the fact that he was only a junior minister, the 1831 bill was fundamentally his creation.

Inevitable as the Reform Act appears to modern eyes it had a torturous path through both Houses, encountering ferocious opposition before eventually becoming law. The bill brought before the House of Commons in 1831 proposed the electoral extinction of 60 boroughs that had populations of less than 2,000 and the redistribution of 97 seats to the counties and – crucially - the industrial metropolises such as Manchester, Leeds and Birmingham. In addition, 47 boroughs that were represented by dual MPs would now have a sole representative. In regards to the voting franchise the proposals were less dramatic - the boroughs would now have a flat £10 household value as the voting qualification whilst the counties embraced £10 copyholders and £50 leaseholders as well as those who held a 40 shilling freehold. In real terms this meant an increase in the franchise from 500,000 people to 700,000 – or from 5% to 7%.

As expected it was a deal aimed squarely at the middle classes rather than a radical bid for universal suffrage but the bill was still far too lenient for most Tories. It squeaked through the Commons by a single vote but was, unsurprisingly, defeated in the Lords. This led to a further upsurge in violent disturbances around the country, although there is a certain irony to the fact that these were mainly working class rebellions – exactly the section of society that the Act would still exclude from the franchise.

The following year Grey tried again. Once more the bill passed the Commons but looked set to be blocked by the Lords. But this time Grey took precautions, persuading a reluctant William IV to create sufficient Whig peers for the bill to be passed. In the end the mere threat of an upper chamber heaving with Whig lords proved enough for Wellington and a hundred other Tories to abstain. The 1832 reform bill had passed into law.

In terms of the level of actual reform delivered the Great Reform Act is dwarfed by the subsequent legislation of 1867 and 1884. Its significance lies more in the fact that - as the strongly anti-reform minded Robert Peel warned at the time - it opened the door for greater policy changes further down the line. Considering the stubborn insistence from the Tories that any change to the constitution, no matter how small, risked violent revolution it was remarkable that any legislation on Parliamentary reform had wound up on the statute books at all.

But it did not take long for the working classes to realise that they had been tricked. In 1834 a group of farm workers were sentenced to transportation after pressing for an increase in wages. The judgement outraged not just the working class but many liberal-minded members of the middle class also. The six men became known as the Tolpuddle Martyrs and provided a symbol of the continued injustice suffered by those excluded from the vote.

The subsequent Chartist movement - inspired by the London Working Men's Association of William Lovett - claimed that the working classes were actually worse off than they had been before the Great Reform Act. Since the middle classes had now joined the aristocracy in the gilded tower of enfranchisement the oppression and persecution of the working class was compounded. The six points of the 1838 People's Charter harked back to the Levellers of the Civil War - universal manhood suffrage, annual Parliaments, payment for MPs, abolition of property qualifications for those same MPs, the secret ballot and equal electoral districts.

Whilst undoubtedly a valuable outlet for disaffected members of the working class and a precursor to the modern trade unions the Chartist movement was brushed aside contemptuously by the ruling elite. Three petitions were presented to the government between 1839 and 1848 and all were completely disregarded. This was a risky strategy from successive governments as there was a distinct possibility that such a high handed attitude would result in widespread rioting. But in the end the Chartists could never quite bring themselves to follow through on their threats and the movement had fizzled out by the 1850s.

The Whig governments of Grey and Melbourne probably felt secure enough given the raft of reforming legislation that had been implemented and, indeed, this had been the plan all along. A substantial amount of reform had been inevitable in the wake of the Napoleonic wars and if

Parliament were seen to be doing their bit then the measures that would irrevocably alter the landscape of the electorate – measures such as those demanded by the People's Charter – could be unequivocally abandoned. Yet the aloof, detached style of government that the Whigs embodied was already becoming outmoded as the focus of Parliamentary life began to switch inexorably from the Lords to the Commons.

But we should not be too cynical of the Whigs' motivations. After all, the most welcome piece of reforming legislation that they passed was the total abolition of slavery throughout the British Empire. The outlawing of slavery had been progressing piecemeal for a number of decades, first in Britain and then in terms of the specifics of the trade. The 1833 Abolition Act brought a sense of closure to the process – literally, for its most longstanding and fervent campaigner.

William Wilberforce died one month before the bill passed into law but he had already been assured of its success by Parliament. A cheerful and considerate man by nature he converted to evangelical Christianity in 1785, a decision which committed him to a lifetime seeking reform and alleviating human suffering. His overt religiosity was frowned on at a time when, although the nation was overwhelmingly Christian, worship was viewed as a respectful, sombre activity rather than an emotive and impassioned one. Wilberforce had worked tirelessly for the abolitionist cause since meeting a naval officer called James Ramsay in 1783, who related tales of the dreadful treatment that slaves were subjected to in the West Indies. It was largely due to Wilberforce's influence that abolitionism remained a live issue for so many years. He is now justly celebrated as a Christian hero and a pioneering campaigner for human rights.

Compared to the abolition of slavery the other reforms that the Whigs pushed through necessarily look smaller. In theory the Factory Act of 1833 was an enlightened piece of legislation that worked to ameliorate another social evil - that of child labour. It banned the employment of children under nine and limited the working hours of those aged nine to 13 to eight hours per day. In practice, however, the Act proved impossible to enforce with an inadequate supply of inspectors and cunning factory owners crafting various ingenious methods to get around it. The same was broadly true of attempts to limit the working hours of young children in the mining industry.

But if the Factory Act was a well-meaning but ultimately unworkable attempt to improve the lot of the poor then the 1834 amendment to the Poor Law – the benefits system of its day - served only to compound the misery of those in dire poverty. After a royal commission reported that the existing system was open to too much abuse the government cracked down on those seeking poor relief by making the only alternative to employment - the workhouse - as unattractive as possible. It is from this point that the Dickensian vision of the workhouse as a vicious, filthy hell on earth comes into the culture and there was outrage at the time over the brutality of such legislation from a supposedly compassionate government. The Whigs viewed it as one of their crowning achievements.

The years 1834-5 were something of a watershed, however, and once more it was Ireland that proved the flashpoint. The issue of appropriation of Irish church funds for secular purposes was both indirectly responsible for Grey's resignation and directly responsible for the sacking of his successor Lord Melbourne by an increasingly agitated William IV. When Robert Peel's royally sanctioned ministry inevitably lost the 1835 general election the sheepish monarch had no option but to recall the quietly authoritative Melbourne. But now Melbourne had a bargaining chip and refused to budge on the matter of Irish church fund appropriation. William IV caved and handed the new Whig administration exactly the kind of autonomy that his meddling had been designed to avert.

Suddenly there were marked successes. The 1835 Municipal Corporations Act was a microcosm of the Great Reform Act at local government level and resulted in the ending of self-electing aristocratic monopolies in local councils. The act also legislated for the devolving of certain responsibilities for sanitation and public health as well as the rights of councils and JPs to form their own police forces. Reforms of the Church of England were also long overdue and the Ecclesiastical Commissions Act -

also of 1835 - centralized and tightened up the disparate financial situations of individual dioceses as well as providing a raft of new civil rights for dissenters. Reductions in stamp tax and the introduction of the penny post made news and newspapers more accessible to the masses than they had ever been.

Yet by the end of the decade it was apparent that the Whigs had run out steam. The Lichfield House Compact of 1835 - engineered by Lord John Russell - had bound radical and Irish MPs into a Parliamentary voting bloc against the newly fashioned Conservatives. What had seemed like a smart move at the time looked more and more like desperation as Whig reforming zeal began to dissipate. Poor harvests had also bumped the issue of the Corn Laws up the agenda and Melbourne's advocacy of their repeal alienated the vast majority of aristocratic voters.

The Whig pre-eminence came to an end at the general election of 1841 when Peel's new look Conservative ministry, which had cannily presented itself as the true party of reform, swept into power. It was perhaps the misfortune of Melbourne to come up against such a strong and perceptive opposition leader as Robert Peel, a man who understood better than anybody of the period the vital importance of public image. The Whigs would reclaim power in 1846 but by then the unofficial moniker 'Liberal' was starting to be employed to describe them. By the late 1850s the Whig party would be dead and the political landscape of Britain would look totally different.

7

CORN AND CONSERVATISM

As the Whigs celebrated their return to power in 1830 the Tories were not just licking their wounds, they were gleefully re-opening them. Wellington's support for Catholic emancipation had driven a wedge through the party that appeared terminal. The hard right 'ultra' Tories saw any concessions to the Catholics as closet Jacobitism and were appalled by what they viewed as a betrayal of principles from the otherwise firmly traditional Iron Duke. Faced with such perceived treachery the Ultras, led by Edward Knatchbull, opted to bring down their own government. Perversely they sided with the Whigs over the issue of Parliamentary reform, thus making Wellington's position all but untenable - although he did himself few favours by sticking to his dogmatic assertion that any kind of reform of the current system was completely unnecessary. At a time when the Whigs were portraying themselves as enlightened harbingers of progressive change the Tories had shown themselves to be petty, blinkered and even more inflexible than their reputation proclaimed.

At war with themselves and deeply unpopular in the country they may never have recovered. Fortunately for the party their new leader was a skilful student of Parliamentary practice, shrewd enough to realise that the now toxic Tory image had to undergo a massive ideological overhaul and dextrous enough to take the majority of his fellow MPs with him. However, this same boldness in policy making would ultimately be his undoing. As many a future Conservative leader has come to appreciate, underestimating the right-wing of the party is folly of the highest order.

The son of a wealthy textile manufacturer Robert Peel was a product of middle class aspiration at the time when the Industrial Revolution was threatening the hegemony of the landed classes. His sharp political brain could not have been more at odds with the empty headed aristocrats with whom he shared the Parliamentary sphere. He entered politics in 1809 as MP for Cashel in Tipperary, Ireland - a rotten borough secured for him by the Duke of Wellington who would become Peel's closest professional ally. After a stunning maiden speech in the House of Commons the following year he served his political apprenticeship diligently in a number of junior posts before becoming Home Secretary in Lord Liverpool's more reform-minded cabinet in 1822.

Whilst his bond with Wellington was strong Peel possessed a greater ability to play the political game than his friend. He instinctively knew when to hold to a firm line and when to subtly adapt his position. For example, Peel was just as firm a supporter of Catholic emancipation as the Duke but was able to avoid the ire of the Ultras as his previous position was not regarded as so intractable. On the issue of Parliamentary reform he wisely chose to stick to his guns when Wellington accepted the argument for limited change in 1832. Such a stand may have run counter to the prevailing political wind but it both shielded him from the accusations of hypocrisy levelled at his comrade and endeared him to the powerful right-wing of his party. Two years later, as Prime Minister and party leader, he would change his public opinion but by that point the Great Reform Act had been passed and the furore had abated. This Machiavellian talent was not inexhaustible, however, and Peel's attempt to juggle the requirements of party leadership with the aspirations of statesmanship would ultimately do more damage to his party than Wellington ever could.

When William IV controversially selected a Tory ministry in 1834 it was Peel who was nominated Prime Minister. In truth, the position at that time was a poisoned chalice, with the Tories simply not ready to reclaim power. Their operating as a minority government quickly proved unworkable and yet the episode was highly important in one very specific sense. In the general election of early 1835 Peel himself was to contest the constituency of Tamworth and, although he was standing unopposed, took the opportunity to publish a manifesto which effectively rebranded the Tories as a party of moderate reform.

In one of Peel's many deft changes of ideological course he - and the Tories - now recognised the legality and authority of the changes to the electoral system made in the Great Reform Act. This was a cleverly timed U-turn which forced the Ultras into a corner. In addition to the specific acknowledgement of the Great Reform Act the Tamworth Manifesto also spoke of embracing change in a general manner not even hinted at in any Tory document hitherto. It was beginning to look for all the world as though the Tories were trying to turn themselves into the Whigs. It was here that Peel was at his most politically astute. He accepted the fact that the mood of the nation was strongly in favour of reform and that if the Tories continued to be the party of stasis and tradition they would be obliterated. But the dilemma was how to present a more liberal side to the party that didn't just look like a sudden volte face to steal Whig voters - which is essentially what it was. Peel skilfully emphasised his own reforms as Home Secretary in Liverpool's government and managed to convey the impression that the Tories had always been supporters of gradual reform as a method of strengthening the established system. This was Whiggism in all but name but the party - presumably recognising that they had no choice if they ever wanted to regain sustained power - swallowed it.

The manifesto was not enough to swing the general election - which saw the Whigs comfortably returned to power - but it signalled a crucial moment in the history of the Conservative party. For that was the term that was being used ever more frequently to describe this new brand of Toryism and even when the hard-right regained control of the party the name stuck. From 1834 onwards the word Tory slips out of common usage as an official title, surviving only as a nickname - derogatory or otherwise.

It would be another six years before Peel's Conservatives would find themselves back in government as the reforming measures of the Whigs gained them a great deal of support and goodwill amongst the voting public. They also enjoyed the unexpected support of the opposition leader in a number of matters, for Peel voted with them on policies such as the amendment to the Poor Law and the Municipal Corporations Act. Effectively keeping your opponents in power for long periods might seem like a wilfully perverse action to take but here again Peel demonstrated the kind of strategic genius that marked him down as the first truly modern politician.

Having dragged his party into a position where they were seen as moderate reformers it would have been highly inadvisable for them to then oppose all the reforming legislation that the Whigs proposed. It was playing a very long game but Peel considered it more advantageous to bide his time in rational opposition and simply wait for the Whigs to run out of ideas. Then, when that time came - as, of course, it did - the Conservatives' record as sympathetic to moderate change would be unblemished and they would become eminently electable.

Once more in power Peel continued to keep a cool head and displayed admirable judgement and foresight, particularly in his handling of the economy. His belief in the principle of free trade governed his decision to reduce - and in some cases entirely remove - tariffs on a considerable number of imports. The consequent revival in trade coupled with the controversial reintroduction of income tax helped to reduce the national deficit that the Whigs had let drift out of control. Additionally, the strengthening of the Bank of England and the enforced registration of companies tightened up a decidedly baggy financial sector.

But by 1844 it was not just the Ultras who were beginning to get restless. Having united the disparate interests of the party for so long – as well as attracting a considerable number of middle class voters that had defected from the Whigs – the Prime Minister found himself under attack from a variety of different factions. On the one hand there were the increasingly embittered landed gentry and aristocracy - who formed the majority of the Ultras' ranks - who saw their entire philosophy and way of life being steadily eroded by some metropolitan arriviste. On the other were the Young England group who pined for an idyllic agricultural nation with a rigid yet harmonious social hierarchy. Both of these groups had a reactionary nostalgia for a so-called 'golden age' wiped out by the Industrial Revolution, but a third faction opposed Peel for more progressive reasons.

For all of his undeniable economic acumen Peel had always been less concerned with remedying social problems. Whether from a belief that improving the overall economic situation would necessarily lead to humanitarian benefits or simply from a lack of interest in the minutiae of social reform little had been done during his ministry to alleviate the suffering of the poor. His most vociferous critic on this issue was Anthony Ashley Cooper, 7th Earl of Shaftesbury and descendant of the Whig agitator who had tried to excise James II from the royal line. Shaftesbury was the founder of the Ten Hours Committee which sought to limit the working day for women and children in textile mills to ten hours, a proposition that Peel had conspicuously refused to countenance.

The trouble with the Prime Minister was that his image of himself was of a statesman rather than a party leader. After the self-destruction of his friend Wellington Peel was reluctant to take responsibility for the party leadership and his open acknowledgement of preference for the national good rather than party advantage was an added source of resentment to his more partisan colleagues. At the same time these fundamentally noble motives led to a grandiose desire to tackle huge, abstract issues and thereby lose any empathy for the individual. He would rather play God than a social worker.

A prime example of the disconnect between executive power and party allegiance was his attitude towards Ireland. Enhanced rights for Catholics and the perceived denigration of the Anglican Church in Ireland were thorny problems for a succession of 19th century British Prime Ministers - as we have already seen in the cases of Wellington, Grey and Melbourne -

and Peel's apparent sympathy for the Catholic cause aroused considerable dissent within the government. In reality Peel was just trying to temper the belligerence of the pro-independence Irish MP Daniel O'Connell. But Ireland's exemption from income tax, a commission into the examination of Irish grievances and – particularly - a threefold increase in funding for the Maynooth Catholic Seminary seemed inherently contrary to Conservative ideology for more traditionally minded party members.

For a while Peel's natural brilliance forestalled any crisis. But, as an avowed supporter of free trade, there was one piece of legislation that he passionately believed must be repealed. His attempt to force this through Parliament would split the Conservatives irrevocably and lead to the formation of the other great political party of the next 70 years. The political landscape would be forever altered by the issue of corn.

For aristocratic landowners the end of the Napoleonic Wars brought serious concerns about renewed imports of grain. The 1815 Corn Law - which prevented the release of imported corn until the home price had reached 80 shillings per quarter - had been passed to protect these producers from the threat of economic ruin that cheap foreign corn posed. But, by keeping prices artificially high, this practice did little to help the masses struggling to adapt to a depressed peacetime state. The Law not only cut to the heart of inequality in nineteenth century Britain - the landed classes were to be aided at the expense of everybody else – it highlighted the clash between old fashioned mercantilism and the global business of free trade.

None of which would have mattered quite so much had the Corn Law worked, but the combination of unpredictable harvests and erratic foreign supply led to precisely the kind of fluctuations in price that the Law was enacted to guard against. Rather than scrap them altogether two further revisions in 1822 and 1828 first added a fixed and then a sliding scale of duties. These measures were supposed to make the system more flexible but ended up just making its workings even more impenetrable.

But protection of corn ran deep into the psyche of Britain's ruling elite. Peel may have won his party around to a primarily free trade policy but grain was one of the fundamental products for any nation and this lent it an almost sacred air - tamper with British corn and you tamper with the bedrock of the country. This was, after all, the issue that had finally seen off Melbourne's Whigs and with so many Conservatives also landed gentry it was one matter of self-interest that was too precious to sacrifice upon the altar of reform.

But if he did not have the support of his party then Peel did possess considerable backing in the country as a whole. The Anti-Corn Law League, set up in 1838, was arguably the most successful British pressure group formed in the entire 19th century. Tellingly, it was not an organisation of working men - unlike the worthy but ineffective Chartist movement - but a specifically middle class concern, led by businessmen, merchants and manufacturers. These champions of industry had the resources to hire solicitors, establish regional operations and run a highly efficient national campaign that took in everything from fundraising bazaars to the launch of their own specialised newspapers.

It helped that their argument was so cogent and logical. Britain, they stated, was no longer a predominantly agricultural society and to snub foreign markets because of a romantic hankering for a declining way of life was cutting the nation's nose off to spite its face. The complete opening up of Britain to global trade would also lead to growing cooperation between the nations of the world and hence the mutually beneficial propagation of lasting peace. In addition to this spirit of internationalism there were obvious advantages for the country's poor - if the price of grain fell then wages and living conditions would descend with it leading to a more contented and less irksome working class.

In contrast the confusingly named Anti-League - established to combat the growing effectiveness of the Anti-Corn Law League - was badly organised and could only put forward arguments that either reeked of self-interest or had already been disproved. It was patently obvious that the existing laws had failed whilst the acceptance by industrial manufacturers of the principles of free trade undermined the agricultural producers' claim that an example was being made of them. Also, the Anti-League only came into being in 1844, by which time the impressive progress achieved by the Anti-Corn Law League in the previous six years had already inflicted mortal blows.

Yet the fact remained that the bulk of the Conservatives would never consider voting for repeal and without their support Peel would be gambling on an alliance between the Whigs and the more radical members of his own party to force it through. His hand was forced by a humanitarian crisis across the Irish Sea which even the arch intellectual could not fail to be moved by.

The potato had been the staple crop of Ireland for several decades and bad harvests had triggered famines in 1817 and 1839. But these were as nothing to the devastation wrought by the crop failure of 1845 which resulted in the halving of the population either through starvation or emigration. The artificially high price of grain, cranked up due to the existence of the Corn Laws, made it virtually impossible to get the required help through to the country in time. Taking this as incontrovertible proof of the pernicious nature of the Corn Laws Peel set his mind to repeal them.

After a long battle he managed to persuade the majority of the cabinet to back repeal but over two thirds of the Conservative party remained unshakeable in their support of the existing system. So the Prime Minister crossed his Rubicon and, with the minority of his own party, formed a coalition with the Whigs which saw the bill passed and the Corn Laws repealed.

Four days later the government was defeated on an Irish Coercion Bill and Peel, disgusted by the intractability of the party that he had transformed in the mid-1830s, resigned, taking his band of remaining loyalists with him. They became known as the Peelites and made it their mission to contest previously safe Conservative seats, which they did with considerable success. The split was permanent - never again would Peel or his followers combine with the Conservatives. The division would forge a new party that would subsume both Peelites and Whigs and become the dominant political force for the next 40 years.

8

THE LIFE AND TIMES OF LORD CUPID

On 1st April 1818 Henry John Temple, 3rd Viscount Palmerston was striding up the steps of the War Office - his workplace as Secretary at War for the previous nine years - when a bullet passed through his coat grazing his back. In an eerie echo of Spencer Perceval's assassination the gunman, David Davies, was an unhinged lieutenant aggrieved about a pension application. Davies fared rather better than John Bellingham however - when Palmerston discovered that his assailant was insane he paid the legal costs for his defence.

It is difficult to imagine any other nineteenth century politician behaving in a similar fashion towards their would-be murderer but then Palmerston was one of the most singular public figures of the age. He entered Parliament in 1807 at the age of 23 and remained in office until 1865 when he died during his second stint as Prime Minister. A Tory in Perceval's wartime government he defected to the Whigs when they embarked upon their reforming ministries of the 1830s and wound up leading the conglomeration of Peelites, Whigs and Radicals that became known as the Liberals. As this party political flitting suggests Palmerston's ideology and beliefs were in a constant state of flux. His university education at the hands of a Whiggish moral philosopher inculcated a basic liberalism but his father's traditionalist connections meant a political apprenticeship with the Tories. As a result he was a curious mix of liberal Tory (like Canning) and disinterested reformer (like Grey). His dash and impetuosity made him a darling to the Great British public yet the jury is still out on whether he was a maverick statesman of rare stature or a womanising Regency relic who was all flash and no substance. In reality it is highly probable that he was both.

The first unpredictable thing that he did as a young MP was to turn down Perceval's offer of Chancellor of the Exchequer in 1809. Thinking himself too green for such a senior position he buried himself in the War Office for the next twenty years, supporting the more reforming measures of Liverpool's government from the side-lines. When George Canning began his short-lived administration Palmerston finally secured a seat in the cabinet, only to resign on principle when Wellington took over as Prime Minister and antagonised his friend William Huskisson. Increasingly disillusioned with the direction that the Tory party was heading in Palmerston sided with the Whigs and, upon Earl Grey's ascension to Prime Minister, was rewarded with the Foreign Office. It was a field he was to dominate for the next two decades.

If William Pitt the Elder personified the buccaneering bravado of the United Kingdom in the 18th century then Viscount Palmerston was his 19th century equivalent. He made unilateral decisions on foreign affairs of great importance, exasperating all those who were his nominal superiors, and pursued British interests with such ferocity that the term 'gunboat diplomacy' was coined to describe his uniquely aggressive style.

Yet, unlike Pitt, he had no interest in expanding the British Empire. Thanks in large part to Castlereagh and his concern for the balance of power there had been no pan-European conflict since the end of the Napoleonic Wars. That fundamental harmony would hold until the Ottoman Empire declared war on Russia in 1853, kick-starting the Crimean War. There were numerous smaller conflicts, of course, as well as bursts of revolutionary activity in 1830 and 1848, but there was nothing to match the Seven Years War or the irresistible force of Napoleon at his zenith. Consequently Palmerston saw Britain's international role much as the United States viewed hers in the early 21st century, namely that of a global policeman or trouble-shooter. She would employ her might to slap down any unwelcome scuffles between less civilized nations whilst sternly wagging a finger at her fellow superpowers should they get too ambitious . It was a matter of British prestige rather than conquest.

Yet - much like the former Foreign Secretary George Canning - Palmerston combined aggressive protection of British interests with genuinely held liberal beliefs concerning the autonomy and independence of small nations. He despised the kind of despotism prevalent in Eastern Europe and was determined to preserve freedom and liberty in the west. This standpoint resulted in increasingly bellicose sabre rattling to ensure that major conflict was averted. Palmerston's brinksmanship was brazen and frequently outrageous, yet he hardly ever blinked first and often won the day. And, what was more, he always made certain that the public knew every last detail about his achievements.

From the first he was decisive and unequivocal but also utilised a goodly amount of tact and subtlety that would desert him as he became more established. The 1830 Belgian Revolt against union with Holland was a rebellion that Palmerston the inchoate Liberal broadly approved of, but the issue was complicated by France also seeking to support the Belgians with a view to installing a puppet monarch. Whilst the Belgian cause may have been noble any attempt by Britain's old enemy to profit from it had to be quashed. Palmerston's solution was ingenious and eminently diplomatic. Britain simply clung like a limpet to French movements, closely allying with her in naval action at the mouth of the Scheldt and effectively neutralising any untoward attention towards the region. Britain and France never came to blows but there was no disputing who had come out of the situation better. He employed similar tactics to avert French and Russian gains in vulnerable Turkey throughout the decade, playing them off against each other expertly and not only preserving but strengthening the Sultan's regime.

These successes emboldened Palmerston when he returned to the Foreign Office under Lord John Russell's leadership in 1846. Always a handsome, charismatic bon viveur with a constantly rotating collection of mistresses - hence the nickname 'Lord Cupid' - he now began to cast himself as a kind of political folk hero. In so doing he became the first high profile MP to actively court the common man rather than the landed and aristocratic classes. In his manipulation of journalistic media he was as adept at public relations as Boris Johnson and he reaped similarly huge rewards. Many of his most famous speeches were available to the public in pamphlet form and he embarked on numerous sell-out speaking tours of the country. Whilst there can be little doubt that Palmerston was the most popular politician of the 19th century with the man in the street, this carefully stage managed image was not mere self-aggrandisement. Palmerston married flagrant showmanship to a sincere belief in a politician's responsibility to represent the interests of the people. While no fan of democracy in the conventional sense he nonetheless felt passionately about the duties of Edmund Burke's enlightened ruling elite.

Yet the corollary of painting yourself as a larger than life character is – as BoJo knows equally well – that it tends to lead to inadvisable statements, inappropriate jokes and just plain cringe-worthy gaffes. Hence Palmerston's disastrous attempt to avoid a marriage union between France and Spain, where he dictated to the two nations exactly who should marry whom and when, whilst simultaneously making no bones about his determination to scotch an alliance between the superpowers. Such arrogance and presumptuousness had a predictable effect on King Louis Philippe, whose eldest son was one of the betrothed. He turned the tables on Palmerston, seeming to agree to British demands before reneging at the last minute. On the other hand Palmerston's unguarded comments celebrating the beating up of an Austrian autocrat in a London brewery only further endeared him to the British people. Lord Cupid was certainly different to the parade of stiff, unapproachable politicians that they were used to.

If one incident typified Palmerston's infamous 'gunboat diplomacy' at its most spectacular it was the Don Pacifico affair of 1850. Pacifico was the Portuguese diplomatic consul in Athens and was also both of Jewish descent and, being from Gibraltar, a British subject. So when an anti-Semitic mob attacked his home and destroyed sensitive documents Pacifico sought compensation from the Greek government. When this came to nought he appealed to Britain instead.

To say that Palmerston lent his support to Pacifico would be something of an understatement. Without consulting either the French or the Russians (who also had considerable stakes in Greece), the Greek judiciary or even his own Prime Minister Palmerston felt that an ostentatious show of military power was required. He took it upon himself to dispatch a Royal Navy squadron to forcibly claim Greek property to the value of Pacifico's losses. Naturally, a British court had decided upon the wildly overestimated amount beforehand. The affair ended after two months when the Greek government - exasperated at the squadron's blockade of Athens' main port - compensated Pacifico in full.

Palmerston justified this outrageous exploit by stating – in a five hour Parliamentary speech – that it demonstrated that Britain would always come to the aid of her subjects wherever in the world they may be. His popularity with the nation soared but the government was livid. Palmerston's patriotic populism had nearly triggered a diplomatic incident with two of the largest powers in Europe and from then on the much embarrassed Russell was looking for any excuse to offload his rogue Foreign Secretary. Lord Pumice Stone – to give him his freshly created nickname - charged ahead regardless, playing into Russell's hands in 1851 by recognising the new French regime of Louis Napoleon without prior consultation with either the Prime Minister or Queen Victoria.

But instead of the anticipated slide into mediocrity his new role at the Home Office appeared to reinvigorate him. The scope of his reforming measures recalled the heyday of Grey's Whig ministry and was all the more surprising considering that Palmerston had only been a moderate supporter of social reform in the past. Factories, prisons and public health were all addressed positively whilst he showed astonishing prescience in his drafting of the Smoke Nuisance Abatement Bill of 1853, arguably the first piece of environmental legislation passed by a British government. Indeed, Palmerston's time at the Home Office had the opposite effect to the one Lord John Russell had desired. The Prime Minister – driving force behind the Great Reform Act -portrayed himself as a great Liberal pioneer and saw Palmerston's mass appeal as a direct threat to his authority. Yet far from neutralising Palmerston by dumping him in the Home Office the slew of reforming legislation that came out of that department painted him rather than Russell as the true father of liberalism. It was a turn of events that would have profound consequences in the near future.

Tellingly, the most all-encompassing military conflict since the Napoleonic Wars began when Palmerston was safely ensconced as Home Secretary. Russia's insatiable desire for imperial expansion finally came to fruition over a dispute with the Ottoman Empire concerning the rights of different Christian denominations in the Holy Land. Whether or not Palmerston would have been able to salvage the situation is a moot point but before long the Crimean War had dragged in the French and the Sardinians as well as the British. Initial setbacks culminated in the legendary military fiasco of the Charge of the Light Brigade at Balaclava and the Prime Minister, the Earl of Aberdeen, resigned amidst general dismay early in 1855. Despite Victoria's deep misgivings about Palmerston's flagrant libertinism and dangerous impulsiveness it was obvious that there was only one man for the job.

In truth Palmerston's influence on the course of the war was negligible in all but one crucial respect. On March 2nd 1855 Tsar Nicolas I died and his successor Alexander II was eager to sue for peace. Palmerston wanted to fight on but the French, who had suffered more losses than any of the other allies, were desperate for a speedy settlement. With characteristic chutzpah Palmerston persuaded Napoleon III to delay negotiations until the capture of Sevastopol as control over the Black Sea would put the allies in a superior position when it came to talks. The gamble paid off and Sevastopol fell to the allies in September. The following year's Congress of Paris resulted in a considerably more humbled Russia than would otherwise have been the case.

Feted as a war leader of genius Palmerston's popularity was at its peak. His reputation as protector of British interests around the globe was further enhanced by his abrasive conduct over the 'Arrow' affair. The 'Arrow' was a cargo ship of dubious activity which the Chinese seized in

Canton on suspicion of piracy. Although its fourteen crew members were Chinese the ship was registered as a British vessel, and when the Chinese Commissioner refused to apologise for this affront to the Crown Palmerston's response was to shell his compound. This led to a series of tit-for-tat exchanges between the two nations culminating in 1856 in the Second Opium War. Four years later - and with the aid of France, India and the United States - Britain forced the surrender of the humiliated Qing dynasty. Palmerston was proving as adept at winning wars as he had previously been at averting them.

It was, however, all downhill from there. Despite his success at the Home Office foreign affairs had always been his passion and his domestic achievements as Prime Minister were desultory. Indeed, he seemed more concerned with blocking as much legislation as he could. The same man who had reformed factories and prisons as Home Secretary was now stubbornly battling against any further reform of Parliament. His first term as Prime Minister ended with a whimper with defeat for his proposed Conspiracy to Murder Bill, which outlawed murder plotted in England but perpetrated overseas.

But - much like Pitt the Younger at the turn of the century - Palmerston so overwhelmed political life that it was inconceivable to have him rot on the backbenches. After the Conservatives proved incapable of winning a majority the 1859 general election returned a Whig government and the defeated Conservatives now tried to lure Palmerston back as party leader. Their reasoning that he had switched allegiance once in his career and, if his vanity were flattered enough, he could be tempted to do it again was sound enough. But Palmerston did not bite. Instead he did the extraordinary, which is exactly what everyone had come to expect of him by now.

Back in the days of the Glorious Revolution and Walpole's Peace politics had been a purely upper class affair. By the end of the eighteenth century a handful of professionals such as Henry Addington had forced their way in to the aristocratic club but Parliament remained overwhelmingly dominated by the landed gentry, with the voting franchise limited to the most affluent of society.

The 1832 Reform Act opened the door to the upper middle class whilst successful pressure groups such as the Anti-Corn Law League were peopled by self-made industrialists of ever growing standing and resources. The Tories/Conservatives had always been the unabashed defenders of upper class privilege and deeply hostile to any attempts at diluting aristocratic power. Whilst the Whigs were in favour of gradual progress and the amelioration of human suffering they were still a party of wealthy, titled gentry condescending to share their wisdom with the masses. The importance of a middle class manufacturer's boy like Robert Peel rising to become such an influential Prime Minister should not be underestimated. But the dynamic, creative middle classes - whose skills and money industrial Britain was built on - were still shamefully under-represented in nineteenth century party politics.

On 6th June 1859 Whigs, Peelites and Radicals convened in the Willis Rooms in St. James Street, London and officially merged into the Liberal Party. The term had been used by Lord John Russell as early as 1839 but only now did it relate to a unified political entity rather than a nebulous assortment of splinter groups from disparate parties.

The most striking aspect of the amalgam was that it gave a stronger voice to Radicals such as John Bright, co-founder of the impressive Anti-Corn Law League and ferocious advocate for the new Northern industrial hubs. As the son of a Lancashire cotton mill owner he embodied the new middle class entrepreneurs whilst as a committed Quaker he had the streak of religious reforming zeal that Wilberforce had possessed. Considered the finest Parliamentary orator since Fox Bright would wield greater influence in William Gladstone's first ministry. But it was to accommodate MPs like him that the Liberal Party came into being.

Yet however middle class and worldly its base may have been the leadership of the Liberal Party was just as rarefied as the Conservatives. The 3rd Viscount Palmerston decided to accept the position of leader and, as the election-winning Whigs had effectively been dissolved, sauntered nonchalantly back into Number 10 Downing Street as well. Other than a vague inclusiveness of the middle classes and a predictable desire for further reform it was quite difficult to piece together this new political entity's identity. There was something a little uncomfortable about the aristocratic Russell and Palmerston occupying key positions within a supposedly more egalitarian party. Yet Palmerston undoubtedly shared the belief in self-help and education that became the hallmark of Gladstone's first truly Liberal ministry, even if he disagreed about the need for Parliamentary reform.

Sadly this timely revitalisation of his political career did not seem to stem the tide of poor luck and judgement. When the American Civil War broke out in 1861 Palmerston tentatively supported the Confederacy, partly because of the Northern states' stronger dislike of the British and partly because he had one eye on the South's lucrative cotton trade. Blunders such as the sailing of the British-built Southern warship 'Alabama' despite a strict armaments embargo led to the sinking of numerous Union ships and indignant compensation claims from the North. Palmerston's pig headedness had got him into trouble before but this was just barefaced incompetence. When the Union triumphed in 1865 the ageing Prime Minister was forced to sheepishly admit he had backed the wrong side and opened stilted trading negotiations with the North.

But the fundamental problem with Palmerston's conducting of foreign policy in his twilight years was that his cherished 'gunboat diplomacy' was now an empty threat. In 1863 he responded to the Polish revolt against Russia with promises of pro-Pole military intervention which he had no intention of following through on. Then, later in the same year, he tried to pull exactly the same trick over the tussle for Schleswig-Holstein between Denmark and Prussia. Unambiguous support was declared for the Danes, only for any practical assistance to be voted down by the rest of the cabinet. On both occasions Palmerston had relied on the aggressive brinksmanship that he had used to such devastating effect earlier in his career, but, in Alexander II's Russia and Bismarck's Prussia, he found himself confronted with super-states that would not allow themselves to be browbeaten by a pompous old bully on his last legs.

As these humiliations show Britain was no longer the global powerhouse that she had been during Palmerston's glory days. His period of influence coincided perfectly with the high Victorian era, that clutch of decades where Britain was the biggest economic force in the world with a diverse and stable empire to match. It was a period of innovation both industrially and artistically with novelists such as Dickens, Trollope and Collins producing their finest work and iconoclastic figures like Ruskin and Darwin challenging the sacred cows of art and religion. Whilst Queen Victoria is rightly seen as the intelligent steadying influence on this golden period of British history it is Palmerston who arguably symbolises it more accurately - bold, enlightened and intensely patriotic yet arrogant, bullying and maddeningly impulsive. When he died in office in 1865 the world was already moving on. A formidable German state was on the rise which would soon sweep all before it and the United Kingdom could no longer afford to be the self-appointed, swaggering policeman of Europe.

But, for all his bombastic, magnetic qualities, Palmerston was never the greatest politician. He only had one concrete technique in conducting foreign policy and, as his later record shows, it was one that was soon found out and turned against him. The new generation of political leaders on both the Liberal and Conservative sides would prove to be considerably more subtle and skilful operators, as the Parliamentary battleground became bloodier than ever before.

9

THE LION AND THE UNICORN

In 1871 British party politics managed to infiltrate its way into children's literature. Sir John Tenniel's illustrations for 'Through the Looking Glass' - Lewis Carroll's characteristically absurd sequel to 'Alice's Adventures in Wonderland' - featured the two most recognisable politicians of their day cast as a slow and ponderous lion and a duplicitous, insecure unicorn. Whether or not it was Carroll's intention to satirise the Liberal leader - and then Prime Minister - William Ewart Gladstone as the lion and his Conservative counterpart Benjamin Disraeli as the unicorn, Tenniel's subversive pictures give some indication of the extent to which the intense rivalry between the two men had permeated the popular culture.

Gladstone and Disraeli's hatred of each other put even Pitt and Fox's feuding in the shade. Aside from their non-aristocratic origins they had nothing whatsoever in common and the vitriolic political discourse between them would become more and more personal as the years went on. Each fitted a Victorian stereotype to a tee. Gladstone was the stern religious moralist firmly convinced of his belief in libertarian self-help whilst Disraeli was the slippery Jewish novelist, full of charm and ingratiating words but ultimately unprincipled and selfish. The truth may have been a little more complex but their personal divisions remained immense even when their political viewpoints broadly coalesced.

Both had started out as staunch Tories but, under Peel, Gladstone had become converted to laissez-faire economics and the merits of free trade. Always a man who put great store by ethical principles he followed Peel into the political wilderness when the Prime Minister was forced to resign over the repeal of the Corn Laws. Disraeli, by contrast, was one of the leading members of the Young England group who lambasted Peel for his embracing of industry and commerce. His critics would argue that Disraeli never held a genuinely principled belief in his life and it is interesting to note that when he became party leader he was quick to break all ties with the agricultural elite. In this instance it was undoubtedly Peel's refusal to advance Disraeli's career that caused the latter to create such problems. As his future policies demonstrated Disraeli was considerably more radical than Peel, particularly in matters of Parliamentary reform.

But, in the wake of Peel's departure and yet more suicidal infighting, the Conservatives desperately needed him. Comfortably the most able politician amongst the rump of remaining MPs - all the talent having followed Peel out of the party - Disraeli became leader in all but name, managing to do what Peel never had and get the rest of the party to accept the demise of protectionism. His reward for dragging the Conservatives out of their self-induced torpor was the position of Chancellor of the Exchequer in Lord Derby's woefully inexperienced and predictably short-lived 'Who? Who? Ministry.' With no real economic grounding or financial expertise Disraeli's budget was all smoke and mirrors and attracted the full fulminating ire of Gladstone, who considered himself the true Chancellor elect. From this point on the two rising Parliamentary stars would be at permanent loggerheads.

Gladstone was only too happy to show his lightweight rival how the job should be done when he became Chancellor later in the year, in a Whig-Peelite coalition headed by Lord Aberdeen. Gladstone was precise and definitive where Disraeli had been flighty and confused, and with the mercurial Jew now firmly back in opposition for the foreseeable future the Chancellor must have felt that he had dealt his enemy a mortal blow.

But he had reckoned without Disraeli's ruthless ambition. Despite what people said about him Disraeli *did* have an unwavering and consistently held cause - it was called Benjamin Disraeli. He would do whatever it took to climb what he termed the 'greasy pole' to Parliamentary power, revelling in the discomfort and embarrassment of his fiercest competitor as he did so. In the short term that meant, paradoxically, trying to woo Gladstone back to the Conservative fold as he acknowledged that his rival's undoubted ability would be key to re-election.

Gladstone frustrated him, however, by joining the newly formed Liberals and consolidating his unassailable record at the Treasury under the maverick Palmerston. It was Gladstone who transformed the office of Chancellor from glorified accountant to the second greatest office of state. His financial rectitude and sheer capacity for hard work established a department that oversaw the minutiae of all government spending and had a significant hand in the drafting of legislation. When Palmerston – who Gladstone detested almost as much as Disraeli – died in 1865 the eminently capable Chancellor was widely seen as the Liberal heir apparent. Yet Palmerston's great rival Lord John Russell snatched the premiership instead, determined to push Parliamentary reform back to the top of the political agenda.

Calls for further change to the electoral system had become more muted during the 1850s as Britain basked in the high Victorian summer of global prestige and economic might. But as soon as the 'Palmerston Show' was over there was a renewed flurry of earnest debate about the limitations of the voting franchise. Having let the middle classes creep through the door in 1832 there was now serious talk of extending the vote to the upper echelons of the working class also. Palmerston had steadfastly obstructed this but Russell and Gladstone were all in favour and in 1866 Russell introduced a bill that gave the vote to £7 borough householders and £14 county tenants.

Whilst the Conservatives were limbering up to attack the bill for being too extreme the Radical element within the Liberals stole a march on them by savaging it for not being extreme enough. Disraeli then employed all his Machiavellian genius to form an alliance with the more right-of-centre Liberals, diluting the proposals to such an extent that Russell resigned in disgust. Once again finding himself as Chancellor in a minority government led by Lord Derby, Disraeli set about one of the most audacious conjuring tricks in British political history.

Rather than abandoning the very idea of further reform Disraeli persuaded the weak-willed Derby to introduce a Conservative bill that went even further than that proposed by Russell's Liberals. This bill, which extended the franchise to include all borough householders, looked as though it had been drawn up with the sole intention of pulling the rug from under Gladstone's feet. Worse was to come for the Liberal lion. As he raged against the bill during its arduous passage through the Commons Disraeli was giving the performance of his career, gleefully accepting countless Liberal amendments from anybody other than Gladstone. By the time the bill had passed the Lords in August 1867 it had enfranchised more than double the number of new voters proposed by its Liberal forebear.

Disraeli had triumphantly achieved all that he had set out to do. The defeat of Gladstone had, of course, been delicious but it was actually secondary to Disraeli's key intention of switching the association of reform from the Whigs/Liberals to the Conservatives. Quite how Disraeli managed to get such an incredibly radical reform bill past his own deeply reactionary party remains something of a mystery. It speaks both to a creative skill possibly acquired in his secondary career as a novelist and an unparalleled ability to twist every situation to his advantage.

With the resignations of both Russell and Derby in late 1867 and early 1868 respectively, Gladstone became leader of the Liberals whilst Disraeli - astonishingly considering his background and religious origins - rose to the position of Prime Minister. It was, however, to prove something of a false dawn. His minority government was defeated in the 1868 general election after Gladstone, the devout adherent of the Church of England, had questioned the Anglican Church's supremacy over predominantly Roman Catholic Ireland. Disraeli's ignorance was painfully exposed and Gladstone replaced him as Prime Minister with a majority of over 100.

It was the first of Gladstone's four ministries that epitomised the curious dualism of 'Gladstonian Liberalism.' Whilst a muscular Anglican of the highest order he was surprisingly tolerant of other denominations and faiths. Gladstone viewed religion as an individual expression of free will and whilst he fervently believed in Christian doctrine as preached by the Church of England he recognised that he had come to that belief through his own personal journey. Everybody had the right to their own specific religious quest and given time, he believed, the masses would embrace God of their own volition rather than by being persecuted into false faith.

The corollary of this religious tolerance was its emphasis on free will and individual choice. Gladstone may have supported reform and had an instinctual love for 'the people' but the poor and destitute were required to help themselves at least as much as the state aided them. There would be enlightened, moral legislation under a Gladstonian government but there would be no free rides. In addition to this small state ethic Gladstone's Peelite heritage inculcated the virtues of free trade into the Liberal doctrine, an economic formula that would be co-opted by the Conservatives in the following century.

The 1870 Education Act is emblematic of Gladstone's approach. The organisation of the country into school districts under the control of separate boards devolved power to local government – although they had very strict guidelines on the minimum educational levels expected – whilst the increased literacy of the nation's schoolchildren would, in theory, enable them to better themselves both intellectually and morally. Whilst Gladstone put significantly more store by the moral than the intellectual aspect the establishment of education as compulsory - effectively a human right - and its subsidisation for the poorest in society remains a noble policy for the improvement of the younger generation.

The case can be made equally for Gladstone's empowering of the middle and lower classes. Like the good middle class liberal that he was Gladstone detested arbitrary privilege and his reform of the civil service in 1871 introduced grading and public examination to ensure that the most competent man was found for each position regardless of wealth or heredity. Thus the aristocratic chaff was eliminated and the system became as close to a meritocracy as was possible in 19th century Britain. A similarly egalitarian philosophy was also introduced into the army. And now that Disraeli's audacious reform bill had enfranchised some strata of the working classes it was necessary to appeal to the common man as well. Here, however, Gladstone's approach was a little fudged. For while he legalised trade unions and recognised the right to strike he also banned picketing, although this was perhaps consistent with his firm views on individual choice.

Yet there was one issue which overrode all others in all four of Gladstone's ministries and that was Ireland. The resolution of Irish unrest became an overarching personal obsession for the morally crusading Prime Minister and his first government alone saw a flurry of legislation aimed at redressing the balance between the Catholic majority and Protestant minority. Whilst the dramatic, complex story of the Irish question will be examined separately in this book, it is important to understand why Gladstone made it his life's work to rescue Ireland from conflict and hate.

As previously stated Gladstone did not believe in ramming his own personal Anglicanism down the throats of those of different denominations and this extended to the Roman Catholics who dominated the Irish population. The power and authority of the Church of England - and by extension Protestant landowners - in a predominantly Catholic country was fundamentally unjust and required remedy. In addition the Liberals were still a young political party searching for a big issue to unify the ragbag of former Whigs, Peelites and Radicals and in the complicated and emotive Irish struggle Gladstone believed they had found it. Therefore a torrent of bills was decisively introduced tackling a broad range of contentious issues. Religious inequalities were addressed via the 1869 Disestablishment of the Irish Church Act, which toppled Anglicanism from its perch as the country's official religion. Abuses by Protestant landlords were covered by the First Irish Land Act of 1870 -which stopped landlords from charging exorbitant rents and protected evicted tenants - and educational prejudices were tackled head on by the creation of a Catholic university in 1873.

Needless to say that these reforming measures were not welcomed by the Anglican elite. Naturally Disraeli seized on every opportunity to criticise and belittle Gladstone's Irish policies, combining his argument with an attack on the Prime Minister's weak stance on global affairs. Gladstone's foreign policy was directly influenced by Castlereagh and the preservation of the balance of power, although to some extent he agreed with Palmerston's conception of Britain as a peacekeeping European policeman. The trouble was that by 1870 the other European superpowers were beginning to stretch their muscles again. The freshly unified Germany was now the most formidable nation-state on the continent, making great economic and technological strides that the fading Britannia could not hope to match. Additionally the Franco-Prussian War, Russia's aggressive denial of Black Sea neutrality and the Paris Commune were all dark portents of the carnage to come. Gladstone's United Kingdom failed to either avert or capitalise on these flashpoints, providing the Conservative leader with precisely the ammunition he needed to paint his rival as an unpatriotic and ineffective excuse for an international statesman.

The effect was cumulative rather than immediate but by 1874 Disraeli had secured a general election which he micromanaged with obsessive brilliance. Returned to power with a comfortable majority the low born Jewish arriviste could finally implement a governmental programme of his own and - possibly of greater importance to him - rub salt in Gladstone's wounds on a daily basis.

Once again Disraeli took delight in adapting Gladstone's cornerstone policies to his own ends, frequently taking them further than the Liberals had when in power. In an early triumph of nebulous spin the new Prime Minister unveiled 'One Nation Conservatism', an ideological platform that broke with old style 'Tory' philosophy quite spectacularly. With both eyes fixed keenly on the new working class base of the electorate he rebranded the Conservatives as the party of the common man, emphasising the betrayals and half measures of previous Whig and Liberal governments. In fairness to Disraeli this radical reinterpretation of Conservative ideology was broadly consistent with the opinions that he espoused as leader of the Young England group in the 1840s, when he railed against Peel's veneration of the commercial middle class at the expense of the lower orders.

And for all its rank opportunism 'One Nation Conservatism' became Disraeli's greatest gift to the Conservative party. Its crafty repositioning of the party as representative of the working classes capitalised on the hugely expanded electorate that had resulted from Disraeli's astounding Reform Act. Undoubtedly it rescued the Conservatives from electoral oblivion in a more lasting way than Peel's rebrand managed and, despite its explicit rejection by Disraeli's successor Lord Salisbury, the concept continually reappeared in Conservative governments through the years.

Disraeli wasted little time in reversing Gladstone's ban on picketing and introduced the Employers and Workmen Act of 1875 which levelled the legal playing field between employers and employees in instances of breach of contract. Factory reform was also instigated by cutting the working day by 30 minutes to ten hours and raising the minimum working age from eight to ten. Small factories were also brought under the control of the government rather than local authorities. It is hard to know to what extent these were just ad hoc, vote winning manoeuvres but they made a calculable difference to the working lives of countless people.

Having criticised Gladstone's ineffective foreign policy Disraeli also made sure to play the Palmerston card in his overseas dealings, managing to pull off two great coups in the process. Firstly, in 1875 he contrived to purchase the majority of shares in the Suez Canal from under the noses of the French, who had had a hand in the canal's construction. This acquisition provided a far more efficient and cost-effective trading route between India, Australia and New Zealand as well as sending clear signals to the other European superpowers that Britannia was still a force to be reckoned with.

Disraeli's second great achievement was the bestowing of the title Empress of India on Queen Victoria in 1876. His ability to credit his monarch with this title cemented the bond of tremendous affection between the Queen and the Prime Minister and was yet another slight inflicted on Gladstone. Of the two political titans it was clear whom Victoria preferred. Disraeli flirted with her and made her feel his equal whilst Gladstone treated her with the humourless respect that his uptight morality dictated. Disraeli appeared to be living a charmed political life - saviour of the working man on the one hand and the darling of his ruling monarch on the other.

His stance on the crisis in the Balkans was more ambiguous, and a classic case of choosing between humanitarian and strategic ends. In 1876 Christian peoples in the Eastern Mediterranean were being persecuted by the ruling Turkish regime in increasingly extreme ways. The dilemma for Disraeli was that Ottoman influence held the ever expansionist Russians at bay and that overthrowing the Turks could allow Alexander II in through the back door. Such a diplomatic headache was made infinitely more awkward for the Prime Minister by his deadly rival's dramatic return from self-imposed exile.

Gladstone had effectively retired from political life after standing down as Liberal leader following the 1874 electoral defeat. He proffered opinion on weighty topics as party grandees are wont to do but he was far removed from the cut and thrust of Westminster. The Balkan crisis, however, stirred up his Old Testament rage and brought him back into the political limelight. Depending on your point of view Gladstone's tract 'The Bulgarian Horrors and the Question of the East' was either an impassioned call for Christian justice or a shockingly racist dissection of Turkish stereotypes. The Liberal heavyweight was unequivocal about the correct course of action. As he saw matters the Turks had committed appalling atrocities and a combined force of Britons and Russians must extinguish their rule in the region, regardless of the long-term benefits to the Russian empire. Disraeli procrastinated for as long as possible - with Gladstone denouncing him all the while - until Russia eventually declared war on Turkey in April 1877. Forced to respond the Prime Minister sent the British fleet through the Dardanelles and deployed Indian troops in Malta, acts which Gladstone now railed against as illegal. When peace was declared in March of the following year Disraeli was instrumental in brokering the Treaty of Berlin which limited Russian designs in the region at the same time as controlling the excesses of the Ottoman Empire. Whilst the ramifications of the agreement would ultimately play a large part in the prelude to the First World War, at the time Disraeli appeared to have triumphed once again at the expense of his indignant, blustering rival.

Which is why his defeat to Gladstone in the 1880 general election came as such a shock to him. There were a number of factors that contributed to this reversal - from a lengthy economic slump to a paucity of new ideas in the last few years of the ministry - but perhaps the single biggest mistake Disraeli made was accepting the title of Lord Beaconsfield and moving to the upper chamber. The elevated position of a peer deprived him of the right to engage in the bear pit of Parliamentary debate and thus left him powerless to defend himself from Gladstone's trenchant attacks. A peerage may have satisfied the personal pride of the vilified Jewish boy but it effectively neutered the most incendiary political rivalry of the century.

But for all the delight ousting his old rival must have given him Gladstone's second ministry was almost entirely devoid of merit. The one undisputed positive of his government was the Reform Act of 1884, which brought the county franchise into line with the boroughs and added about six million new voters. Yet even this development was somewhat inevitable - as demonstrated by its comparatively easy passage through Parliament - and there is certainly not the sense that only Gladstone could have pushed it through.

Elsewhere, Ireland was increasingly weighing on his mind and yet the legislation passed had little practical effect. His domestic policies were essentially non-existent. But Gladstone's greatest weakness still lay in foreign affairs and it was strikingly noticeable, considering how hands on he was elsewhere, that he kept any major decisions in the diplomatic arena at arm's length. One of the consequences of the 1884 Berlin Conference had been to open up Africa to a frenzy of European colonisation, a 'scramble' that the pious Gladstone heartily disapproved of. Nevertheless battle was joined with Egypt in 1882 - ostensibly to protect the Suez Canal that his old foe had so audaciously procured - and within a couple of months the country was in British hands.

But it was reaction against British control in Egypt that would lead to Gladstone's downfall. Nationalist forces led by the self-proclaimed Islamic prophet Muhammad Ahmad revolted against British and French rule, necessitating the mass evacuation of Egyptian subjects from Sudanese Khartoum in early 1884. General Charles Gordon - the former Governor General of the Sudan - was charged with the operation, successfully evacuating 2,500 Egyptians and managing to hold the city for the best part of a year. Whilst the public demanded that Gordon be feted as a hero and receive immediate support Gladstone stalled, not wishing to become embroiled in a costly stalemate. When the Prime Minister finally bowed to public pressure and sent back-up into the Sudan it was too late - Khartoum and Gordon fell two days before the troops arrived in January 1885. The backlash against the government was vicious and - after he was defeated on a minor amendment to the Budget - Gladstone had no other option but to hand in his resignation to a relieved Queen Victoria.

One wonders whether Gladstone's second ministry would have been as desultory had Disraeli been at the forefront of opposition, needling him and keeping him forever on his toes. But his new position in the Lords only allowed him limited influence and, in any case, Disraeli died in April 1881 before Gladstone's ministry had a chance to gather a head of steam. Gladstone would return to power barely a year after the fall of his second ministry but his conversion to the cause of Irish home rule split the Liberals and ushered in the Conservatives almost immediately. His fourth and final ministry - 1892-4 - was similarly monomaniacal in its obsession with Ireland, another failed home rule bill bringing it to its knees.

The palpable animosity between William Ewart Gladstone and Benjamin Disraeli had fuelled some of the key reforming legislation of the 1870s and laid the foundations of the modern British political system. The emphasis on personality, the primacy of general elections and dog-eat-dog adversarial jousting all stem from the innovations of these two titans of

Westminster. It is just a shame that few modern politicians can play the game with such eloquence or dreadful passion as they did.

10

THE END OF ISOLATION

On 31st August 1907 Great Britain signed a convention with Russia which irrevocably shattered any lingering hopes that she could remain aloof from European entanglements. The nation was now locked into a Triple Entente with the Russians and the French that effectively divided the continent into two massive power blocs. The Triple Alliance of Germany, Austria-Hungary and Italy had been in force since 1882 although that did not halt the internecine attempts at subsidiary coalitions and convoluted alignments hastily drawn up in an era of ever worsening tension and paranoia.

The fragile balance of power that had just about held - save for a few notable skirmishes - since the Napoleonic Wars was crumbling in the face of irresistible nationalism. The German Empire, under the ruthless control of Chancellor Otto von Bismarck, had subsumed the mighty Prussia within its collection of territories and was threatening to carry all before it. Its victory in the Franco-Prussian war of 1870-1 was a turning point in 19th century power politics both in terms of German hegemony and French indignation. There was a widespread fear that Napoleon III would seek to reclaim territory lost in the conflict thus triggering another pan-European war. Meanwhile the mass production of weaponry and armaments was growing ever more sophisticated and efficient. A dark mood of foreboding hung over Europe which Britain was by no means immune from.

The period of Britain's 'splendid isolation' from diplomatic alliances lasted from 1895 to 1902 and was sold as a conscious decision made from a position of economic and imperial strength. In reality there was nothing splendid about the growing unpopularity of a nation that had swaggered around the world with entitled arrogance in the 1850s and 60s and was now being rapidly superseded by more advanced super-states. Russia and France had waited for decades to twist the knife into the United Kingdom and now, with the riches on offer from the partition of Africa, they were in a position to cut Britain off from key trade opportunities and dent her fading prestige. Bismarck was similarly keen to bar Britain from the European high table, confidently identifying Germany as her natural successor in terms of global power.

In Westminster this era coincided with the return of the Conservatives to power under Lord Salisbury, the last peer to assume the role of Prime Minister. He was a figure perfectly suited to his times - anxious, suspicious and intensely pessimistic about the march of progress. Yet whilst he was undoubtedly the most reactionary Prime Minister since Lord Liverpool there was more to him than mere aristocratic solipsism. A thoughtful essayist and political philosopher he shared the same obsessions as Karl Marx, albeit viewed through a crystal clear looking glass. According to Salisbury class warfare was inevitable at some point in the near future and the job of the Conservative party - as keepers of the aristocratic flame - was to hold it at bay for as long as humanly possible. Thus his governing philosophy was almost entirely negative, having no desire to create new legislation but rather to strangle any potential reform at birth.

Had Salisbury been faced with Gladstone in his prime rather than the old, increasingly deluded and obsessional moral crusader that the Grand Old Man had become, the Conservatives' incredibly cynical ideology would have struggled to find an audience. But the Liberals played into Salisbury's hands perfectly, not least in the area of foreign policy where Gladstone's dithering and uncertainty could be convincingly painted as unpatriotic cowardice. Opposition to the Liberal obsession with Irish home rule also provided a strong rallying point for those frightened by any devolution of power from Westminster and it has to be said that Lord Salisbury exploited such weaknesses and their accompanying inter-party divisions brilliantly.

Salisbury was British Prime Minister for a total of 14 increasingly dispiriting years, yet despite his intelligence and Machiavellian ability to neutralise all opposition, it is hard to find him either inspiring or commendable. There is one figure, however, who captured the zeitgeist for good or ill during this period and cut a swathe through the limp, frightened nobodies inhabiting Parliament - the radical-turned-imperialist serial party-splitter, Joseph Chamberlain.

*

There have been few political conversions more extreme than that undergone by Joe Chamberlain between 1866 and 1886. The son of a shoemaking firm owner he had marched through Birmingham in support of Russell's doomed reform bill, a classic middle class idealist with a fundamental faith in the wisdom of the masses. Appointed Liberal Mayor of the city in 1873 he transformed its facilities and conditions. He eliminated slums and a toxic water supply and created libraries and green spaces in the most impressive burst of creative civic energy seen in the 19th century. Thrust into the political limelight Chamberlain was persuaded to stand for Parliament and - after failing to secure the Sheffield seat in 1874 - he filled the vacancy left in his beloved Birmingham by the previous candidate's retirement. He then set about reorganising the Liberal party with the same restless vigour that he had utilised as Mayor. By reinvigorating the radical party voices that he considered to have been muted by the moderate Gladstone he was instrumental in discrediting Disraeli's government and returning the Liberals to power in 1880. His reward for this work was the cabinet position of President of the Board of Trade. Yet whilst he toiled diligently in this role Gladstone's sudden conversion to the cause of Irish home rule set the young firebrand on a collision course with his leader.

However reform-minded Chamberlain may have been at home he was still an old school imperialist at heart. He baulked at Gladstone's proposed home rule bill - which would have given Ireland a separate Dublin Parliament and substantial self-governance - sharing the Conservative view that home rule was the start of a slippery slope to full independence and the undermining of the British empire as a whole. Chamberlain also correctly identified the Irish issue as Gladstone's Achilles heel. Far from being a cause to rally the entire Liberal party behind it had become a divisive and poisonous wrangle which Gladstone was incapable of leaving alone. The cherished reforms that were so close to Chamberlain's heart were being abandoned in favour of an unwinnable personal crusade.

Chamberlain felt so strongly that when the bill came before Parliament in 1886 he split the party, taking 80 like-minded MPs with him to form the entirely separate Liberal Unionists. This was a hammer blow to both the bill's chances of success and the survival of the Liberal government. Gladstone's humiliation was complete when Chamberlain and a handful of his new party took positions in Salisbury's Conservative government, elected later the same year. Aside from their views on empire the two men had little in common and it was a strange kind of alliance. Yet Chamberlain - with his distinctive dandified dress and customary monocle - revelled in his celebrity and reputation for making the political weather.

The alliance suited the new Prime Minister also, since despite the Liberal malaise the Conservatives had still not secured enough votes for a majority. Salisbury embraced the Liberal Unionists with a typical mixture of personal foreboding and public support. Concessions were made to the Liberal Unionist position and one member of the fledgling party, George Joachim Goschen, was even appointed Chancellor of the Exchequer. Yet Chamberlain was still wary of this unexpected political marriage and it was only after the landslide election victory of 1895 and the subsequent formal coalition of Unionists and Conservatives that he felt truly at home in Salisbury's government.

Whilst domestically the pace of change ground to a standstill British imperial ambition would become the dominant theme of the last years of the 19th century. Salisbury realised that the best way of forestalling reform at home was to be bold and bellicose abroad and, fortunately for him, the timing was perfect for a spot of good old fashioned conquest. The European superpowers were jockeying for position in the race to acquire new colonies. Nowhere was this more apparent than on the African continent, where the 'Scramble for Africa' showcased western venality and repression at its most heinous.

From having been almost totally ignored by the major western powers for most of the century Africa rapidly became the most hotly contested area on earth in the mid-1880s. The reasons for this are many and varied - from persistent exploration of the few remaining uncharted locations to increasing awareness of the commercial benefits of the continent's raw materials. But ultimately the partitioning of Africa was brought about by intense competition between the European superpowers and the need to avert serious military conflict.

The Berlin Conference of 1884 was convened by Bismarck in an effort to halt the aggressive claiming of various parts of the continent for different nations. This practice had been set in motion by the cloak and dagger imperial machinations of King Leopold II of Belgium, who had hired the British explorer Henry Stanley to aid him in establishing the Congo Free State. This ruse was discovered by the French who wasted no time in pressing their own claims to the region alongside Guinea and Tunisia. This in turn drove Portugal, Germany and Britain – who acquired Egypt in 1882 - into the manic rush for territory.

As British possessions began to mount up imperialism was promoted back home as a moral imperative. Whilst some, such as the future Prime Minister David Lloyd George, were disgusted by such crude jingoism the nation as a whole was swept away on a wave of renewed prestige and patrician smugness. The education and religious conversion of noble savages was part and parcel of good Christian values, the people of Britain told themselves. But such self-satisfaction and moral conviction often lead to dark places. When the government backed the scheme of entrepreneur and Cape Colony Prime Minister Cecil Rhodes to build a rail-route from Cape Town to Cairo they reawakened the fury of the Boers of independent Transvaal. The state, which lay directly in Rhodes' path to Southern African domination, had won its freedom from Britain in the First Boer War of 1881. But Rhodes and British colonial statesman Leander Jameson thought that it was about time Transvaal returned to the imperial fold. The Jameson Raid of 1895-6 was thwarted, however, and provided the Boers with just the fillip that they needed to begin an organised resistance. Conflict was inevitable and in October 1899 war was declared.

It was a war that Britain was expected to win and win swiftly. She was, after all, fighting a force comprised predominantly of farmers who were vastly inferior in both numbers and expertise. But, as the Americans would later discover in Vietnam, a smaller army is far more mobile and elusive and can make brilliant use of their knowledge of local terrain. It took two and a half years for the British - under the command of Lord Kitchener - to triumph, and it was only through unspeakably brutal treatment involving the establishment of the first concentration camps that she won at all. Opinion back home turned to embarrassment and revulsion. The squalid, shameful confrontation was duly noted elsewhere in Europe.

But the legacy of the Second Boer War was economic as well as diplomatic. Controversially, corn had been taxed during the conflict in direct opposition to the laissez faire principles established by Peel in the 1840s. Now Chamberlain wondered whether the era of free trade should come to an end altogether. Constantly looking over his shoulder at Britain's European rivals - and also the United States of America - he noted that all the major powers had built up higher and higher tariff walls and were doing very well for themselves off the back of it. Free trade had been beneficial when Britain was the world's primary producer exporting to a predominantly peaceful global market. But the technological rise of Germany coupled with the febrile atmosphere within Europe meant, to Chamberlain at least, that the United Kingdom was alarmingly open to exploitation.

But the reinstatement of protectionism raised two worrying issues, one practical and one psychological. The historic argument against high tariffs had always been that they led to soaring prices which badly hit the welfare of the consumer. It was ironic that Chamberlain the champion of reform was calling for a measure that would shield landowners from foreign competition but have a deleterious effect upon the poor. The second problem was that a retreat from the precepts of free trade and laissez faire would send the message to Britain's competitors that she was a fading power in desperate economic trouble. At the very least this would be a bitter blow to British pride.

Another Conservative politician by the name of Winston Churchill had the foresight to predict that the abandoning of free trade would adversely affect the nation's relationship with the ever more powerful United States. Simultaneously the charismatic Liberal David Lloyd George employed all his rhetorical skill in repudiating the spurious logic of Chamberlain's claims.

Yet at the same time as he was advocating trade protectionism Chamberlain was also pressing for an end to the diplomatic isolation that threatened to expose Britain in case of war. Germany, France and Russia were all busily building up their naval capabilities with a view to challenging Britain's traditional maritime supremacy. Negotiations for alliance were opened with Germany but neither power was ultimately willing to accept each other's terms. Chamberlain was therefore forced to look further afield in his search for a useful political ally. As one of the key threats to British security was the insufficient number of ships deployed in the China Seas he hit upon the novel idea of forming an alliance with Japan to safeguard British interests in the Far East.

However, as the 1902 Anglo-Japanese Alliance did not tie Britain to coalition with a fellow European power it was still possible for Chamberlain and his new Prime Minister Arthur Balfour to claim that 'splendid isolation' remained in force. The complication came from the wording of the act, which committed Britain to intervene on her new ally's behalf should more than one other nation declare war on Japan. Therefore when the Russo-Japanese War broke out in 1904 Britain was determined to do all she could to prevent France from joining Russia, thus necessitating British intervention. To this end the Anglo-French Entente was hastily signed, ostensibly to curb colonial aggression in Africa but in reality to keep both parties out of damaging wider conflicts.

Meanwhile, back in Westminster Chamberlain's campaign for tariff reform was starting to run out of steam. His critics were winning the people around ahead of the 1906 general election whilst the improvement of the economic climate negated the urgent requirement for drastic action. The debate split the Conservatives just as Irish home rule had split the Liberals 20 years previously and when the results of the election came in the government had been routed. Henry Campbell-Bannerman's Liberal Party won a landslide on a mandate for reform and the reactionary imperialism of the Salisbury/Chamberlain years was over.

But there was no let up on the diplomatic stage. Russia had been frustrated by the Japanese and was now looking elsewhere in Asia to satiate her imperial desire. Once again Britain's wisest course of action was to attempt to neutralise the threat by making a formal alliance. And so in 1907 the Triple Entente between Britain, France and Russia came into existence and the battle lines were effectively drawn throughout Europe. Now there was no disguising the fact that Britain was enmeshed in the specifics of European diplomacy and, whilst no longer isolated, was inextricably bound up in a network of agreements that could lead her into places unknown. Few could imagine exactly how dark those places would prove to be.

11

WORKING CLASS HEROES

Whilst the British government was busy 'civilizing' Africa and shoring up dubious alliances with foreign powers a movement was gathering force back home that would change the face of Britain's party political system. Vulgar nationalism was all very well while the going was good but the Conservatives' obsession with empire and isolation meant that domestic reforms of any note were placed firmly on the backburner. Since the passing of the 1884 Parliamentary Reform Act thousands of working class voters had been enfranchised yet neither of the two main political parties had any first-hand experience of the working class experience.

In theory the Liberals were the party most sympathetic to the working class cause but despite the presence of Radical MPs within their ranks they were still firmly the party of middle class interests. Equally the Liberal emphasis on individual freedoms and self-help conflicted with any realistic claim to represent 'the masses.' Yet for the Liberals to ignore the demands of this newly politicised sector of society would have been suicidal at a time when their traditional voting base was losing faith with the direction that Gladstone and his successors were taking the party in. In fact the Liberals had fostered small numbers of working class MPs on the party's fringes since 1868. Running on a Labour ticket they were both part of the Liberal Party and separate from it but any electoral gains were recorded as Liberal and the influence of the Labour politicians - known as Lib-Labs - was always negligible.

Considering the effort and resources that would be required for a completely new political party to break the duopoly of the existing system many working class voters - and middle class sympathisers - considered it a waste of time to try and infiltrate Parliament. Instead they proposed more militant trade union activity. The existence of trade unions was a major bone of contention to governments of the early to mid-19th century, with organisations such as Robert Owen's Grand National Consolidated Trades Union playing a key role in the political agitation of the 1830s. By the late 1860s, however, industrial unrest had eased to the extent that a Royal Commission of 1867 advocated the legalisation of trade unions, stating that they were mutually beneficial to both employers and workers. The iconic Trades Union Congress was founded the following year although its tenor was considerably less antagonistic than it would later become.

The union militancy of Ben Tillett was thus a break with the superficial harmony that had reigned in industrial relations for the previous two decades. Tillett was a bullish and combative leader who was prepared to follow through on industrial action no matter how strongly the odds were stacked against him. The London Dock Strike of 1889 was a pivotal moment in British labour relations with Tillett leading 100,000 workers out over a dispute in pay for the swift unloading of ships. Whilst there had been other industrial walkouts in previous years the scale of the Dock Strike was unprecedented and forged what became known as New Unionism. Hitherto union activity had been the preserve of the skilled craft unions but after the dockers' victory it became predominantly associated with casual, unskilled labourers instead.

Tillett went on to found the Dock, Wharf, Riverside and General Labourers' Union - later to morph into the Transport and General Workers' Union - which saw membership skyrocket in the closing years of the century. Yet whilst some Lib-Lab candidates were supported by trade unions the Parliamentary distance that union leaders preserved left them with limited opportunities to set the political agenda. For a coterie of idealistic intellectuals there was a third way. While the Lib-Lab experiment and New Unionism were both groping around for a foothold in power a motley assortment of radical societies were also carving out their own visions of Socialist utopia.

Britain's reputation for political tolerance attracted many radical emigres in the middle of the 19th century and none were more notorious than Karl Marx and Friedrich Engels. Whilst based in London the pair set up the first Marxist party anywhere in the world, the Communist League, whose manifesto would prove to be a great influence on a frustrated would-be politician called Henry Hyndman.

Hyndman had stood for Parliament as an Independent in the 1880 general election but attracted next to no electoral support. A chance reading of 'The Communist Manifesto' then converted him to the Marxist cause and within a year he had founded the Social Democratic Federation. For the time their modus operandi was strikingly progressive. Alongside the customary Marxist tropes of nationalisation of the means of production and redistribution of property they called for a reduction in the working week to 48 hours and equal rights for women. However, the cause of internal strife was not the radical nature of the party's programme but the inordinate personal influence of Hyndman himself. By 1884 a faction - which included the textile designer and novelist William Morris and Marx's youngest daughter Eleanor - had left to form the splinter group the Socialist League. Whilst the ideals of the League lived on in Morris' celebrated utopian novel 'News From Nowhere' the organisation was quickly overrun by anarchists and disbanded acrimoniously in 1901.

The more genteel end of the Socialist spectrum was represented by the intellectual Fabian Society, in particular Beatrice and Sydney Webb. Founded in the same year as the Socialist League, the Fabians held to the view that human society was in a constant state of evolution and merely required the right sort of enlightened technocrats to guide it in the most socially beneficial direction. They did not, unlike the Social Democratic Federation and elements of the Socialist League, advocate revolution but rather the gradual change and adaptation of society into a democratic utopia. Like the Socialist League the Fabian Society attracted writers and artists and numbered George Bernard Shaw and Virginia Woolf amongst its membership.

Lastly there were the Christian Socialist societies who stressed the anti-Capitalist nature of Christ's teachings and sought to address issues of social inequality through extensive charity work. The Methodism of John Wesley formed a strong plank of the Labour party's foundations and would continue to exert early influence in the uniquely religious dimension to British Socialism.

The proliferation of these various societies demonstrates the groundswell of opinion that an engagement with working class issues was urgently needed. The trouble was that - in a prefiguring of the future civil wars of the left - all of these groups were convinced that they alone had the answer to society's ills and consequently loathed each other with a righteous indignation that bordered on the farcical. It would take a voice from within Parliament to begin the arduous process of uniting the disparate base of the Socialist movement.

Keir Hardie's upbringing was so deprived as to be almost parodic. Born a bastard in a Lanarkshire turnip field he was working 12 hour days delivering bread before he was ten years old. When his age reached double figures he started work as a 'trapper' in the mines, opening and closing a door for ten hours so that miners received a steady supply of air. Through determination and hard work he taught himself to read and went on to become a miners' union leader in the early 1880s, before founding the Scottish Labour Party in 1888.

Elected to Parliament for West Ham South in 1892 Hardie outraged the Commons by flouting the formal dress code of the age. His plain tweed suit, red tie and deerstalker hat marked him out as a working class rebel with no respect for the archaic traditions of the constitutional process. His radical agenda, which included votes for women and the abolition of the House of Lords, greatly alarmed both the reactionary majority and those in favour of more gradual reform. But Hardie believed passionately in the primacy of Parliament to bring about change for the working classes and to this end formed his second political party in 1893, the Independent Labour Party.

The timing was judicious as by now the Lib-Lab candidature agreement was breaking down. The Liberals were becoming ever more reticent to sanction Labour candidates of working class origin, at the same time as the Liberal cause was at its lowest ebb since the party's inception. Trade unions were now less likely to back a Lib-Lab candidate and suddenly the formation of a major new party to challenge the wounded Liberal giant did not seem like quite such a hopeless endeavour.

Yet this was not quite the glorious revolution that Hardie and others had predicted. There was disagreement over exactly how Socialist the ILP should be, with some members arguing that not all workers were sufficiently politicised to embrace ownership of the means of production and just wanted their rights protected by a political party. Trade union support was lacking also, with union leaders still convinced that agitation outside of Parliament was the most productive course of action. The ILP took a hammering at the 1895 general election with even Hardie losing his seat and as the century drew to a close it appeared that the nation was simply not ready for a party that chiefly represented the interests of the common man.

But as radical as Hardie was perceived to be by the establishment his brand of Socialism was positively cosy compared to the rabid Marxists of the SDF and other extremist societies. Hardie's doctrine eschewed the violent imagery of class revolution and reinterpreted Marx's teachings in a more progressive light. The system did not necessarily have to be smashed, just bent towards proletarian use through the adaptation of constitutional methods. And just as later British Socialism would differentiate itself from the secular Bolshevism of Lenin so Hardie's pioneering ideology would embrace both Methodism in particular and the institution of the Church as a whole.

Hardie was still startlingly progressive on a broad range of weighty issues. The tragedy of mass unemployment became his signature cause, and whilst this was no great surprise considering his impoverished background the vehemence and eloquence that he utilised brought the issue to far higher Parliamentary attention than it would have merited otherwise. He was also in the vanguard of women's suffrage - a position that earned him much mockery and opprobrium - and racial equality. The rights of black South Africans and Indian self-government were deeply unfashionable issues at the turn of the 20th century but Hardie championed them both, becoming something of a folk hero on the Indian subcontinent for his efforts.

Yet Hardie was also a pragmatist who realised that as long as the cross-society bickering was allowed to continue a Socialist party had no chance of making any impact in Parliament. Whilst it was a union member called Thomas R. Steels who first proposed the consolidation of all left-wing organisations into a single body Hardie was instrumental in setting up the Labour Representation Committee of 1900. It was his motion to create a unified Labour group in Parliament that was passed by 129 delegates and saw the warring factions of the left finally brought together into one political entity. The LRC comprised seven trade unionists, one Fabian and two members apiece from the Independent Labour Party and the Social Democratic Federation.

And they soon had a specific incident to rally behind. In 1901 John Ewington, a signalman at the Welsh village railway station of Taff Vale, was threatened with displacement to another station after arguing with the company manager for higher wages. The Amalgamated Society of Railway Servants took up Ewington's cause, not merely coming out on strike but also greasing rails and uncoupling carriages in a sustained campaign of industrial sabotage. Negotiations were joined and the strikers returned to work, but the company subsequently sued the union for damages. Accepted wisdom held that unions could not be sued but, controversially, Judge George Farwell held in favour of the railway company and they were awarded £32,000 in damages. To add further class antagonism to the mix the ruling, having been reversed by the Court of Appeal, was restored by the House of Lords.

Whilst there was widespread working class outrage at this judgement the Taff Vale case brought the position of the trade unions into stark relief. Those who claimed that union militancy had the power to reform working conditions were forced to acknowledge that, in this instance, the union in question had been comprehensively defeated. Maybe Hardie and his ilk were right and the only way to bring about constructive change was from within Parliament itself.

Suddenly the unions were falling over themselves to back the LRC, approximately 127 of them - including the first mining unions - signing up to the Parliamentary cause. As the Socialist movement gathered pace the future Prime Minister Ramsay MacDonald was able to reverse the Lib-Lab dynamic and secure Liberal support for Labour candidates standing in solid working class constituencies. This unofficial coalition against the Conservatives paid off spectacularly for both parties. Whilst the Liberals won a landslide in the 1906 general election 29 Labour MPs were also elected to the Commons. They may have still been in the vast minority but at last the Socialist agenda could now be fought for in Parliament.

The party's first political act was to ditch the unwieldy title of Labour Representation Committee for the snappier Labour Party - or specifically the Parliamentary Labour Party in Westminster - and elect Hardie as their first leader. 1906 also saw the effective reversal of the Taff Vale judgement with the passing of the Trade Disputes Act, which outlawed the suing of striking unions. The legislation has passed into Labour myth as the act that definitively bound the party to the trade union movement. In decades to come such a close tie would prove distinctly troublesome to Labour Prime Ministers.

The Liberal government had strong reservations about this bond at the time, making the funding of election campaigns by trade unions illegal in 1909. This development provoked concerns over Labour's performance in the forthcoming general election yet, under Hardie's successor Arthur Henderson, Labour seats rose to 42 in 1910 and the Liberals were forced to pass a bill allowing the payment of MPs to sweeten the pill of union exclusion. It is a mark of Labour's growing influence that by 1913 the calls for reinstatement of trade union funding could no longer be ignored and the provision was made legal again.

By the eve of the First World War Labour had made astonishing progress from the hotch-potch of intellectual societies, militant unions and Lib-Lab compromises of 30 years previously. Yet they were sandwiched between a resurgent Liberal government and a resilient Conservative Party, struggling to make themselves heard on key issues and mocked and patronized by the traditional elite. Many wondered whether this was the end of the line. Where could the Labour Party possibly go from here?

12

THE WELSH WIZARD AND THE WAR TO END ALL WARS

The assassination of the Archduke Franz Ferdinand of Austria was so nearly a botched operation. Seven members of the Black Hand Gang - a Serbian terrorist organisation committed to the relinquishing of Slav states by the mighty Austria-Hungary - lined the Sarajevo route due to be taken by the visiting dignitary on the 28th June 1914. A grenade thrown by one conspirator hit the wrong car, seriously wounding a number of bystanders. The visit's schedule somewhat thrown out by this event the Archduke and his entourage made a politically expedient visit to the hospital to console those injured in the blast. En route the Archduke's driver took a wrong turning and stalled directly in front of the startled young revolutionary Gavrilo Princip, who was standing outside a local cafe. The 19 year old strode up to the car and fired twice. Both Franz Ferdinand and his wife Sophie, Duchess of Hohenberg were killed.

Upon such quirks rest the fate of nations. Once an Austrian ultimatum had been rejected by Serbia the network of alliances that had been painstakingly built up in the preceding decades clicked into place, committing the European superpowers to the bloodiest conflict yet fought in world history. The British Prime Minister Herbert Henry Asquith formally declared war on Germany on 4th August, ostensibly in defence of Belgium but in reality over fears of German invasion of Britain's triple entente ally France. Asquith, like many in government, little realised the devastating effect the conflict would have on the country and the appalling scale of the loss of young life.

Asquith had led the nation since 1908 after his Liberal predecessor Henry Campbell-Bannerman retired due to ill health. In the following six years he presided over the most radical reforming government yet seen in the British Isles - a calm, patrician presence nodding through a tidal wave of legislation that paved the way for the modern welfare state. Yet the demands of war leadership would break him, crippling his reputation and contributing to the obliteration of the Liberal Party as a credible political force. In his place would come the eternally contradictory figure of David Lloyd George. Corrupt, womanising and narcissistic yet principled, frighteningly astute and utterly dazzling he is undoubtedly one of our most complex and fascinating political titans.

The period from 1906 to the end of World War I is packed with exhilarating incident and landmark moments, taking in both the high-Edwardian era of gathering agitation and the brutal age of mechanized mass slaughter. At the same time as social and economic reforms were flying out of the Treasury the government was dealing with the triple threat of the suffragette movement, increased industrial unrest and the powder keg of Irish revolution. The tale of the last British Liberal government to date is a gripping potboiler with the darkest of twists.

From the outset of Asquith's tenure it was clear that Edwardian Liberalism was to be markedly different from its Gladstonian ancestor. The emphasis on self-help that the schoolmasterly Gladstone had viewed as integral became a more subsidiary concern in Asquith's government, replaced instead by a far greater level of state support and intervention that bordered dangerously on the Socialist.

The majority of significant reforming legislation came from the Chancellor, Lloyd George. Whilst he would later mythologise the extent of his lowly upbringing his origins were relatively humble and defiantly Welsh. He empathised with the plight of the nation's impoverished and destitute - at the time a subject for much handwringing study and research – yet his flagrant disregard for party loyalty first surfaced early on in his political career. In 1895, inspired by the cause of Irish home rule then championed by his hero Gladstone, Lloyd George campaigned vociferously for Welsh self-government and attempted to transmute the Welsh Liberals into his own Cymru Fydd movement. The plot failed but it would serve as sufficient warning of the young outsider's lack of respect for conventional political process.

The first legislative missile launched from the Treasury was the Old Age Pensions Act of 1908, arguably the bedrock of the modern social welfare system. Under the act persons over 70 years of age would be entitled to 5 shillings a week and, although the overall level of benefit was low, it aided half a million people for whom no such provision had previously existed.

Yet Lloyd George was by no means alone in his passion for social reform. The support garnered within the Conservative Party for Joseph Chamberlain's protectionist tariff reform depressed Winston Churchill to such an extent that in 1904 he crossed the floor and joined the Liberals. It would not, of course, be the last time that the great statesman would switch party allegiance, but the energy and ideas that he brought to his role as President of the Board of Trade demonstrated a genuine desire to implement socially beneficial legislation. Between them Lloyd George and his adoring protégé introduced labour exchanges, free school meals, maintenance for divorced mothers and improvements to workhouses.

Lloyd George and Churchill adapted much of their legislation from German welfare templates, a stark reminder of just how advanced Kaiser Wilhelm II's state had become. The conspicuous shipbuilding that Germany had been engaged in for some time led to excited calls for Britain to step up her production of dreadnoughts. The building of warships was highly expensive and Lloyd George had opposed the Second Boer War on the grounds that money spent on armaments was money taken from the poor and needy. His position had not changed and he proposed to cut the number of new dreadnoughts from six to four. However, when the public responded with cries of 'we want eight and we won't wait' the Chancellor grudgingly acquiesced.

Yet covering the cost of dreadnought production gave Lloyd George the perfect opportunity to launch the grandstanding attack on the upper classes that he had been dreaming of for years. His 1909 budget was unlike any other the Treasury had thus far produced. Aiming to raise a total of £18,000,000 so that social reform could continue alongside the enhancement of the navy he unleashed a budget teeming with taxes on everything from alcohol and cars to land and estate duties. And just in case the target of these swingeing measures was not obvious enough he threw in a super-tax to directly hit the incomes of the richest in the land.

There was the inevitable outrage - mainly from Conservatives MPs and peers but also from many landowners within the Liberal Party - who would be hit hard by these taxes. It is quite probable that this was precisely the Chancellor's intention. Like the mercurial demagogue that he was Lloyd George took his budget to the people, passionately pontificating on class war to an entranced crowd of 4,000 in Limehouse, East London. King Edward VII joined the chorus of disapproval as pressure began to mount on the government from the nation's most influential aristocrats. Lloyd George, supported by Churchill and his Prime Minister Asquith, stood his ground and readied himself for battle with the Lords.

That the upper chamber would reject the budget was on the one hand wholly predictable. They had already blocked a number of the more radical Liberal measures such as the Education Bill, the Plural Voting Bill and the Licensing Bill and none of that legislation was half as damaging to their wealth or prestige as the 'People's Budget.' Yet there was an unspoken agreement that the - predominantly Conservative - Lords would never stand in the way of a strictly financial bill and it was probably this that Lloyd George and Asquith were banking on. The budget was, however, far too rich for the Lords' deep blue blood and was comprehensively kicked into touch. With the nation without a budget there would have to be a snap general election to either reaffirm the government's mandate or sweep the Liberals from power. The result was the former, although only just. The huge majority that the Liberals had won in the 1906 election was wiped out and Asquith only clung on with the help of the Irish Nationalists. However narrowly, the Liberals had won the day and through gritted teeth the Lords passed the People's Budget.

But there was now a wider issue at stake. Lloyd George detested the peerage system and would have dearly loved to abolish the House of Lords altogether. Whilst such an extreme measure was not possible he was determined to curb what he saw as their disproportionate and excessive powers. The 1911 Parliament Bill was introduced, formally barring the Lords' right to block a finance bill and limiting them to three attempts at killing any other legislation. Such a bill would give the Commons unquestioned supremacy over the Lords for the first time in Parliamentary history.

It would also necessitate another general election which the government won in an almost identical manner to the first. The bill passed slowly through the Commons and the stage was set for the government's final showdown with the reactionary yet increasingly harried peers. But just as battle was about to be joined the Prime Minister dropped a bombshell. He had persuaded the new king, George V, to create 500 extra peers to swamp the Lords with those sympathetic to the bill. This was too much for 234 Conservative peers who reluctantly admitted defeat but a great many others remained undaunted. They became known as the 'ditchers,' prepared to 'die in the last ditch before giving in.' But die they – metaphorically – did, as the Parliament Bill passed the Lords and became law, a great initial victory for Britain's burgeoning democratic state. Yet there was plenty of pressure for reform from outside Parliament as well as inside.

On the 4th June 1913 an intelligent, middle class woman named Emily Davison stepped onto the race track during the Epsom Derby and was trampled to death by the King's horse Anmer. She may - or may not - have been attempting to pin a 'Votes for Women' rosette onto the animal as a means of publicising the suffragette cause that she had embraced since 1906. At the time more people were concerned for the condition of the horse than the woman.

Davison had been a member of the Women's Social and Political Union, the leading militant suffragette organisation founded by Emmeline Pankhurst and her two daughters Sylvia and Christabel in 1903. The suffragette movement was predominantly middle and upper class, with educated and privileged women frustrated and angry at their lack of influence in political affairs - primarily their inability to vote. The methods that they employed to get their message across were formidably brave and incredibly violent, encompassing window smashing, firebombing and armed assault alongside more familiar actions such as chaining themselves to railings.

The issue of votes for women was a thorny one for MPs of the time. A surprising number supported the idea in principle, although the notion that the franchise could be extended to working class women was almost universally unacceptable within Parliament. The complication came – predictably enough - from party self-interest. Liberal and Labour politicians were convinced that upper and middle class women would vote overwhelmingly Conservative and in 1912 Asquith himself pulled back from giving the vote to affluent females over the age of 30, fearing that they would betray him in the following election. Whilst the Parliamentary dithering continued the violent nature of the campaign was ramped up, resulting in mass arrests and imprisonment.

This incarceration of suffragettes gave the government another headache when Emmeline Pankhurst lobbied for her imprisoned colleagues to be classed as political prisoners, thus granting them certain rights and privileges that they would not enjoy as ordinary convicts. When this status was denied the decision was taken for imprisoned activists to go on hunger strike. Since the prison was liable should a suffragette die whilst they were incarcerated a practice of force feeding was introduced which inflicted considerable physical pain and injury on the subject. Realising rapidly that this practice was inherently inhumane an increasingly desperate Home Office then passed the Prisoners Act of 1913. This policy legalised the bizarre procedure of releasing a prisoner when they were dangerously unwell and then re-arresting them when they had returned to acceptably healthy levels. Unsurprisingly it became known as the 'Cat and Mouse Act'.

Ironically it was not the concerted campaign of the suffragettes that persuaded the government to grant property owning women over the age of 30 the vote in 1918, but rather the indispensability of female workers during the First World War. Nevertheless, the militancy of the movement sparked the flame of modern feminism and proved that respectable women from affluent homes were not content to just be homemakers or trophies for their powerful husbands. The shockwaves that the suffragettes sent out in the Edwardian era can still be felt in the 21st century.

But it was not just politicised women who were making life difficult for the government. A wave of industrial unrest was sweeping through the country affecting everyone from dockers to miners to jam factory workers. From 1910 until the outbreak of World War One a succession of strikes and riots crippled local economies and nearly brought the country to its knees. It started in the Welsh town of Tonypandy in 1910 where a three day riot broke out amongst striking miners and the local constabulary. The blustering King ordered military intervention but Churchill - fearing another Peterloo - opted instead to deploy more police officers from the capital thus containing the disorder and neutralizing the strike.

He attempted to use the same methods the following year when dock workers in Liverpool came out on strike, but this time the militancy filtered through to other industries - such as railway workers - and the violence escalated to alarming levels. The army and a lone warship were eventually called in to stop what had become a deadly mini-revolution on Merseyside. London - scene of the great 1889 Dock Strike - was not to be outdone and, in 1912, Ben Tillett once more led out masses of dockers in a dispute over pay. The atmosphere was considerably more bellicose than it had been 23 years previously with armed resistance and calls for the murder of Lord Devonport, chairman of the Port of London Authority. This time, however, the strike failed.

In the background to this rising unrest and violence David Lloyd George was drafting the revolutionary National Insurance Bill, which would provide a raft of insurance benefits on health and unemployment paid on a compulsory contributory basis. Health insurance was a direct progenitor of the post-war National Health Service whilst unemployment insurance removed the reliance on begging and charity that had hitherto been the recourse of those left without a job. There is a certain irony to the fact that the most farsighted piece of workers' legislation that the Liberals introduced coincided with the most militant union agitation for a generation.

Ireland also saw its fair share of industrial action with a brutal transport workers' strike in Dublin in 1913 which left five dead and many others wounded. But Ireland in the run-up to the First World War was a basket case, atrociously mismanaged by Westminster. The twin issues of independence and home rule were bringing Protestant and Catholic activists to boiling point and the appallingly violent release that was the 1916 Easter Rising was the bloody result.

But all of this domestic agitation and militancy paled into insignificance the second Gavrilo Princip fired his two shots into the Archduke's car. Europe - and later the world - was plunged into an unknowable war, a conflict of more sophisticated technologies and inhuman mechanization than had ever been seen before. It was now possible to mow down thousands of men in seconds and lay waste to entire towns and cities. And one man in particular was completely unequipped to deal with it.

Although the dynamic reforming zeal within government had come primarily from Lloyd George and Churchill the Liberals needed a solid, unflappable figurehead to provide gravitas and reassurance whilst nation-changing legislation was whirling all around. Herbert Henry Asquith had played that part to perfection, reacting to crises with marvellous sang-froid and defusing tension with delicious understatement. It should be remembered that he was one of the finest peacetime Prime Ministers this country has ever had but - unfortunately for both him and that same country - he was also required to be an effective and inspirational war leader.

From the start of the war Asquith showed no sign that he understood the severity of the conflict. In his defence he was most certainly not alone, many respected politicians and military commanders assuming that the majority of the ground fighting would be done by the French and viewing Britain's role as primarily naval. But the lack of urgency or initiative he displayed was worrying, especially as Lloyd George was already making economic provisions with his customary energy and elan. In swift order the Chancellor increased the bank rate, issued the first £1 and 10 shilling bank notes and doubled income tax, restoring faith in the financial system at a time of national crisis. Aside from passing the Defence of the Realm Act - which granted government exceptional powers of state control - the Prime Minister appeared to be doing very little.

When he did condescend to act it invariably had negative consequences. Although at the time the appointments of Lord Kitchener as War Secretary and John 'Jacky' Fisher as First Sea Lord were hugely popular with the nation they would prove to be disastrous. Both were self-regarding maverick heroes from a bygone age who had no conception of working as part of a government machine.

Kitchener was the imperial hero of the 1898 Battle of Omdurman - which reinstated British rule in the Sudan - and had for the past three years been in effective control of Egypt. He may have been a national favourite but he was also a pompous, single-minded relic of the golden days of empire with no respect for politicians or understanding of the new nature of the current conflict. He began promisingly enough, correctly identifying that the war would be a long, drawn out battle of attrition and recognising that the British army would need to grow spectacularly from the tiny professional British Expeditionary Force. To this end he lent his face to a profoundly effective and historically iconic recruitment campaign which resulted in huge numbers of volunteers. However, his misunderstanding of the correct type of shells that the army needed - high-explosive rather than shrapnel - and his subsequent refusal to acknowledge his mistake cost an untold number of lives. The inflexibility that had been a virtue in the days of Victorian imperialism had become a tragic flaw. When he drowned en route to Russia in 1916 Britain lost one of its major impediments to victory.

By that point the other celebrity loose cannon had self-destructed. Jacky Fisher was second only to Nelson in British naval lore, a perceptive innovator and military strategist with a glorious career behind him. One thing he was not used to was playing second fiddle which - under Churchill as First Lord of the Admiralty - he was now required to do. Churchill was enjoying the war a little too much and was coming up with ever more creative strategies for naval attack, a task that Fisher thought he was better suited to. The latter was proved right over the disastrous 1915 Gallipoli offensive - although the operation was not Churchill's first choice either – but his reaction to the impending slaughter was to have an almighty hissy fit quite unbecoming of a key figure in a wartime government. Disappearing from his post at a time of supreme national crisis he refused to return until Churchill had been removed. In addition to this he informed the Conservative and Unionist leader Andrew Bonar Law - the Liberal Unionists having formally merged with the Conservatives in 1912 - of his machinations and then sent a letter to Asquith demanding that he assume total control of the war at sea. Needless to say that he did not get his wish. It was an ignominious end to such a distinguished military career.

Both of these very public scandals combined with Asquith's languid leadership, to bring the Liberals to crisis point. The Prime Minister now succumbed to pressure to include Conservative/Unionist and Labour politicians in a wartime coalition government and, equally importantly, created a new role for the only minister who had responded effectively to the war thus far. Now Minister of Munitions David Lloyd George outstripped even his own previous achievements. Not only did he cajole and threaten both unions and companies into unheard of levels of compliance, coordinate and oversee the mass production of armaments across a broad range of industries, enthusiastically promote the employment of women in munitions factories and speed up weapons production to incredible levels but he also managed to shoehorn his cherished social reforms in along the way. His department built thousands of houses, flats and other forms of accommodation for workers, alongside canteens and children's play areas. It seemed that even in producing instruments of death Lloyd George was able to improve the welfare of the living.

By now it was becoming only too clear who should really be in charge of the country's war effort. The press had begun questioning Asquith's suitability for his role and were playing up the Munitions Minister as his obvious successor. Lloyd George himself - once a staunch supporter of the PM - was drifting away from his Liberal colleagues and into the arms of the coalition Conservative and Unionists, particularly their leader Bonar Law. At this point the war was going from bad to worse. The 1st of July 1916 saw the darkest day in British military history as nearly 20,000 of her troops were slaughtered in the bloodbath of the first day of the Somme. The government appeared listless and defeated, Asquith having blundered yet again by holding off on introducing conscription until the start of that year. When Lloyd George virtually demanded the position of War Secretary in June 1916 the Prime Minister meekly agreed, all but acknowledging his lame duck status and the Welshman's claim to his title.

But he did not relinquish power just yet. Whilst they had worked well together before the war Asquith had always fundamentally mistrusted Lloyd George, probably for good reason. There was also an element of class snobbery in Asquith's opinion of his populist colleague which led him to fight to the last. Unfortunately everybody else could see what was blindingly obvious and Asquith just came off looking petty and ungracious.

The final showdown came in November 1916 over an unseemly squabble about who should form the government's war cabinet. Bonar Law initially proposed a council of four – himself, Asquith, Lloyd George and Edward Carson, the leader of the Unionists – but the Prime Minister, uneasy about the power this would give Lloyd George, rejected the proposal. Lloyd George then rashly suggested a triumvirate that excluded Asquith which was unsurprisingly vetoed as well. Asquith then countered with a council of five but Lloyd George absolutely refused. Back and forth went this schoolboy tantrum whilst thousands were dying in the trenches, until Asquith was finally persuaded to accept the war cabinet of three. He then reneged on his agreement the following day when a newspaper article claimed that it was evidence he was being side-lined. Now the Prime Minister attempted to call Lloyd George's bluff by resigning, gambling on the Welshman being unable to form a government. But by now even Asquith's core supporters recognised that he had to go and Lloyd George - the rough diamond from rural Wales - became the most humbly born PM since Benjamin Disraeli.

The change was instantaneous. Instead of the lackadaisical hands-off approach of Asquith Lloyd George directed every aspect of the war effort personally, blatantly ignoring Parliament and assuming near dictatorial powers over the nation in the process. It was precisely what was needed. His five man war cabinet was the hub of government, meeting multiple times a day and responding to each new development with speed and intelligence. Not everything the new Prime Minister touched turned to gold. His decision to replace the controversial Field Marshal Douglas Haig as Commander of British troops in France with the French general Nivelle had to be reversed when the latter proved hopelessly out of his depth. But gradually Britain's fortunes began to change and the Germans who had looked so indestructible a few months previously started to falter.

And, despite Parliament's subservience to the demands of the war effort, Lloyd George also managed to steer through a landmark reform act which effectively completed the transformation of Britain into a democracy. The Representation of the People Act is most well-known for introducing women to the franchise – all women over 30 who owned property or were graduates in university constituencies, at least – but it also vastly increased the number of men who could vote. The heroics of the nation's young Tommies had to be seen to be rewarded and so the franchise was extended to all males over the age of 21. The process begun by the cautious pragmatism of the Great Reform Act of 1832 had culminated in the transference of electoral power to the masses.

By late 1918 the Americans had joined the allies, the Kaiser's troops were mutinying and Communists were agitating on the streets of Berlin. The armistice that was signed on the 11th November condemned Germany to global humiliation, and the subsequent Treaty of Versailles inflicted punishing reparations payments on a shattered and resentful nation. Everybody knows the poisonous nationalism that was unleashed as a result.

But all that was in the future. For now Britain had proved victorious and David Lloyd George was a hero to a grateful nation. The Liberals, however, saw Lloyd George's presidential style of government rather differently. Lloyd George's effervescent genius as a war leader had squashed the very concept of party politics. The Welsh Wizard was a force of nature whose titanic ego demanded he be seen as a one-man-band rather than the figurehead of a group of self-interested politicians. The issue came to a head when Asquith half-heartedly moved a vote of confidence against his successor over governmental duplicity concerning the nation's military capability. Lloyd George's emphatic defence not only won the day but irrevocably split the Liberals into pro-Asquith and pro-Lloyd George camps. For all Asquith's weaknesses as war leader, to many of the party faithful he still represented true Liberal values. In their eyes Lloyd George was a narcissistic demagogue with no principles whatsoever.

Lloyd George then set about proving his critics right. Cut off from the base of Liberal support he fought the 1918 election on a 'coupon' with the Conservative and Unionists, effectively extending the wartime coalition into peacetime. The mongrel coalition won a massive and decisive victory, securing 473 seats in total. For Lloyd George this was glorious vindication but for the Asquithian Liberal party it was a disaster, winning a mere 30 seats and losing their leader into the bargain. The aftermath of the 1918 general election is crucial in understanding what happened to the Liberals after World War One. For whilst the result sent the official Liberal party into a freefall from which – excepting the aberration of 1923 when Stanley Baldwin's misguided calls for protectionism briefly raised the party's profile – they have never recovered, it also put the increasingly hubristic and volatile Lloyd George in a highly vulnerable position. He may still have been Prime Minister but his 'party' was dominated by Conservative and Unionists who were growing weary of their leader's tiresome messiah complex.

And that was the problem with Lloyd George after the Great War. The total power that being a war leader had bestowed upon him had turned him from a borderline Socialist reformer into a lazy autocrat who believed his own hype. There was still a trace of the old reforming spirit in his housing and pensions policies but now his sleazier side - always apparent - began to dominate. He was by no means the only leading politician to sell honours for cash but he was the only one to treat it as a legitimate business, establishing tariffs and accepting money from just about anyone - including convicted criminals. In addition, his fixer in the cash-for-honours scandal was a thoroughly unsavoury character known as Maundy Gregory - profiteer, violent anti-Semite and quite possibly murderer. Whether or not Lloyd George knew the full scale of Gregory's misdemeanours their association, when combined with the brazen nature of the Prime Minister's honour selling, damaged his career fatally. He might have survived the scandal had his management of the economy been better, but, having been a restless crusader for change all his political life, he now just sat back and let the worst recession in decades take its punishing course. The embryonic welfare state that he had improvised in wartime now fell into abeyance and the British public were hung out to dry.

By 1922 the Conservative and Unionist backbenchers had had enough. Worried that Lloyd George's behaviour was tarnishing the image of their party they revolted against their superiors, decreeing that the

132

Conservatives/Unionists should break away from the coalition and fight the forthcoming election on their own terms. It proved to be an inspired decision. That year's election returned the Conservatives - who soon dropped the Unionist appendage despite the merger officially lasting until 1965 - to sole power for the first time since 1905, and with an enormous majority to boot. The Liberals, shorn of any coherent identity thanks to the Asquith-Lloyd George haemorrhage, were decimated. When Asquith, still party leader, decided to back Labour in forming a minority government in 1924 rather than attempting some sort of coalition for his own party the game was well and truly up.

The Conservatives, under Bonar Law, had never looked stronger. With the Liberals quashed and Labour still young and inexperienced their path seemed clear for a generation. Yet Bonar Law was a weak Prime Minister, already seriously ill and perpetually anxious. When he was diagnosed with terminal throat cancer the King's choice of successor, Stanley Baldwin, appeared equally uninspiring. Yet Baldwin was a deceptively complex character who would come to dominate the inter-war period. Cultivating a homely, self-consciously 'ordinary' image he was ideally suited to the consensus politics of the era.

And what of David Lloyd George? There was still life in the Welsh firebrand yet - he reclaimed the party leadership and made a peace of sorts with Asquith too. But he badly misjudged the emergence of Hitler, considering him a kind of revolutionary hero throughout the thirties and then becoming fatalistic and defeatist during the Second World War. It was a sad end to such a staggering political career, but, despite the vices, hypocrisy and naked greed, he will always be remembered as one of the greatest reforming politicians of the 20th century and the man who turned an unthinkable military defeat into the most exhilarating of victories.

13

THE BATTLE FOR IRELAND

Roger Casement, a retired consular official turned Irish revolutionary, presented the British government with a not inconsiderable problem. He had been sentenced to death for his role in the Easter Rising of 1916, a disorganised fiasco whose intention had been to liberate Ireland from British rule. But the terms of the 1351 Treason Act confined the definition of treason to activities carried out in Britain and, since Casement had made his preparations for the insurrection whilst in Germany there was a real worry in Westminster that he would escape the noose.

Asquith's ministry then did two things which encapsulated the whole tawdry, pernicious nature of the British government's treatment of the Irish people since the act of union in 1801. Firstly, they reinterpreted the archaic Norman-English text of the Treason Act to suit their purposes and provide legal justification for Casement's execution. As if that wasn't enough, they also elected to expose his homosexuality - which was at the time regarded as both morally reprehensible and highly illegal - by publishing explicit diaries which may or may not have been faked. One way or another they would get their man.

The irony is that in hanging Casement alongside 18 others - many of whom had nothing to do with the uprising - the Liberals appalled the Catholic majority of Ireland. They not only made martyrs of the executed men but exploded a sense of grievous injustice that had previously been confined to a gaggle of religious fanatics and serial agitators. The years to come would see the inexorable rise of Sinn Fein and militant Irish nationalism, culminating in bloody civil war and eventual, hard won independence for the South. Then a period of relative stability would give way to the relentless sectarian terrorism of the Troubles in Northern Ireland, a political and humanitarian crisis unparalleled in post-war Britain. The story of Britain's vexed relationship with its oldest colony is tragic, embarrassing and ignominious, yet ultimately hopeful and cathartic. It runs parallel to some of her greatest successes and most enlightened achievements - a constant reminder that the famed British constitution should not always be the envy of the world.

*

In 1801 - after she had been cajoled into becoming a part of the United Kingdom - Ireland's population, particularly in the South, was predominantly Catholic whereas England's was predominantly Protestant. The fact that British governance was essentially Protestant governance was bound to cause a certain amount of friction, especially considering that - although Catholics had been enfranchised in 1797 - Catholicism remained a bar to entering Parliament itself.

This was the issue that Pitt the Younger had resigned over and it also created the original Irish radical folk hero, Daniel O'Connell. A product of the revolutionary upheavals of the 1790s O'Connell won the County Clare by-election in 1828 but, as a practising Roman Catholic, was prohibited from taking his seat in Parliament. O'Connell made it clear that he was determined to exercise his political right and, via his Catholic Association, bombarded Wellington's government with speeches and propaganda that threatened violent retribution if he was prevented from doing so. Wellington - with Peel at his side - caved in and passed the Catholic Emancipation Act of 1829 which finished him politically.

Now that O'Connell was a fully-fledged Member of Parliament he led the more reform-minded Irish representatives in campaigning for improved primary education for Catholics, reform of the Board of Works and a major overhaul of the Anglican Church of Ireland. After the successful resolution of these issues O'Connell became more extreme and in the early 1840s started lobbying for repeal of the Union and Irish independence. The then Prime Minister Robert Peel responded to this pressure with a confused mixture of repression and appeasement which did little to calm the rapidly heightening nationalist mood amongst the Catholic South of Ireland.

The sense of bitterness towards British rule was intensified by the catastrophic potato famine of 1845-6. The loss of significant numbers of smallholders led to the buying up of large amounts of land by speculators, leaving many of the remaining natives destitute and impoverished. Whilst Peel and his successor Lord John Russell did put policies in place to attempt to alleviate the suffering caused by the famine, the insistence on the continuation of laissez faire economics meant that vital food was still being exported out of the country at the height of the tragedy. In addition, despite Peel's vociferous opposition to the infamous Corn Laws his unwillingness to simply suspend them during the crisis rather than arguing for permanent repeal led many within Ireland to speculate that their suffering was being used for political leverage. The concomitant mass emigration - primarily to the United States - fostered a vigorous anti-British movement overseas that heavily publicised the Catholic Irish cause.

O'Connell's death in 1851 left the protesting Irish without a dynamic leader to rally behind. Just as it seemed like opposition would crumble into apathy the republican Fenians emerged to fill the void. The Fenians - or the Irish Republican Brotherhood as they became known from 1860 - were a new breed of Irish radical. Founded in American exile by the Gaelic scholar John O' Mahony they preached open revolution and unequivocal separation from the United Kingdom through armed insurrection. Their most provocative act was the double murder of Lord Frederick Cavendish, Chief Secretary for Ireland, and his permanent undersecretary Thomas Burke as they walked through Dublin's Phoenix Park in May 1882. With the IRB there was no room for negotiation or reform and it was from the Fenian ideology that later extreme organisations such as Sinn Fein and the Irish Republican Army were birthed. But at the tail end of the 1860s their primary effect was to frighten the bulk of the Irish into pursuing more moderate methods for autonomy. The key initiative became home rule, which would obsess Gladstone for much of his time as Prime Minister.

Despite passing voluminous legislation aimed at pacifying the discontented Irish it was not until the mid-1880s that Gladstone accepted the idea of home rule as a viable option for resolving the ongoing problems. The contentious concept would mean a separate Irish Parliament based in Dublin but the retention of the common government of the United Kingdom. It felt to many at the time like the most sensible compromise available.

The most passionate Irish advocate of home rule was Charles Stewart Parnell. A formidable Irish Nationalist MP he was leader of both the Land League and the Home Rule League, which morphed into the dominant political party for Irish nationalism, the Irish Parliamentary Party, in 1882. Whilst Parnell was radical enough to associate with the Fenians and had served a sentence in the monolithic Kilmainham Gaol, he was also sufficiently canny to advance more moderate views on the Irish situation. His condemnation of the assassinations of Cavendish and Burke earned him the respect of many political heavyweights of the time, including Gladstone.

But Parnell's hopes were to be dashed by the House of Commons, who threw out the first Home Rule Bill in 1886, contributing to the fatal split in Liberal ranks that saw Chamberlain and his band of Unionists decamp to the Conservatives. The Conservatives then surged to power and held it for the majority of the next two decades. At least Parnell did not have to suffer the agony of the Second Home Rule Bill of 1893 crashing in the Lords, having died of pneumonia two years previously.

Despite the advent of a Conservative government bolstered by virulent Liberal Unionists the Irish Nationalist cause was surprisingly subdued in the closing years of the nineteenth century. This was due in large part to ideological infighting centred on support for and disaffection with the Parnellite home rule position. The Liberal resurgence in 1906, however, brought fresh hope and confidence of a satisfactory outcome. The traditional Liberal sympathy for a degree of Irish self-governance was shared by Asquith who proposed a third Home Rule Bill in 1912.

The crucial difference between the Third Home Rule Bill and its two unsuccessful predecessors was that the position of the House of Lords had been irrevocably altered in the interim. The Parliament Act of the previous year had neutered the upper chamber's ability to cast aside legislation it did not approve of, limiting its powers to that of finite delay. It was no surprise that the Lords blocked this incarnation of the bill but now that would not mean incontrovertible defeat. The Nationalists would have to wait a further couple of years for a Dublin Parliament but, considering the decades that they had spent fighting for a measure of autonomy, two more years barely seemed a hardship. Ireland, however, was not an exclusively Catholic country and in the North in particular the Protestant population were preparing to assert their identity just as forcibly.

*

The Ulster Unionists were formed in 1905 as a response to the disparate nationalist groups that were determined to sever links with Westminster. However, it was the accession of the Dublin born Edward Carson to the party leadership in 1911 that really galvanized opposition to home rule in the northernmost counties of the country.

A brilliant barrister who had played a significant part in the conviction of Oscar Wilde for sodomy, Carson viewed the imminent passing of the Third Home Rule Bill as a green light for Catholic persecution of the Northern Protestant minority. To this end he created a muscular militia called the Ulster Volunteer Force to combat the more zealous strands of the nationalist movement. The trouble was the UVF also attracted the attention and fear of Parliament. The British government reacted to the raised profile of Ulster unionism with a muddle-headed pre-emptive strike in the summer of 1914 that alienated huge numbers of its own subjects.

Nervous of rumours of Ulster Unionists stockpiling arms Asquith told the army to prepare to intervene should events take a violent turn. The problem was that many British Army soldiers shared the Ulster Unionists

Protestant faith and had a good deal more in common with Carson's men than with the Catholic agitators that they were supposed to be defending. There were fears of mass mutiny among the ranks should these troops be called upon to suppress the Ulster Volunteers. Secretary of State for War Sir John Seely decreed that soldiers with connections to Ulster were exempted from serving against Ulster Unionists only to discover that his most senior officers were also determined not to fire on Ulstermen who they regarded as good British patriots.

It was not just the army who were disgusted by the government's attitude towards Ulster. To many in England the granting of home rule looked suspiciously like the first step to abandoning empire and smacked of a defeatism that gravely insulted Britain's imperial history. Faced with such steadfast military and public opinion Seely and the British Army's Commander in Chief Sir John French were humiliated into accepting that home rule would not be enforced by the army in the North of Ireland. It was an astonishing display of insubordination from a military that prided itself on unquestioning loyalty and devotion to Crown and Parliament. And it worked.

The outbreak of the First World War was a further nail in the coffin of home rule. Just as the technicalities of the process were being ironed out in Westminster Gavrilo Princip assassinated the Archduke Franz Ferdinand and tore the existing global order asunder. Britain now had a far more pressing crisis to deal with and Ireland would have to wait. To a significant number of Catholics in the South this was simply unacceptable.

Both the Nationalist and Republican causes in the South and the Unionist cause in the North gathered pace and aggression. The Fenian-derived Irish Republican Brotherhood that had lain dormant for years attracted more passionate young activists as did Sinn Fein, a republican political party founded in 1905 whose name translates as 'Ourselves Alone.' By 1916, with the Allied powers floundering on the battlefields of France, the republican movement felt that their moment had come.

Enter the disillusioned, Irish born, former government apparatchik Roger Casement. Ever since the declaration of war he had been lobbying for German military assistance for an Irish uprising, an action which would be mutually beneficial since it would draw significant numbers of British troops away from the European theatre of war. At the same time and unbeknownst to him the IRB were laying the foundations for their own revolt, martialling their forces and infiltrating more moderate Nationalist organisations.

Both rebellions were doomed to fail. This was a fact that the Kaiser realised only too well, resulting in a paltry offer of 20,000 rifles and no men. The arms were intercepted before they even reached Ireland and Casement himself was captured upon landing at Tralee Bay. Yet the IRB and Casement's improvised band of terrorists were in too deep to back out and pooled their meagre resources into an insurrection in Dublin over Easter weekend 1916.

The Easter Rising has gone down as a flashpoint in the battle for Irish independence and an event of talismanic importance to those who believe that all of Ireland should be free from British rule. But at the time it was a bloody disaster for the Republican cause resulting in the slaughter of over 250 civilians and the execution of all their leaders and key figures. This crushing defeat was inevitable considering the feeble resources at their disposal, although the British reacted unaccountably slowly and fought with bizarre incompetence. Over a hundred British soldiers died needlessly before waves of reinforcements made further Republican opposition untenable. The rising had lasted for five days.

And that should have been that. The British Army had hardly covered itself in glory but the rebellion had been comprehensively quashed and any uppity notions of Irish independence should have evaporated at the same time. But now the British government made a horrendous error of judgement which only served to turn many more Irishmen and women against Westminster. Despite Sinn Fein's singular lack of involvement in the Easter Rising 3,500 of its members and supporters were rounded up by the British and 15 brutally executed. The Republican cause now had a ready-made band of political martyrs and an unequivocal symbol of British cruelty and injustice. In the aftermath of the executions Sinn Fein's membership soared. After the 1918 general election and aided by the government's threat of Irish conscription, they became the dominant Irish party in Parliament.

Issues of republicanism and unionism became further complicated by the heroic actions of the 36th Ulster Division at the Battle of the Somme in July of 1916. Both the incredible bravery demonstrated by the division and the huge casualties that they incurred meant that any idea of forcing Ulster to accept a form of home rule became unthinkable. For the British it polarised the argument even further - the Unionists were gallant, patriotic heroes willing to lay down their lives for the mother country whilst the Republicans were psychotic terrorists only too happy to do deals with the Kaiser. Conciliation appeared impossible.

Sinn Fein continued to stir the pot by refusing to allow its 73 new MPs to take up their seats at Westminster. Instead they set up the Dail Eireann - an alternative Irish Parliament in Dublin – in 1919 and elected the fanatically religious Eamon de Valera as their inaugural President. They backed up their proclamation of independence with guerrilla violence against British soldiers and police, chiefly carried out by the newly formed Irish Republican Army and the president of the IRB Michael Collins. Backed into a corner by the escalating levels of bloodshed Lloyd George, exhausted by waging war against the Kaiser, had no option but to declare the Dail and Sinn Fein illegal. The Prime Minister's action ushered in the Irish War of Independence.

This vicious little war saw tit for tat violence perpetrated by both the IRA and government-sanctioned demobbed troops known as Black and Tans. Desperate for a speedy resolution to the conflict - particularly after the devastation wrought by World War I - the Prime Minister proposed the Government of Ireland Act in 1920 which partitioned the country into Southern and Northern Ireland. The latter was comprised of six of the nine Ulster counties and retained its place as part of the United Kingdom.

However, whilst the South became a separate Irish state it was still under overall control from Westminster. Unsurprisingly the Protestant Northern Ireland was happy to accept the Act whereas the rest of Catholic Ireland was most definitely not.

Talks began the following year to attempt to reach a settlement that all sides could accept. De Valera, keen to secure a political scapegoat should compromise be required, sent Collins to negotiate with the British. The best offer on the table was for Southern Ireland to be renamed the Irish Free State, according it dominion status. She would govern herself but would still ultimately be a British possession. Collins accepted this Anglo-Irish treaty and the Dail grudgingly voted in favour but all parties knew that it would not be good enough. The IRA split into the pro-treaty Free State and anti-treaty Republican factions. By 1922 the Irish Civil War had replaced the Irish War of Independence as the senseless, brutal conflict du jour.

The fighting dragged on for a year and became increasingly cold-blooded and sickening. Collins was one of many who would not live to see its conclusion, gunned down on a County Cork road in August 1922. The final stages of the conflict were characterised by the summary executions of prisoners on both sides, until eventually the Free State gained the upper hand. After the Republican leader Liam Lynch became the latest high profile figure to be ruthlessly dispatched his successor Frank Aiken decided that enough blood had been shed and called an immediate ceasefire. It was not until 1949 - following studied neutrality during the Second World War that appalled many outside observers - that the Irish Free State would finally shrug off the last vestiges of British control. Yet the freshly created Republic of Ireland still clung on to a constitutional claim to the North of the island thus proving that unification of North and South was still very much alive in many people's hearts and minds.

Meanwhile in Northern Ireland a separate government, headed by Sir James Craig, had been set up at the Stormont Estate. Although technically a part of the Irish Free State under the terms of the Anglo-Irish treaty, the wording gave Northern Ireland dispensation to opt out of the State and remain a British province. This was a right which she duly exercised.

Although this pleased Northern Ireland's Protestant majority there was still a significant Catholic population resident in the province who quickly realised that greater devolved power meant the strong likelihood of remorseless persecution. So it proved, with anti-Catholic prejudice rife in public housing and employment as well as frequent physical attacks carried out by various Loyalist gangs. But the violence was never quite severe enough to direct Westminster's gaze away from the 'red threat' of Stalin's Russia or the numerous collapsing parts of Britain's far flung empire. The bigotry, bullying and hatred festering within Northern Ireland may not have been officially sanctioned by the British government but, so long as it remained low-level, successive ministries were more than happy to turn a blind eye.

And then, one summer day in 1969, a Loyalist organization elected to process along the same route that was being taken by a Catholic civil rights march. The results were incendiary. A notoriously wild section of the Royal Ulster Constabulary known as the B-Specials laid into the civil rights activists with incredible ferocity, leaving over 75 marchers injured and all right thinking members of the public horrified. The Northern Irish government made conciliatory noises and promised long overdue reforms aimed at fairer treatment of Catholic citizens. But the genie was now out of the bottle and the sectarian antipathy that had been lurking beneath the surface for the past four decades exploded in a series of bloody clashes across Belfast.

Fearing a return to the brutal civil war of the 1920s Britain's Labour Prime Minister Harold Wilson made the fateful decision to send in the British Army. Ostensibly there to protect Catholics from potential Protestant pogroms they were trusted by neither side, and the resurgent IRA persuaded the Catholic faithful that they were the only organization that

143

would fight for their interests. It is a measure of the febrile atmosphere of the times that even the IRA came to be seen as too soft, splintering in late 1969 and creating the Provisional Irish Republican Army or Provos. The struggle to forcibly unite Ireland was back on again.

The next year the Conservatives were returned to power in Britain under Edward Heath. Heath understood the urgent need to get both the Republic and Northern Ireland talking and to thrash out a deal which would bring an end to the escalating bloodshed. His favoured idea of a power-sharing executive between Catholics and Protestants appeared to be gaining traction when events in the embattled city of Londonderry overtook any attempted negotiations.

Following the introduction of a policy of internment without trial in 1971 the Catholic Northern Ireland Civil Rights Association planned a demonstration through the streets of Derry to protest at what they saw as inhumane treatment. The events of 30th January 1972 are hotly disputed but, although the protest was intended to be peaceful, there may have been a small faction within the NICRA who began throwing stones. What happened next stunned the world. The British Parachute Regiment opened fire shooting 26 unarmed civilians and killing 14 of them. 'Bloody Sunday' instantly became infamous, a shocking atrocity that served as the best recruitment material for the Provos imaginable. The Provisional IRA had always said that the British Army were treacherous and here was the bloodstained proof. Heath's government could only fan the flames, arresting over 300 suspected IRA members and sympathisers. The number of sectarian murders skyrocketed and by the end of March direct rule from London had been imposed. A staggering 479 people were killed in 1972 alone.

Now mainland Britain was seen as a legitimate IRA target for bombings, assassinations and other atrocities. Atrocity bred outrage with the mass murder of civilians in Guildford and Birmingham leading to dreadful miscarriages of justice from a British legal system desperate to secure convictions. In a last throw of the dice the first Secretary of State for

Northern Ireland Willie Whitelaw attempted a double whammy of desperate diplomacy. Firstly he tried to persuade the Republic of Ireland to abandon its traditional constitutional claim to the North before encouraging the implementation of the Sunningdale Agreement. This optimistic piece of 1974 legislation proposed a power-sharing executive between Unionists and the moderate Social Democratic and Labour Party. Both gambles failed.

The Troubles remained at fever pitch for the rest of the seventies with yearly death tolls in the hundreds. In March 1979 Airey Neave, the Shadow Secretary of State for Northern Ireland and close friend and adviser to Margaret Thatcher, was assassinated by the IRA just outside the House of Commons. A bomb had been planted in his car. Later the same year Earl Louis Mountbatten of Burma, uncle of the Duke of Edinburgh, was blown up on board his fishing boat whilst holidaying in County Sligo. The IRA claimed responsibility, insinuating that the attention this one high profile death would attract highlighted the hypocrisy of a government supposedly apathetic to the deaths of hundreds in the province.

Margaret Thatcher's attitude towards these and subsequent terrorist atrocities in the 1980s was typically robust. Conservative policy aimed at integration of Northern Ireland into the United Kingdom and would brook no compromise with the IRA, Sinn Fein or any other aggressively nationalist organisation. The IRA responded in 1984, attempting to wipe out the Prime Minister and her cabinet by detonating a bomb in the Grand Hotel in Brighton, scene of the Conservative party conference. She survived unscathed but five party members were killed. Six years later another car bomb dispatched Ian Gow, a Conservative MP who had had a hand in drafting Northern Ireland policy with Airey Neave many years earlier.

Meanwhile in the province itself Republican martyrs were being created. A horrendous hunger strike was instigated in 1981 in the notorious Maze Prison by the IRA member Bobby Sands. Centred on the right of Sands and his fellow terrorist inmates to be classed as political prisoners rather than common criminals, the strike attracted widespread publicity and resulted in Sands being elected to Parliament as MP for Fermanagh and South Tyrone. The Anti H-Block/Armagh Political Prisoner party was hastily created as his platform. Sands died in May the same year amidst global condemnation of his treatment at the hands of the British government.

Whilst the numbers of casualties in the conflict had dropped from their terrifying early-70s peak the yearly death tolls were still a devastating testament to the depth of hatred and refusal to compromise that the Troubles had instilled. But by the 1990s there was a chink of light that would, after much more heartache and suffering, grow to become a glorious new dawn for Northern Ireland.

It may be easy to criticize the limp, listless administration of John Major but in terms of furthering the Northern Ireland peace process he achieved considerably more than his predecessors had done. By talking the language of conciliation rather than belligerence he paved the way for Tony Blair's Labour government to bring the saga's protagonists round the negotiating table.

Major's key message was a dramatic shift in Conservative policy toward the province. The British government was now ready to accept a unified Ireland should that be what both sides in the conflict really wanted. Hitherto Margaret Thatcher and her successive Northern Ireland ministers had preached steadfast commitment to the United Kingdom and Northern Irish integration. What was more the Prime Minister promised legitimacy for the IRA if they were prepared to lay down their weapons for good. The timing was still not quite right to bring the Troubles to a conclusion but without Major's intervention the end would have been considerably longer coming.

When Tony Blair surfed into Downing Street in 1997 on a wave of public adoration he was determined that peace in Northern Ireland would be a major part of his legacy. Blair's presidential view of himself demanded

146

that he address the big issues head on and there was no more pressing problem than the Troubles. There can be no doubting the time, effort and resources that the new Prime Minister put in to solving Northern Ireland. But there is equally no denying that he was immeasurably aided by his fearless, compassionate Northern Ireland Secretary Mo Mowlam, one of the finest female politicians that Parliament has thus far produced.

The negotiations behind what became the Good Friday Agreement were arduous, infuriating and frequently appeared to have fallen apart. That they eventually succeeded was down to a sheer will not to give up on the part of the government. Blair and Mowlam took huge risks in their pursuit of the ultimate goal, the former inviting Gerry Adams and Martin McGuinness of Sinn Fein to Downing Street and the latter entering the Maze prison to converse with convicted terrorists. The delicate balancing act of keeping both Republicans and Unionists on side led to accusations of favouritism and leniency toward both camps, in particular towards the Republicans who secured the release of considerable numbers of political prisoners. But Blair was prepared to do whatever it took to get the right result and on the politically significant Easter weekend of 1998 a deal was finally struck.

Ireland would continue to be partitioned with the North remaining a part of the United Kingdom and the South surrendering its contentious constitutional claim to the province. The practicalities proved a good deal harder to ensure than the legislative niceties. The establishment of the longed-for power-sharing executive was complicated by fresh elections which returned the hard-line Sinn Fein and Democratic Unionist Party at the expense of their more moderate equivalents. Also predictably troublesome was the stipulation that both sides surrender their arms.

Tragically it took the single worst atrocity of the entire conflict to persuade the central protagonists to compromise. On 15th August 1998 a car bomb ripped the heart out of Omagh in County Tyrone killing 29 civilians. An IRA splinter group calling themselves the 'Real IRA' claimed responsibility but this time there was nothing but condemnation from all sides. The group were forced to apologise for the atrocity and a little while later Gerry Adams and the DUP leader Dr. Ian Paisley finally accepted the urgent need for conciliation.

The subsequent 18 years have been by no means a bucolic utopia. There have still been sectarian deaths but they have drastically decreased in number and are no longer tacitly sanctioned by larger political parties or pressure groups. Northern Ireland is still haunted by its bloody, divisive history but in the 21st century it has become a largely peaceful, more prosperous place to live. It can only be fervently hoped that it will long remain so.

14

AMBLING TOWARDS THE ABYSS

On 30th September 1938 the Prime Minister Neville Chamberlain stood on the landing strip of Heston Aerodrome and delivered one of the most infamous speeches in British political history. His confident assertion that the agreement he had signed in Munich with the German Chancellor Adolf Hitler was 'peace for our time' has become synonymous with British complacency and diplomatic hubris.

Ever since Hitler had seized power in 1933 his succession of aggressive nationalist manoeuvres had been met with inactivity and appeasement by the British government. Eventually his demands for the annexation of the Sudetenland – a part of Czechoslovakia but with a substantial German population - to the Reich in May 1938 forced the hands of both Chamberlain and his French counterpart Edouard Daladier. The Munich Agreement acquiesced meekly to practically all of Hitler's stipulations in the vain hope of preserving the precarious peace that had been under threat ever since the Nazis came to power. The German Chancellor had given his word that he would curb his rapacious desire for lebensraum – or living space – and to a decent, unimaginative Englishman like Neville Chamberlain a gentleman's word was his bond.

But in the increasingly dark and ruthless inter-war years Britain's traditional belief in 'playing the game' put her at odds with the prevailing ideologies of the rest of Europe. The collapse of the Liberals in the early 1920s left a void which was filled by Britain's first major Socialist political party and the new duopoly that Labour shared with the Conservatives sharply divided the electorate along class lines. Many feared that such a stark dichotomy could bring the nation to the brink of revolution, with the catastrophic financial crises that were currently rocking the world acting as the perfect catalyst. That it didn't happen is testament to a deep seated deference to authority present in the working classes. Despite industrial unrest and class resentment, the lower orders refrained from the kind of insurrectionary behaviour that gripped the rest of the continent in the 1930s. Britain in the inter-war years was a place where consensus ruled and little got done, but it was also one of the most politically stable countries in the developed world.

After a conflict as unprecedented in its brutality and wholesale destruction as the First World War the last thing that Britain needed was more excitement. Lloyd George may have been a dazzling statesman in his prime but now that his star had faded the British people craved stability, consistency and a quiet life. Stanley Baldwin was just the man to give it to them. In reality he was no more the affable country gent than Robert Walpole had been. Indeed he had demonstrated considerable steel in leading his party's backbenchers in the 1922 coup against Lloyd George. But Baldwin, whilst never the most dynamic politician, possessed a genius for manipulating image and message that would have today's legions of spin doctors drooling in admiration.

His meteoric rise to power alone gives the lie to his carefully honed persona of Pooterish ordinariness. He had gone from President of the Board of Trade to Chancellor in quick succession before becoming the Conservative Prime Minister in May 1923. Baldwin made numerous mistakes throughout his three spells in the top job but his uncanny knack for telling the public exactly what they wanted to hear ensured that he survived where many a bolder but less perceptive politician would have crashed and burned.

The first of these errors of political judgement resulted in the Conservatives losing office and came after Baldwin had been PM for a matter of mere months. Searching for ways to fix the country's broken economic model he revived the hoary old issue of protectionism, becoming so convinced that this was what the nation wanted that he called a snap general election to provide him with a mandate for its implementation. But the public did not want it and the Conservatives haemorrhaged votes, finishing well short of the numbers required for a majority. Yet despite Baldwin's colossal misjudgement he was canny enough to make the best of it. Recognising that a coalition with Labour - who had finished second for the first time in a general election – would provide plenty of ammunition for the Socialists he sat back and offered the Liberals the chance of coalition with the Labour party instead. When the Liberals refused – as Baldwin knew full well they would – Labour would be left with the mixed blessing of forming a minority government. Baldwin correctly surmised that the Labour ministry would be short-lived and that when it inevitably fell the Conservatives, rather than the Liberals, would be best placed to take advantage.

The first Labour administration may have been prevented from achieving anything of note by the combined opposition of the Conservatives and the heavily depleted Liberals but, considering Labour's Parliamentary infancy, it was an astonishing development. This was a political party formed by the working class for the working class and they were now – at least in theory - running the country. Baldwin's replacement as Prime Minister was Ramsay MacDonald, one of the firebrands of the left instrumental in the party's formation, and there was a genuine horror from large sections of society that Britain was about to slide into Bolshevik revolution.

Yet the flamboyant MacDonald's greatest skill in his early political career had been the forging of alliances between the party and both the trade unions and the Liberals. He was a committed Socialist but, like Keir Hardie, one who recognised the need to cultivate goodwill and trust. MacDonald, therefore, was too aware of his government's need to earn respectability for any radical measures to even be proposed. Yet this did not stop Lord Rothermere, the reactionary press baron and owner of the Daily Mail, from publishing a forged letter from Soviet heavyweight Grigory Zinoviev on the eve of the 1924 general election. The letter purported to be urging British Communists to revolt and implied strong links between the Russian hierarchy and the Labour government.

Rothermere's scare tactics did the trick and Labour was ousted in favour of a knowing Baldwin and his Conservatives.

The Prime Minister now set about instilling his vision of a country where everybody knew their place and rubbed along with each other agreeably. A key part of his stratagem was to subtly emphasise the potential dangers of the new democracy and inculcate a sense that he was the man to marshal it responsibly. He was also keen to appear sympathetic – even indulgent – to the Labour party as a clever way of neutralising their threat and fostering a broad, safe political consensus.

Courtesy of the self-destructing Liberals and a discredited Labour the Conservatives appeared to have an unassailable claim to power for years. Baldwin's idea was to solidify this single party hegemony into a society where the different classes collaborated willingly for the national good. Crucial to this utopian inter-class teambuilding was the relationship between the trade unions and the captains of industry. It may have been a laudable concept in principle but the reality was that the lower and middle classes had practically nothing in common in the mid-1920s and treated each other with mutual bafflement and suspicion. This disparity was only emphasised at a time of economic hardship for the Industrial Revolution's Northern powerhouses whilst the affluent South enjoyed something of a consumer boom.

But the biggest threat to Baldwinian class consensus was almost entirely of his cabinet's own making. It was an all too frequent example of British self-importance getting in the way of common sense, and it provoked the only general strike that Britain has ever endured. The government was about to be seduced by the glitter of gold.

Winston Churchill had been unceremoniously dumped out of government in 1915, sacrificed for the unity of the wartime coalition. Seething at repeated snubs from Lloyd George and increasingly aeriated over the rise of Socialism he defected back to the Conservatives at the 1924 general election. To everyone's surprise - including Churchill's own - Baldwin appointed him Chancellor of the Exchequer.

This was rather a poisoned chalice during the depressed post-war years. As we have seen, Baldwin's gamble on reintroducing protectionism had backfired on him badly but something radical had to be done to try and break Britain out of the financial doldrums. The maverick, impulsive Churchill – entirely unsuited to the sober mathematics of the Treasury – looked backwards to Britain's pre-war policies of free trade and the gold standard. Ever the nostalgic romantic he recklessly disregarded the shifts in the global order that the First World War had wrought and wildly overvalued sterling against the rampant US dollar.

The gold standard fixed the currency of a particular country against a set amount of gold thus simplifying the process of trade between member nations. The downside of this streamlined trading tool was that the currencies of economically ailing nations could be readily exchanged for gold by their investors. Therefore valuing your currency too highly was an act of potentially ruinous hubris. This was precisely what Churchill did in 1925 by reinstating the pre-1914 rate of sterling against the dollar, taking no account of the United States' dramatically altered financial and political position.

When cheap imported coal from Germany began to flood Britain Churchill's folly was exposed. The mining industry was hit with lower wages and longer hours by owners desperate to cut costs, resulting in 800,000 miners going out on strike in May 1926. The Trades Union Congress then called on all their members to support the aggrieved miners, thus kick-starting Britain's one and only general strike.

The striking workers' cause was undermined by two key factors. Firstly, the strike leaders were too timid in their threats should they not receive the assurances that they were seeking. They openly declared that they had no desire to overthrow the government or even hamper its effectiveness therefore rendering their bargaining position weak from the outset. Secondly, their intention to bring the country to a complete standstill was thwarted by scenes reminiscent of the communal spirit of the First World War. Huge sections of the middle class 'mucked in' by running makeshift transport services or shovelling coal and, whilst there were a handful of altercations between strikers and volunteers, it quickly became clear that the anticipated widespread disruption of the strike was being neutralised highly effectively.

After nine days the TUC's Arthur Pugh called off the general strike, much to the relief of Stanley Baldwin who had been characteristically reasonable and conciliatory throughout. The miners carried on alone until they were starved back to work in November. The mine owners retained every measure they had originally imposed on their workers and - to add insult to injury - the government passed the Trade Disputes and Trade Unions Act the following year which outlawed sympathetic strikes. Baldwin's dream of harmonious worker-owner collaboration lay in tatters.

The nation was still combating the chaos caused by the return to gold when a fresh economic crisis enveloped the entire globe. It had originated in America where the consumer boom had seen vast amounts of goods purchased on hire-purchase credit and legions of fraudulent investment and property schemes launched. The inevitable happened on October 24th 1929 with the collapse of the US stock market, and whilst its reverberations were not felt as keenly in Britain as in many other western nations, the effect on the country's finances was devastating nonetheless.

The Wall Street Crash coincided with the formation of the second minority Labour government of the decade, once more under the leadership of Ramsay MacDonald. The 1929 general election had been the first to be fought with a full franchise - Baldwin having extended the vote to women over the age of 21 the previous year – and so the rejection of the studiedly cautious Conservative government was a reflection of what the entire nation felt. The defeat of the general strike had softened fears of Bolshevik takeover and many voters simply wanted a change from Baldwin's avuncular inactivity. Yet had they known the severity of the economic collapse on the horizon they may not have been so magnanimous in the polling booth.

Unfortunately the Labour government did not prove up to the task of rescuing the economy. Their inexperience in government coupled with too many differing economic standpoints within the cabinet led to chronic indecision and confusion. MacDonald favoured public works schemes to bolster employment whilst his uncompromising Chancellor Philip Snowden advocated blind faith in the precepts of free trade. When the monolithic Creditanstalt Bank of Vienna collapsed in May 1931 the European financial situation went from desperate to catastrophic. The only option remaining for MacDonald's beleaguered government was a package of swingeing cuts which would hit trade union unemployment benefit particularly hard. For many senior figures in the cabinet such measures went against everything the Labour party stood for. In the late summer of 1931 the cabinet sensationally split over enormous proposed cuts to public spending, thus bringing the government to its knees.

The logical next step would have been to call for Baldwin. Instead George V appealed to MacDonald to head up an inter-party National Government to pool resources and save the economy. This was a crucial moment not only for the Labour leader but for the immediate future of the entire party. MacDonald's Socialism may have been tempered by an awareness of electability but his track record more than proved his commitment to the cause. By retaining the position of Prime Minister in a government shared with the Conservatives he laid himself open to accusations of selling out his principles for the sake of personal power. On the other hand, if he stayed true to his political ethics and walked away was he then abandoning his country at a time of national emergency? It is a dilemma that a certain Liberal Democrat leader of the 21st century may sympathise with.

MacDonald felt compelled to accept the King's offer but soon realised that he was now effectively a puppet leader. The Conservatives dominated the new coalition with Baldwin himself Prime Minister in all but name. MacDonald and Snowden were vilified by the Labour faithful and thrown out of the party. Their reputations have never recovered. Britain came off the gold standard that September - thus ending Churchill's ignominious financial experiment - and the protectionism that Baldwin had called for eight years earlier was eventually installed in 1932. The 1931 general election was a ringing endorsement for the National Government but the overwhelming majority of MPs returned were Conservative – 473 to Labour's paltry 52.

The green shoots of recovery were felt relatively quickly but only by those in work and living in the South. The devaluation of the pound resulted in a marked fall in prices and this, combined with a housing boom, meant that the consumer Britain of motor cars and cinema trips made a surprise comeback in the lower half of the country. The situation in the North by contrast was desperate. Industries that had been the bedrock of the Industrial Revolution such as textiles and shipbuilding crumbled and, with no modern welfare state in place to protect them, unemployed workers and their families were forced to beg for handouts or starve. A series of hunger marches took place throughout the 1930s, of which the 1936 Jarrow March is the most famous. These heart-breaking processions involved hundreds of impoverished Northerners walking to London for an inevitably fruitless meeting with largely uninterested politicians.

Yet the workers' revolution still did not come. However, this is not to say that there were no voices of dissent in the political landscape of the 1930s. The formation of the National Government effectively neutered party politics in Britain until the conclusion of the Second World War. The nominal opposition was the ragbag of Labour MPs who had not been absorbed into the National Government. Led by the Christian pacifist George Lansbury their calls for unilateral disarmament sank steadily in public opinion as the power of Fascist Germany and Italy rose in global affairs. Given Labour's suicidal political position Baldwin - hiding behind MacDonald until the latter's resignation in 1935 - had a free hand to do whatever he wanted. But alongside literary left-wingers like George Orwell and JB Priestley a number of parties began to emerge on the political fringes. These disparate radical organisations provided a counter-narrative to the tired Capitalism that had precipitated the worst financial crash in history. Some of these parties were eccentric while some were downright sinister, but they were all a part of the fabric of political life in the lead-up to World War II.

*

The Kindred of the Kibbo Kift were formed by the artist John Hargrave in 1920 as a pacifist alternative to the all-conquering British scout movement. A hotch-potch of paganism, medievalism, Native American and Viking iconography the youth organisation promoted peace, the great outdoors and archaic ritual and were one of the more colourful of the numerous lifestyle fads of the 1920s.

By 1932, however, Hargrave had steered the quaintly esoteric movement in an altogether more political and militaristic direction. Now known as the Greenshirts, what Hargrave and his radically restructured organisation stood for was a controversial new concept called Social Credit, pioneered by an engineer from the North West called Clifford Douglas. Surmising that most workers did not have enough income from their pay packet to buy the self-same products that they had made Douglas proposed a National Dividend which would distribute the profit of the nation equally amongst all of its citizens. This system negated the need for wages or the Bank of England and would, Douglas asserted, result in increased production and national wealth. This economic boon would in turn usher in an age of leisure and spiritual fulfilment.

Douglas' philosophy can be seen as a cosy form of Communism and, indeed, Social Credit gained more traction in the 1930s than the official Communist party. Hargrave's Greenshirts became the movement's cheerleaders, marching through the streets in paramilitary uniforms excoriating the Treasury for its heartless Capitalism. But a large part of the Greenshirts' appeal lay in their sense of theatre and when the government passed the Public Order Act of 1937, which made it illegal to march in political uniform, the writing was on the wall for the survival of the movement. Nevertheless, Social Credit has remained an enticing alternative to mainstream politics in many countries and is frequently wheeled out as the economic Holy Grail in times of punishing recession.

If the Greenshirts were utopian idealists in warmongering costume then the United Empire Party was simply an ego-trip for influential bullies with a hatred of everybody. Set up by press barons Lords Rothermere and Beaverbrook it was the most concerted effort yet seen in British history to assert the megalomaniacal will of the media mogul. The power of the press had been seen to breath-taking effect during World War I when Lord Northcliffe's Daily Mail broke the story of Kitchener's incompetence, provoking the formation of the wartime coalition. Now two of his successors - angered both by the very idea of a Labour government and Baldwin's desire for protectionist tariffs - waged war against the entire political class both in newsprint and at the polling station. Their candidates were remarkably successful in two bi-elections in 1931, forcing Baldwin into his most brilliantly delivered speech wherein the genial man of the people roared like an indignant lion at the disproportionate powers of the press. The speech reversed the government's fortunes and Rothermere and Beaverbrook backed down – never again would a press baron attempt to topple the government so directly.

Yet for all the quirks and chutzpah of the Greenshirts and the Empire Crusaders it was Oswald Moseley's British Union of Fascists that provided the starkest contrast to the sterile, complacent National Government. Moseley's political journey makes even that of Churchill look one-dimensional. He started out as an urbane, well-heeled Conservative before lurching spectacularly to the left after the First World War. An energetic presence in the second Labour government Moseley fizzed with radical, reforming ideas that were curtly dismissed by MacDonald and Snowden, leading him to question the authenticity of his Socialist superiors. After one rebuff too many Moseley resigned to form the imaginatively titled New Party. Whilst this was still ostensibly a Socialist organization its leader was beginning to get drunk on personal power, whilst casting an appraising eye at Mussolini's Fascist Italy.

Given that the world's most powerful democracies were flailing wildly in the wake of a gigantic Capitalist crash it is only logical that restless minds were concluding that the paradigm had failed. They cast about for drastic alternatives. Maybe, they thought, a strong, dictatorial national leader was what was required to counter the fuzzy democratic inclusiveness that had produced such damaging results. Moseley certainly thought so and when the New Party were routed in the 1931 general election he dissolved them to form the overtly Fascist BUF, more commonly known as the Blackshirts.

Moseley had sunk from enlightened Socialist reformer to ugly anti-Semite and, alarmingly, large swathes of the country appeared to agree with his extreme views. Blackshirt membership peaked at 50,000 in 1934 as Moseley acquired the dubious support of Lord Rothermere and the Daily Mail. BUF rallies became increasingly visceral and one in the same year at Olympia attracted the attention of the equally violent Communist Party. The bloodshed and brawling that followed was a watershed moment for the popularity of the party, membership falling away sharply as people realised what an unpleasant gang of thugs the Blackshirts actually were.

But Moseley pressed on, predictably blaming Jewish prejudice for his fall from grace and targeting the predominantly Jewish East End in an effort to stir up confrontation and controversy. Confrontation certainly followed but it was the Blackshirts who came off worst. 1936's Battle of Cable Street is remembered proudly as the moment Britain decisively turned its back on Fascism, with 100,000 expertly drilled counter-demonstrators barricading the eponymous street with bricks and an overturned lorry to prevent a 2,000 strong BUF force from marching through. The Public Order Act of the following year had the same deleterious effect on Moseley's mob as it had on the eminently more endearing Greenshirts, and by the time he was rounded up during the Second World War Moseley had become a ranting curiosity viewed with derision and mockery. The British counted their blessings. In both Hitler and Mussolini they had seen what a narcissistic Fascist leader was capable of and were grateful they had had the good sense to muzzle their home-grown version before it was too late.

Meanwhile Churchill - not content with wrecking the economy - had turned his attentions to the fading grandeur of the British Empire, in particular the 'Jewel in the Crown' that was India. There had been talk of changing the status of Britain's most symbolic colony since 1917 as the financial burden of maintaining it - already severe enough before the Wall Street Crash - was crippling any opportunities to alleviate Britain's domestic woes. Additionally, there had been constant nationalist pressure from within India for a number of years, led chiefly by the charismatic activist Mahatma Gandhi.

In 1920 the Viceroy of India, Lord Irwin, declared that the country should be granted dominion status, in effect calling for Indian self-government. This was a far-sighted, enlightened and realistic assertion to make and a typically shrewd Baldwin agreed with him. Unfortunately, there were plenty of hard-line imperialists who found the idea of relinquishing any amount of power in India wholly unacceptable. Churchill was in the vanguard.

The Indian question displayed the worst aspects of the complex, contradictory Churchillian mind-set. In place of the radical pre-war social reformer came the jingoistic reactionary, making racist remarks about Gandhi's visit to negotiate with Irwin and fighting tooth and nail to preserve absolute control over the empire's Indian subjects. For the second time in his turbulent career he was ejected from the government. Baldwin stopped short of awarding India full dominion status, instead passing the Government of India Act in 1935 - a legislative fudge that promised heightened autonomy for the Indian provinces and the creation of a nebulous Federation of India. The increasingly monomaniacal Churchill railed against it, although the onset of the Second World War rendered it irrelevant anyway. To most sane observers he looked like a busted flush, a deluded old dinosaur consigned to the wilderness.

Which was, as we all now know, a national tragedy. For Churchill was one of the very few politicians who was right about Hitler and the dreadful chain of events that would lead Britain into another devastating global conflict. He spotted the danger early and as soon as the Nazis came to power he was relentless in urging the government to recognise the severity of the threat. In this he laid himself open to accusations of hypocrisy. During his disastrous tenure at the Treasury he had cut defence spending and deliberately slowed down warship production. But at that time the Fascist menace was not nearly so great and he had the backing of a nation who did not even want to consider the possibility of another war.

The trouble was that that was still how the nation - and also most of its elected representatives - thought. Gradually Churchill's non-stop hectoring won enough important people round to convince the government to step up rearmament, but this was in 1935 and was already too late to match the Herculean rate of military production taking place in Germany. Deep down those in power knew that Churchill was probably correct but the admission of this fact was simply too horrific to contemplate.

In 1937 the Age of Baldwin finally came to an end with his aloof and highly competent Chancellor Neville Chamberlain – son of Joseph – replacing him as Prime Minister. By this time Hitler had been acknowledged as a palpable threat to global peace and Chamberlain, backed by the majority of the nation, embarked on the now notorious process of appeasement that still shames Britain to this day. Whilst Hitler may have been going about his business too aggressively there was a general feeling that a lot of what he was striving for was eminently reasonable and a natural consequence of the punitive peace settlement at Versailles. If it avoided another ghastly war then why shouldn't the Germans reclaim what had originally been theirs in the first place? In many quarters Communism was viewed as the more immediate and potentially catastrophic danger.

Alarm bells really started ringing after the Anschluss of March 1938 which subsumed Austria into Hitler's Third Reich. This was followed by the German Chancellor's demands over the Sudetenland which prompted the capitulation of the Munich Agreement. Chamberlain and his chief appeaser Lord Halifax - formerly the Lord Irwin who had been so wise over the Indian question - relaxed slightly, confident that Hitler's hunger for expansion had been satiated.

But then, in March 1939 and following domestic atrocities such as the anti-Jewish pogrom of Kristallnacht, the Nazis marched into Bohemia. It was by now blindingly obvious that Hitler had been mocking all those weak, conciliatory diplomats and had never had any intention of halting his quest for total Nazi domination. With a dark foreboding of what would come next the British government resolved to intervene should Germany invade Poland. Hitler did exactly that on 1st September and war duly followed two days later. It was time to bring Winston back into the light.

15

NEVER SURRENDER

Few countries venerate and mythologise their heroes quite like the British. From Boudica the warrior Queen to Wellington the great commander - albeit, as we have seen, not the greatest politician - these legendary figures are interwoven into the grand narrative of this island, frequently employed as shorthand for the indomitable spirit and pluck that we seem convinced is peculiarly British.

Winston Spencer Churchill is the apogee of this heroic tradition - the resolute, single minded national leader who pulled Britain through her darkest hour when lily-livered bureaucrats were all for throwing in the towel. For many old fashioned patriots Churchill epitomises Britain's bulldog spirit like none other of her rich cast of historical characters, frequently being named the Greatest Briton and having his career pored over in voluminous articles and biographies.

And yet in the general election of July 1945 - held a mere two months after Nazi Germany's unconditional surrender in the Second World War and with national pride and self-confidence at an all-time high - the British people voted in Clement Atlee's Labour government and cast the pivotal figure in the winning of the war into opposition. Superficially this seems like an act of both the grossest ingratitude and stupidity. For not only had Churchill defeated Adolf Hitler he had presided over a radical redesign of governmental infrastructure which led to a more efficient, harmonious and egalitarian political system than had ever been seen in Britain before. The trouble for Churchill was that the system that had worked so well was a fundamentally Socialist one.

In hindsight it had to be. Britain's absolute commitment to victory over Nazism meant that she mobilised more of her nation than any other aggressor, an effort that required not only the democratisation of class and gender but also a vast state-run apparatus to ensure that all the component parts ran like clockwork. Which, amazingly given Britain's chequered history concerning efficiency and equality, it did. Many of the bright sparks who were so vital to the war government's ideological character balked at being referred to as Socialists but the overall effect was undeniably one that Keir Hardie and the Fabians would have recognised and applauded.

It is one of the supreme ironies of British political history that the man whose rabid anti-Socialist opinions led to his demonization by the left should be the same person to usher in the era of nationalisation and the welfare state. Indeed at the outbreak of hostilities it was not just Labour politicians who were dismissive of Churchill, his rose tinted attitude to the Empire made him the subject of much scorn and mockery from Conservatives also. Yet nine months later he was Prime Minister during the greatest threat this nation has ever faced. We should all be eternally grateful.

As recognition of his prescience over the German danger Churchill was returned to the Admiralty in Chamberlain's war cabinet. From the start the rest of the government fretted about how to contain him. Fortunately for them next to nothing happened in the first eight months of the war and the proverbial loose cannon was left kicking his heels, his portentous warnings against national complacency going largely unheeded. Maybe Hitler had finally realised he had bitten off more than he could chew. Maybe it really would all be over inside a year.

And despite his evident misjudgements in prosecuting a policy of appeasement towards Hitler the nation was also confident that, in Neville Chamberlain, it had a strong, authoritative leader with a proven track record as Prime Minister. The parallels between the respective governments of the First and Second World Wars are intriguingly numerous, not least in respect of the merits of Asquith and Chamberlain.

Like his similarly patrician Liberal forebear Chamberlain had shown himself to be a highly efficient and productive peacetime premier, building on the financial rectitude of his time at the Treasury to effectively combat levels of unemployment and improve working conditions in both factory and field. Yet, again like Asquith, he was constitutionally incapable of adjusting to the demands of running a wartime government and was ousted by an inspirational demagogue who motivated the nation for total war.

At the onset of hostilities, however, Neville Chamberlain was busy starting the work that his famous successor would build on. The Defence of the Realm Act that Asquith had inaugurated during the First World War was revived as the Emergency Powers Act, and granted almost total governmental control over the public and personal lives of its citizens. Each and every citizen also received a National ID card and a ration book – the lessons of the previous conflict had evidently been learnt. Governmentally new ministries were established for Food and Information that oversaw imports and propaganda respectively. The mass evacuation of women and children was set in motion which, whilst it had its fair share of problems, ensured the safety of untold numbers of the next generation who may have perished in the Blitz. Domestically at least the Prime Minister appeared to be doing a grand job.

And then, in early 1940, came Norway. Reasoning that control of the massive iron deposits of Scandinavia would prove a vital factor in defeating the Nazis Chamberlain - egged on it should be noted by a typically belligerent Churchill - decided to disregard the region's neutrality and lay claim to her steel. This audacious plan outraged both the Norwegian and Swedish governments - Finland had already been occupied by Russia who, at this point of the war, were allied with Germany - but such niceties were conveniently disregarded as Britain and France argued over the finer points of the operation. Whilst they were doing this Hitler simply attacked Norway himself. Embarrassing misjudgements regarding military equipment compounded the Allied amateurism, and very quickly and easily the Nazis won the first major battle of the war.

For all Chamberlain's foresight on the home front the Norwegian campaign was disturbing evidence of an inability to grasp military procedure on foreign soil. A Parliamentary debate on the issue forced a vote of confidence on the Prime Minister's leadership which saw his majority slashed from over 200 to 81. Now Chamberlain's only chance of remaining in power was to bring enough Labour and Liberal MPs into a Coalition Government to reassert his authority. If he was unable to accomplish this then he would have to be replaced by one of two men - Churchill or Lord Halifax.

Halifax's reputation is now forever tarnished by his conciliatory attitude towards Hitler but at the time he was regarded as the most highly qualified candidate. Churchill may have had flashes of brilliance in his career but his stance on India had lost him the respect of many of his colleagues and he was seen as headstrong and unstable in most quarters. But, crucially, Halifax's peerage officially disqualified him from the post. Had Halifax fought the issue he may well have won the day but, perhaps recognising his unsuitability to lead a wartime government, he used it as a pretext to rule himself out of contention. Everything now rested on the decision of the Labour Party as to whether they would accept positions in a Coalition Government headed by Chamberlain. The response from Clement Attlee, the Labour leader since George Lansbury's resignation in 1935, was that they would not. Chamberlain fell on his sword and in May 1940 Winston Churchill improbably became Britain's wartime Prime Minister.

Churchill's two vanquished opponents were both given places in the war cabinet but it was not long before they were at loggerheads with their new Prime Minister. The issue at stake was about as important as political decision making has ever got in British history, namely should Britain fight on or should she seek a negotiated peace with Hitler. The day Churchill kissed hands with George VI Germany launched an offensive on the Low Countries and, crucially, France. There had been anxiety about French capitulation from the outset of the conflict. Mindful of how much France had lost in the First World War many British politicians, including Churchill, were fearful that she would not want to go through it all again. And so it proved. Caught in the crossfire of the Fall of France was the British Expeditionary Force who started being evacuated from the beaches of Dunkirk on 26th May, the same day that Halifax reported the details of his recent meeting with the Italian Ambassador.

Halifax, now Foreign Secretary, claimed that Mussolini was eager to mediate a peace settlement between Nazi Germany and Great Britain. Given the astonishing success of Hitler's military strategy and the humiliating defeats that the Allies had thus far incurred Halifax reasoned that it was only a matter of time before Germany won the war. To safeguard against the total annihilation of the empire negotiations for peace must be entered into. Chamberlain agreed with him - as did a good number of other senior politicians and diplomats - but there was to be no arguing Churchill around. Halifax had hoped that the matter could be settled within the confines of the war cabinet but the Prime Minister, sensing an opportunity to deliver some rousing and inspiring oratory, took it to the 25 strong outer-cabinet. His passion, eloquence and apocalyptic imagery appealed to the latent never-say-die attitude of the British imagination and cast Halifax and Chamberlain as scared, small men unworthy of the fire and grit of glorious Britannia. Within a few months Chamberlain was dead of bowel cancer and Halifax had been shunted off to the United States to fill the position of British Ambassador. Churchill would not indulge such defeatism again.

Once Churchill had committed Britain to death or glory the handling of the economy was forced into unheard of levels of cavalier recklessness. Public spending soared with no thought for the post-war consequences, leaving the old school economists at the Treasury speechless at such fiscal irresponsibility. Yet the money had to come from somewhere and, due to legislation that would have made Lloyd George blush, it came from the wealthy.

The top rate of income tax rose to a staggering 50% - with surtax not far behind on 48% - whilst the leisure activities traditionally enjoyed by the more affluent were drastically curtailed. Meanwhile the effect of rationing and other subsidies was that prices remained low whilst wages increased. There was therefore a financial levelling out between the classes that went hand-in-hand with the social levelling that extensive volunteer work engendered. And because there was not just a war to be fought but a moral crusade to be won there was barely any complaint from the well-to-do.

In Westminster the old economic rules of balanced budgets and financial prudence were being torn up by a new generation of bold young theorists challenged to improve the organizational efficiency of the nation. The clear-out of appeasers and reactionary figures from the cabinet was combined with the increasing influence of the Liberals and, in particular, Labour in the Coalition Government. This shake-up of personnel led to calls for an ideological break with the complacency of the Baldwin era. Chief among these iconoclasts was the restlessly brilliant John Maynard Keynes.

His keynote work 'The General Theory of Employment, Interest and Money' advocated the theory of aggregate demand – or total economic spending – against the more traditional model of aggregate supply – the total amount of goods that the government expect to sell in a given time-frame. This caused quite a stir as the book was published in 1936, in the dog days of the Great Depression when established economic theories were becoming more and more discredited. His recruitment into the wartime economic 'think tank' gave Keynes the opportunity to develop these ideas in a more practical setting. His great breakthrough - that governments should intervene actively in the national economy and spend more in times of recession in order to stimulate growth – has had a profound influence on - particularly Labour - governments ever since.

The economic radicalism of Keynes was matched by the social reforming zeal of the infuriating and publicity hungry William Beveridge. The totemic Beveridge Report of 1942 into social welfare was only commissioned to give the upper class former social worker something to do so that he would stop pestering the government with his unwanted services. What he came up with was a classic slice of big state Socialism, arguing that the piecemeal benefits that were currently available be assimilated into one giant welfare system overseen by the state. A National Health Service free at the point of use has become the most lauded of Beveridge's suggestions but he also put the case for compulsory social insurance, full employment and the demise of the hated Means Test - a coldly objective method of measuring poverty.

Beveridge's assault on the 'five giants' of Want, Ignorance, Squalor, Idleness and Disease sold over 60,000 copies, making it impossible for the government to ignore. Churchill was too busy with the running of the war effort to make waves about the Socialist timbre of the report and the only grumbling that came from the rest of the government was over the cost of implementing such wide ranging reforms after fighting a hugely expensive war. Ideological indignation was remarkably thin on the ground from Conservative politicians. As the war drew to a close the government officially accepted the report's proposals on social insurance and made encouraging if cautious noises about the idea of a free health service.

Keynes and Beveridge were good, classical Liberals rather than hard-line Socialists but elsewhere in the government Labour party stalwarts were creeping into positions of ever greater power. Clement Attlee, the taciturn Labour leader who had held Churchill's future in his hands, became deputy Prime Minister in 1942 having demonstrated typical common sense and unfussy man-management in keeping the coalition harmonious. With the Prime Minister frequently out of the country on vital military business Attlee found himself de facto domestic leader on many occasions. He rose to the challenge admirably, providing clarity and purpose where Churchill offered fine words but little substance.

Herbert Morrison made a wily Home Secretary, his previous experience on the London County Council proving invaluable during the capital's Blitz. A gifted orator and shrewd administrator he transformed the London Underground, where thousands of people were sleeping rough, into a liveable subterranean world boasting bedding, running water and workable sanitation. In addition he gave his name to the notorious steel table air raid shelters for use indoors and oversaw the restructuring of the London fire service to ensure that blazes caused by German bombing did not spread. The 'Blitz Spirit' that has gone down in national folklore only emerged because the measures that Morrison put in place bred a sense of security and trust in the capital's citizens.

Yet it was the - literally - gigantic figure of Ernest Bevin who proved the single finest politician in the Coalition Government. What makes his stellar achievements all the more remarkable was that he had no Parliamentary experience whatever, having been the head of the formidable Transport and General Workers' Union for the past 18 years. Churchill had been an admirer of the no-nonsense union boss for some time and decided on the potentially risky strategy of parachuting him into government. It was one of Churchill's greatest gambles and it paid off handsomely. Bevin's appointment was arguably the PM's most astute political call throughout the whole war.

As Minister of Labour Bevin demanded – and got – complete control over the direction of manpower for the war effort. By the autumn of 1943 both the armed forces and munitions industries had undergone surges in personnel into the millions, with labour redirected from less essential areas. He also set about transforming the fractious relationship between the unions and business owners. Whilst it is perfectly true that Stanley Baldwin had fervently desired such industrial collaboration he had been coming at the issue from the fundamentally Capitalist viewpoint of accelerating national production. Bevin, the former union supremo, was keen to further the cause of the working man. In key industrial consultations the unions became equal partners with both employers and the government, whilst major private firms were essentially commandeered by the government in the name of the war effort. Both encroaching nationalisation and the rise of the modern trade union movement can be dated from Bevin's time at the Ministry of Labour.

Even those departments that were not overseen by Labour men ran along statist lines. Of the panoply of new ministries two of the most effective were Supply and Food. The Ministry of Supply ensured that the British Army, Navy and Air Force received all the equipment that they needed and liaised with other inter-related ministries such as the Ministry of Works and Bevin's Ministry of Labour. The smooth running of the department was crucial in co-ordinating major military operations and making sure that the armed forces were as equipped and prepared as possible. The Ministry for Food, run by the visionary Lord Woolton, actually managed to improve the diet of most working class children by subsidising milk and school meals. The drab stodge and measly portions that were the effect of rationing may have irked many, but the system was rigorously fair and undeniably necessary to the pursuit of victory.

Comparatively little of this Socialist dynamism can be directly attributed to the Prime Minister - he had other things on his mind. But by sanctioning the creation of these new ministries and giving existing ones free rein to do whatever they thought necessary he tacitly encouraged a big state culture that ran counter to his natural inclinations. True, Churchill had been a reformer in his Liberal days but there had still been a whiff of libertarian self-help about his proposals. The irony for Churchill is that the country he was fighting desperately to save was no longer the country he imagined it to be. And, as made painfully evident by his dealings with the United States of America, the peacetime world was going to be a very different place also.

If you are seeking the perfect example of British delusion and misjudged self-importance then look no further than her cringe-worthy 'special' relationship with the USA. Britain's role in world affairs had been steadily slipping since the glory days of Lord Palmerston in the 1850s and now, potentially bankrupting herself to destroy the Nazis and with a cumbersome, crumbling empire to deal with, she was weaker than ever.

The uncomfortable truth is that whilst Britain's stance during World War Two was genuinely heroic and startlingly brave it fostered a myth about British dominance that ran completely contrary to real events. Yes, Britain had 'stood alone' against the evil might of Hitler and successfully faced him down. But in doing so she shattered her economy and became embarrassingly dependent on a nation that had fought another centuries-old war to extricate themselves from her control. And, to top it all, for a number of years Britain still seemed to view herself as the senior partner.

Churchill - alongside many other of the country's leading politicians - took America to be basically the same as Britain. Both bastions of democracy who shared a common language and sense of fair play it was broadly understood that the two countries would stand shoulder to shoulder, with Britain offering a few sage words of paternalistic advice from the benefit of her experience. Many Americans, however, viewed the idea of such a cosy partnership with horror and disdain. As comfortably the biggest western superpower they held all the cards and would not willingly hand them over to a fading island nation with delusions of grandeur. They had been a democracy from their inception and had a very different view of how the world should be ordered to the British. For example the United States' antipathy to the concept of empire - understandable given their foundation narrative - put them directly at odds with a nation still vainly clinging on to its imperial identity. America preferred to insinuate their values and culture into the rest of the world rather than colonise other countries directly, a policy with which they have had obvious success.

None of which is to say that Churchill was in the least bit wrong to court them so assiduously in the early, skin-of-the-teeth days of the war. Had Britain remained standing alone she could never have hoped to defeat the axis powers and the addition of both Russia and America to the Allied cause in 1941 was integral to overall victory. The Prime Minister's epic charm offensive produced Lend-Lease several months before the United

States entered the war. Made vital by Britain's rapidly dwindling dollar reserves, Lend-Lease involved American payment for British war supplies and their subsequent free transferral. Without it British munitions production would quite possibly have ground to a halt.

Yet for all its undoubted value to a wartime economy on the rack Lend-Lease contained within it certain provisos that amply illustrated America's protection of her own interests. The United States was a nation built on free trade and viewed Britain's emphasis on protectionism and the sterling area as evidence of her imperial insularity. To American minds global trade should not be restricted by any petty barriers or tariff walls just as currency should be universally freely exchangeable. This philosophy would later underpin the 1944 Bretton Woods conference, which also created the monolithic International Monetary Fund and radically altered the shape of post-war Western economics.

Britain, proclaimed Washington, must therefore agree to end discriminatory trade practices with the tacit understanding that the sterling area also had to go. An outraged Keynes managed to turn the harsh demands into more woolly suggestions but he could do nothing about the other conditions the Americans had built into Lend-Lease. Firstly, Britain was banned from exporting any Lend-Lease products or even any that were superficially similar and secondly - and most crippling of all - her reserves were deliberately kept low by the US Treasury so that her exports became almost totally run down, thus fuelling reliance on foreign imports. It was a breathtakingly clinical way of ensuring that her new 'partner' was kept weak and compliant for the foreseeable future.

When the Japanese attack on Pearl Harbour in December 1941 made American involvement inevitable the full extent of US power and self-possession became apparent. The States had the money and the resources and Britain began to realise that they were no longer the ones calling all the shots. Inadvisable strategies had to be either agreed to or subtly waylaid for fear of offending the great cash cow and Churchill, despite his close working friendship with the American President Franklin

D. Roosevelt, was forced to accept that aid from across the Atlantic came at a heavy price.

But, even considering the far-reaching negative effects in post-war Britain, American alliance - as well as Soviet - was essential at the time. Before their arrival Britain had been clinging on, courageously repelling German air-power in the Battle of Britain and stoically enduring the nightly atrocities of the Blitz. Afterwards, American muscle on the beaches of Normandy and the grand folly of Hitler's declaration of war on Russia proved decisive. Combined with Britain's own unlikely victory in the sands of El Alamein the tide had turned incontrovertibly in the Allies favour, forcing Hitler to take his own life and Nazi Germany to surrender on the 4th May 1945. Britain was exhausted, battered and emotional but she had done what Winston Churchill had said she would – 'never surrender.'

16

JAM AND JERUSALEM

It has been remarked that the Conservatives are the natural party of power whereas Labour are the party of principle. Whether or not this statement is true - and there would be many who would struggle to see the principle in Ramsay MacDonald's cosying up to the Conservatives or the Blair government's invasion of Iraq - the fact remains that Labour members like to feel that their party has genuinely held beliefs and acts according to those beliefs. Vulgar political expediency and the gaining or retention of power are often viewed as secondary by the party's grassroots activists, although the same cannot always be said for Labour MPs themselves.

For this reason the first post-war Labour government headed by the spectacularly unspectacular Clement Attlee has a special place in left-wing hearts. It was the first majority Labour government and was elected on a specific mandate to implement the welfare reforms suggested by William Beveridge to make Britain a fairer, more egalitarian society in line with her competitors. It was a platform of reform that the government was determined to deliver on and - whilst the internal and external difficulties that they faced meant that there were failures as well as success stories - the drive and conviction of this group of astonishingly focused men lent them an aura of authenticity and purity that subsequent governments have lacked. For believers in the primacy of the state and the merits of central planning this was a shining example of how things should be done.

But the country was also in dire straits. Bombed out and nearly bankrupt its people had put up with immense privation and suffering during the previous six years and felt that, as the war's victors, they were entitled to enjoy life a little now it was over. But - as we have seen in the aftermath of both the Napoleonic Wars and World War One - winning a war does not make the process of reconstruction any easier. Rationing would not

175

end fully for another nine years - despite the oft-made claim that there would be 'jam tomorrow' - and there was a desperate shortage of housing caused by the ravages of the Blitz. The committed, irrepressible figures at the heart of government may have been bursting with ideas but the economic reality had to be addressed before anything worthwhile could be achieved.

The men – and save for the Education Minister Ellen Wilkinson they were all men – charged with transforming an exhausted nation into the new Socialist 'Jerusalem' were the most dynamic and colourful ensemble of ministers ever assembled in a British cabinet. We have met some of the key players before in the wartime Coalition but now, freed from Conservative interference, they became titans of Socialism with firm - often contradictory - notions of what a Labour government should stand for.

Perversely Attlee's very ordinariness – genuine rather than contrived like that of Walpole or Baldwin - marked him out as a curiosity at the top of the governmental tree. A perceived lack of gravitas prompted an audacious coup against his leadership by the Machiavellian Herbert Morrison, deputy Prime Minister and grandfather of one Peter Mandelson. Yet Attlee's coolness under fire coupled with the incontrovertible fact that he had just won a landslide in the general election saw off the threat comfortably. Attlee did not hold a grudge, appointing Morrison Leader of the Commons and Lord President of the Council with responsibility for pushing through the party's revolutionary legislative programme.

Ernest Bevin, Churchill's big, tireless, no-nonsense Minister for Labour, stepped even further out of his comfort zone as Foreign Secretary. He would prove just as adept at shaping foreign affairs as he had done at directing the domestic war effort. The intense, intimidating Christian former Marxist Stafford Cripps became President of the Board of Trade and Aneurin 'Nye' Bevan - the archetypal left-wing firebrand and earthy Welshman - came in from the cold of opposition to go to Health. Chancellor of the Exchequer was the flamboyant, insecure Hugh Dalton who had also served in the Coalition Government.

Attlee manfully kept these enormous egos in check, the rational foil to the whirling dervishes of passion and unpredictability that danced around him. His first challenge was to confront a sudden economic blow inflicted by Britain's domineering special 'partner.' A week after Japan surrendered on 14th August 1945 President Harold Truman pulled the plug on Lend-Lease stunning the British government. Although the agreement had been put in place to help Britain with wartime supplies huge numbers of those supplies - primarily food related - were still vitally important to a peacetime society where the well had run dry. The Labour government, elected on the promise of a strong, state-run command economy, could not even afford to feed its people.

In an atmosphere of indignation and panic Attlee dispatched John Maynard Keynes to Washington to charm, negotiate and - if necessary - beg the Americans to keep the supply of aid flowing. To start with both Keynes and the government were overconfident and hit a brick wall of American intransigence when holding out for the best deal. Eventually Britain was forced to accept a 50 year loan of £3.75billion at 2% interest, nearly half the amount Keynes brashly predicted he would secure at the outset. The last repayment was made as late as 2006. In addition the abolition of tariff walls that the United States was so keen to achieve was brought a step closer by the proviso that sterling be freely exchanged for dollars from the following year. Britain would therefore be in an extremely precarious economic situation, forever tied to the whim of the US Treasury. It was a deal that set the scene for decades of financial instability, rising inflation and recession. The bedevilment of the UK economy was inaugurated in Washington in the closing weeks of 1945. Keynes, emotionally and physically exhausted by the talks, died the following April.

But at least Britain had her loan and the noble work could commence in earnest. The Beveridge Report was swiftly recast as the National Insurance Act of 1946, providing a unified system of compulsory social insurance for all – well, nearly all as married women and the self-employed were still not catered for. The next project was the one that is widely considered the most enduring legacy of the post-war Labour ministry - the NHS.

A National Health Service free at the point of use had been one of the cornerstones of the Beveridge philosophy and, in Nye Bevan, the Health Department had exactly the sort of minister to push such a controversial proposal through. Like most pre-war British institutions the medical service was hopelessly disorganised and disparate, a conglomeration of municipal and voluntary hospitals all operating under their own rules and processes and varying wildly in quality of care. Without the ability to pay for treatment many unwell people had no option but to remain at home and get steadily worse. There was much head-scratching in Parliament over how centralized a national system should be but Bevan was unequivocal - every hospital in the land, bar a smattering of private ones, would come under the aegis of the state. This not only put him at odds with his near-namesake Bevin, who was a staunch advocate of local government and municipal autonomy, but also with the formidable ranks of GPs who balked at the idea of becoming state apparatchiks and - more importantly - losing their lucrative salaries. But the Welshman would not be diverted and, through a mixture of flattery, concessions and abuse, Bevan secured his National Health Service in July 1948. It has been a source of immense national pride ever since. The initial response was overwhelming, with millions – many of whom had been unable to see a doctor in years - rushing to take advantage of a truly democratic and humane healthcare system. The creation of the NHS was undoubtedly the zenith of the Labour government's achievements.

But it was not just the health service that Labour had pledged to nationalize. The rationalization of industry during the war had been one of the great successes of the Coalition and demonstrated what could be achieved by government taking an active interest in the workings of private companies. Labour would now take this a stage further and bring transport, power, coal and the Bank of England under public ownership. The results varied from an indiscernible change in operation to a wholesale reorganisation of both philosophy and practice.

The railway and coal industries were where the most dramatic changes took place, not least because they were so important to the nation's comfort and stability. The railways were in a unique position in that, whilst they had been rationalized a considerable time ago and competition had essentially disappeared, their national status was so high that the prospect of being subsumed into one gargantuan Transport Commission was greeted with alarm from proud railwaymen across the country. Ultimately the biggest problem in bringing the railways under public ownership was the same one that the government encountered in all of their attempts to nationalize. There was simply no money to pump into the chosen industries to modernize them and exactly the same problems that had plagued them before the war continued after it.

The coal industry was no exception although the conundrums nationalization posed were exacerbated by a spectacular piece of bad luck which soon escalated into another national crisis. The Minister for Fuel and Power Emmanuel 'Manny' Shinwell - one of the more hard-core 'Reds' in the government - delivered nationalization on the agreed date of 1st January 1947 despite having only an obscure old pamphlet written in Welsh as his guide. Yet in the rush to bring the project in on schedule Shinwell had neglected repeated warnings about the depletion of coal supplies. Consequently when the completion date coincided with one of the coldest winters Britain had ever seen the nation was brought to a standstill. Coal was freezing solid in the pits and the archaic machinery was conking out. With no fresh supply the power stations soon shut down and power cuts spread throughout the country, contrary to Shinwell's ill-advised promises that they would not occur. Britain was temporarily returned to a pre-industrial age as factories closed, electric heating was severely restricted and people were forced to walk for miles for (strictly rationed) food due to their cars breaking down in the arctic conditions. March brought apocalyptic floods as many shivering souls began to lose their faith in Socialist democracy.

Whilst a good summer eventually arrived the problems of low investment continued to blight the coal industry and the workers' strikes that nationalization had been designed to prevent reared their ugly heads once more. By the time the iron and steel industries were brought under state control in 1948-9 the gloss of nationalization had worn off and Labour idealism about public ownership looked distinctly hollow.

By that point Attlee's government had already faced down the biggest challenge to their dream of a centrally planned command economy. It was triggered, inevitably, by the clauses converting sterling into dollars in the American loan which kicked in in July 1947. Immediately there was a run on the pound as sterling holders switched to the US currency. This in turn meant a series of enormous cuts on everything from food imports to defence, with an emergency budget from Dalton in November 1947 raising taxes by an eye-watering £200 million. The situation had obviously not been helped by the loss of exactly the same amount in exports due to the national shutdown caused by the harsh winter.

The farce of Dalton's subsequent resignation after leaking crucial details of the budget to a tabloid journalist seemed to exemplify the government's clueless approach to handling the economy. Dalton, like Shinwell, had been guilty of disregarding dire warnings until it was too late to act, although the similar inactivity of his cabinet colleagues led some to the conclusion that the Chancellor was being hung out to dry. Central planning had been the bulwark of Labour's election manifesto but now it felt like an empty phrase, a vague definition of unspecified organisation that could mean whatever the government wanted it to on any given day.

Attlee now faced a second potential challenge to his leadership as the spiky Stafford Cripps mooted the possibility of Ernest Bevin taking over the premiership. Bevin, however, had formed a strong bond with the

Prime Minister and swiftly confirmed he would not budge from the Foreign Office. Attlee once again demonstrated great common sense and magnanimity by appointing Cripps Dalton's successor as Chancellor. Noble ideological terms would have to give way to practical activity, and quickly. Once Cripps was installed at the Treasury - whilst at the same time running the Ministry of Economic Affairs - the whole tenor of the government changed.

Against a rising tide of - primarily middle class - dissent Cripps ploughed single-mindedly on with even harsher cuts than Dalton had introduced. Everything was geared to the reinvigoration of the exports market and if that meant that the public would have to consume inedible food like the tinned fish Snoek then that was what must happen. However betrayed the British people felt at the time – and there were more than a few spirited rebellions against Cripps' policies – the dogged insistence on brutal austerity worked. Cripps was lucky as well, with the unions agreeing to a wage freeze in March 1948. The following month the Americans finally cottoned on to the fact that deliberately keeping her allies in a position of economic inferiority was more likely to drive them into the arms of Soviet Russia. Britain received the lion's share of the Marshall Plan aid package which was instrumental in the financial recovery across Europe. The national finances went from a crippling deficit in 1946-7 to an astonishing surplus the following year, allowing a young minister named Harold Wilson to announce the abolition of scores of restrictions in a 'bonfire of controls' that delighted the nation. Stafford Cripps had rescued the economy by the skin of his teeth.

But Cripps' career would ultimately end in defeat and the reluctant acknowledgement of the flaws of a command economy. In a cruel irony the catalyst for this ideological blow would be an American economy in deep financial trouble, as the US recession of 1949 fatally hit British exports to the States with the result that her dollar reserves were decimated. Serendipitously the Chancellor fell seriously ill at the same time as the crisis peaked and the Treasury was put into the hands of a trio of younger men – Harold Wilson, Hugh Gaitskell and Douglas Jay.

The only solution was the devaluation of sterling by 30% with the concomitant deleterious effect on the exchange rate. Whilst in practice this had a positive effect on the nation's finances it ran counter to everything that the government believed in. Devaluation was a forced response to the vagaries of the market, a game of chance that was precisely what a planned economy was supposed to eliminate. Had Cripps still been in full control of the Treasury at the time his moral objections to devaluation may have had disastrous effects on the UK economy. But Wilson, Gaitskell and Jay were more realistic and recognised – along with Attlee – that the process could not be forestalled. Reluctantly the ailing Chancellor was forced to agree, although he still insisted on putting the announcement off for as long as possible.

The devaluation crisis left Cripps a broken man and by the time of the 1950 budget precious little of his previous Socialist rhetoric had survived. Yet this dominant figure could still make the political weather even if it were not exactly in the manner he intended. His principled refusal to present the 1950 budget before a general election had been called resulted in a surprise slashing of Labour's majority to just five when the country went to the polls. Cripps left office soon after and died in April 1952 of cancer, just over a year after his former cabinet colleague Ernest Bevin.

As Foreign Secretary Bevin ensured that Britain, though battered and bruised economically, would continue to play a significant role in world affairs. It was Bevin who first broached the idea of a 'Western European Union' to protect the fragile peace of the post-war continent and to guard against the twin threats of Stalinist Communism and German revanchism. Recognising that any supranational peace-keeping organisation would have to include the military and diplomatic might of the United States the Foreign Secretary approached Washington with a view to securing a North Atlantic alliance. In April 1949 ten European nations signed a treaty with America and Canada to form the North Atlantic Treaty Organisation.

Alongside the United Nations - which was formed in late 1945 to replace the discredited League of Nations - NATO remains the key intergovernmental body of the post-war world.

It was not the first time that Bevin had demonstrated visionary decisiveness in his new role. When the promise of pan-European financial aid had been dangled by the US Secretary of State, George Marshall, in 1947 it had been Bevin who had taken it upon himself to formulate Western Europe's positive response. Whilst the Marshall Plan did not come into effect until the following year – too late to save the government from the convertibility crisis that did for Hugh Dalton – Bevin's speedy actions ensured that a shattered continent was financially able to rebuild itself. Soviet rejection of Marshall Plan aid marked the beginning of the deep divide between Eastern and Western Europe that would morph into the dread and paranoia of the Cold War.

Yet for all the Foreign Secretary's success in shaping European co-operation and rehabilitation the question of Britain's place in the world proved a far greater headache. In 1945 Bevin was busy trying to sell the nation a vision of Britain as a 'middle kingdom' between the uber-Capitalism of the United States and the uber-Communism of Soviet Russia. After all, Britain had an empire and only truly important world powers had those. In reality it was painfully obvious that if the government were unable to feed and clothe her own people then an unwieldy and grumbling foreign empire was a dubious luxury that she could ill afford.

India was the most logical candidate for independence and had been for some years. The war may have scuppered the Government of India Act but there was a complex jumble of reasons that justified British withdrawal. On the one hand, there was Gandhi's ever-growing saintly reputation and the valiant fighting of Indian soldiers during World War II. On the other there was increased militancy from ordinary Indians and the exploits of the Indian National Army, who had collaborated with the Japanese in the war by guarding British prisoners.

The Labour government's attitude towards empire was equally complicated. They were theoretically anti-imperialist but many in the party - as in the country - still viewed Britain as a great power and were reluctant to let any of her possessions go. Nonetheless Attlee – who had served on a governmental commission into Indian self-government in the 1920s - pressed on with independence only to be stymied by the vicious sectarianism of the Muslim and Hindu populations. After the fighting between Mohammed Ali Jinnah's Muslim League and Jawaharlal Nehru's Hindu Congress Party saw off the melancholic Field Marshal Wavell, the formidable Louis Mountbatten was charged with making British withdrawal from India a reality.

Faced with the possibility of civil war on the subcontinent Mountbatten's solution was to partition the country. Pakistan was created for the Muslims whilst the Hindus would remain in India. The swiftness of Indian independence in August 1947 may have been emotionally devastating for virulently imperialist politicians like Churchill but it was horrific for the many thousands stranded on the wrong side of the border. Widespread sectarian violence resulted in almost a million dead and left many wondering whether it would have been more humane for India to have remained a British possession after all. The situation has never been adequately resolved with Bangladesh splintering off from Pakistan in 1971 and the subcontinent still convulsed in violence and religious hatred to this day.

Yet while 1947 saw Britain withdraw from India the following year the British Nationality Act made it possible for millions of people in the Commonwealth to enter Britain as British citizens. The Act was passed as a sop to the Canadians, who had just passed their own act to separate Canadian citizenship from British nationality, on the assumption that nobody living in an exotic locale would ever want to come to cold, austere Britain. The same year saw the arrival of the 'Empire Windrush,' a former German cruise ship now carrying nearly 500 passengers from the Caribbean to take up residence in the United Kingdom. Given that immigration has proved itself one of the most incendiary political issues ever since it seems astonishing that the whole process was set in motion as an afterthought. It was one of two offhand decisions made by Attlee's government that would have profound repercussions for the future of the nation.

The other came in 1950 when France decided to combine her iron and coal industries with West Germany's and asked Britain whether she wanted to come in on the deal as well. The European Coal and Steel Community was the precursor to the European Union and, had the Labour government said yes, Britain's relationship with Europe may have proved very different to the often fraught and distrustful one that she now 'enjoys'. But the decision was made in the back room of the Ivy restaurant by Herbert Morrison – Attlee being out of the country – and was given little more than a few seconds thought. Morrison's reason for declining to join this nascent European power bloc? 'The Durham miners won't wear it.'

But despite embarrassment over the empire and the sad demise of central planning the shadow that really hung over the Attlee government was America. Economically she was locked in to a series of lopsided loan agreements with the United States that would have dramatic repercussions for decades to come, whilst culturally the Americanization of British life that had begun with the visiting GIs continued apace. Britain was playing catch-up on the global stage as well. The post-war world was one dominated by the threat of nuclear attack and after the devastation wrought upon Hiroshima and Nagasaki by the United States dropping atomic bombs it was clear that there was a direct correlation between nuclear capability and the ownership of global power.

Once again America had reneged on a promise to her supposed ally. During the war Churchill and Roosevelt had come to a mutual understanding that nuclear information would be shared between the two nations but, thanks to the 1946 MacMahon Act, that co-operation was abruptly terminated as the US forged ahead alone. For Britain to develop her own nuclear weapons programme would require huge amounts of defence spending at a time when there was precious little money to go around. Faced, however, with the prospect of an American monopoly on such instruments of mass destruction, it was a price that Attlee - and the intensely patriotic Foreign Secretary Bevin - felt duty bound to pay. It is interesting that, even at the time, there was no real attempt to disguise the fact that this was all about prestige and power-play rather than defence from a palpable enemy threat. Without her own A-bomb Britain could not take her place at the top table with the other global superpowers and that would be an unendurable blow to 'bulldog' pride. Research into the first British atomic bomb began in the summer of 1947, just after Britain had emerged from the big freeze.

And then in 1950 British troops were forced into fighting alongside their American counterparts in the Korean War. Precipitated by the invasion of South Korea by their Communist Northern neighbours and Chairman Mao's Chinese People's Liberation Army this was the first full scale post-war conflict between Capitalist democracy and Communist autocracy. It was a battle that the greatest global superpower had to win. The Labour government agreed and Attlee sent considerable numbers of soldiers and ships to aid the American-led military alliance. The British fought bravely but they were severely hampered by their lack of resources, ending up somewhat predictably as the mere lackeys of the muscular, confident Americans.

The conflict was the beginning of the end for Britain's first majority Socialist government. It was an unpopular war back home with the South Korean regime being seen as equally unpleasant as the Communist Northern one, whilst tales of American military superiority led many to lament the loss of British strategic prowess. But it was the financial cost of the Korean War that really grated and not just on the British public. Cripps' replacement at the Treasury was Hugh Gaitskell, a member of the younger generation regarded as an unprincipled dilettante by the radical wing of the party. When he announced a small charge for dental work and spectacles to cover the cost of rearmament for the war Nye Bevan became incensed at what he perceived to be a betrayal of the principles of his beloved NHS. Bevan, by now Minister of Labour, resigned along with his young acolyte Harold Wilson thus striking the first blow in the interminable, self-lacerating battle between the hard and centre left of the party. The ideological feud between Bevan and Gaitskell would only intensify when both men were vying for the party leadership a few years later.

The government looked - and was – exhausted. Bevin and Cripps would both soon be dead and the other leading figures in the cabinet had all suffered serious bouts of ill-health. Attlee called another election for the following year and this time Labour failed to cling on. The old warhorse Winston Churchill - now in his late seventies - got his revenge for the electoral defeat of 1945, returning to power with a majority of 16. As if sensing that time was running out Labour had just held the Festival of Britain, a quintessentially quirky celebration of Britishness complete with baffling scupltures and a quaint funfair. It was a rare moment of fun and frivolity in the grey post-war years but nowhere near enough to save them.

Yet seventy years on Attlee and his band of Socialist ideologues and obsessive planners are seen by many as the epitome of successful British government. It is ironic considering that a considerable amount of the programme that they implemented failed to work. This was not always their fault of course - they could have done little about the 1947 winter or the American recession – but it does rather highlight the statement at the opening of this chapter. The post-war Labour government wanted to change society and create a new Jerusalem. It may have failed but at least it had a noble aspiration. Sandwiched between the lazy, complacent Little Englands of the 1930s and 1950s that marks it out as rather heroic.

17

THE STAGNANT SOCIETY

In March 1963 John Profumo's world came crashing down around him. Forced to admit a sexual affair with model and call-girl Christine Keeler the Secretary of State for War resigned from the government and lived out the rest of his life in obscurity and shame. Political sex scandals were not unheard of even in early 1960s Britain but what really did for Profumo was the exotic and sordid mix of illicit sex and cold-war espionage. For Keeler was also sleeping with a Russian military attache and spy called Yevgeny Ivanov. The Soviet agent and the cabinet minister had met and played naked water racing in the pool of Lord Astor's Cliveden estate, with both Keeler and her Svengali - society osteopath Stephen Ward - present. Had vital nuclear secrets been let slip during amorous pillow talk? Had national security been jeopardised for the sake of a quick bunk-up in one of Britain's best known stately homes? Such lurid allegations may have thrilled readers of Ian Fleming's popular James Bond novels but in the real life context of a Conservative government that prided itself on old fashioned decency and patriotic values it was too much for the public to bear. It effectively finished Harold Macmillan as Prime Minister and paved the way for the narrowest of Labour victories in the following year's general election.

A large part of the frisson that the Profumo scandal created was down to a clash of class and generation. For over a decade successive Conservative Prime Ministers had kept Britain rooted firmly in the dozing consensus politics of the 1930s. They were a smug, terribly insular establishment clique, doltishly convinced of their role as the ruling elite. And yet it is telling that both Anthony Eden and Harold Macmillan were regarded as dangerous modernisers by certain sections of their own party.

But the country was starting to change. The post-war baby boom had created a generation of youngsters with no conception of living through a world-ranging conflict and, thanks to an economic upswing and a revolution in consumer goods, only a fleeting memory of austerity. They began to question why it was that certain types of people must always hold the balance of power and to openly mock and satirise their leaders in a way that horrified their parents. The Profumo Affair was the tipping point, containing all the elements that a younger, more impudent and less inhibited generation could identify with - sex, spies, drugs and a corrupt and decaying upper class. It felt like the last act of a hopelessly incestuous and out-of-touch government. The times they were a-changing.

All of this hedonistic irresponsibility was a far cry from the staid, self-congratulatory aura of 12 years previously when Winston Churchill had doddered back into Number 10. The mighty war leader was by now frail and delusional, wedded to a romanticised notion of the nation at its imperial height. But for the many millions who had voted him back into office that was precisely the point. After the industrious but predominantly joyless years of Labour austerity they wanted to reconnect with the glorious recent past. There was no more potent symbol of that period than Winston Spencer Churchill. Aged though he may have been the Prime Minister had not lost his ability to create a national mood, although he was considerably helped in this instance by the coronation of Elizabeth Windsor in the summer of 1953. Britain was now living in a new Elizabethan age, proclaimed Churchill, and optimism and creativity were boundless.

Whereas the Labour government stressed the collective ethos over the individual will Churchill's Conservative ministry celebrated the achievements of great men and women and recast them in the light of communal patriotism. Thus Edmund Hilary's conquest of Everest the month before the Queen's coronation was seen as evidence of national adventurousness and endurance. Hilary himself may have been a New Zealander but the expedition was a British one and, besides, New Zealand was in the Commonwealth. Churchill did not have to look too far for proof of British creativity either - Ralph Vaughn Williams, T.S. Eliot and Henry Moore were all major artistic and cultural figures.

Politically the legacy of the second Churchill government was negligible. Despite the Prime Minister's loathing of Socialism he recognised that it would be suicidal to dismantle the nascent welfare state. His - highly effective - lambasting of Attlee's government when in opposition centred on their perceived incompetence rather than the specifics of their policies. He was inclined to let industrial disputes slide as well, frequently giving in to the unions for the sake of an easy life and contributing to the inordinate power and sense of entitlement that they subsequently developed. In truth domestic politics bored him and he only really came alive when wading in to world affairs of weight and import.

There are just two events during these uninspiring years that merit closer attention. The first is Britain's nuclear policy and the unlikely transformation of Churchill from sabre rattling warmonger to sage old peace campaigner. The pragmatist in him acknowledged - like Attlee before him - that British development of nuclear weapons was a grim necessity if she were to retain her international role. However, that did not stop him from trying desperately hard to bring East and West around the negotiating table. Using Stalin's death in 1953 as the spur to re-open talks between the Soviets and the Americans he made numerous appeals to President Eisenhower which all fell on deaf, belligerent ears. Churchill may have had a boyish enthusiasm for military adventure in the past but he alone of all the superpower leaders understood that nuclear conflict was a completely different proposition to the conventional method of troops on the ground. Although his entreaties came to nothing it should be remembered that even as Churchill entered his ninth decade he possessed a perceptive quality that his younger counterparts lacked.

The second issue is a classic case of 'what if?' that casts a fascinating light not only on the economics of the period but also its future echoes. In 1952, with sterling crises becoming a depressingly regular feature of the British financial landscape, Churchill's Chancellor R.A. 'Rab' Butler and a cabal of Treasury bigwigs formulated a radical plan to halt the cycle of boom and bust that they had inherited from Labour. They proposed nothing less than a reboot of the national economy. ROBOT - an acronym of the names of its three architects - proposed the floating of the pound and the convertibility of sterling held outside the sterling area alongside the blocking of virtually all current sterling balances. This would lead to a sudden and dramatic change in the economic lives of millions of British people, forcing up prices and resulting in a marked upturn in unemployment. It would also necessitate the abandonment of many key strands of the burgeoning welfare state. It would be the toughest of medicine for the public to swallow but - so the plan's adherents confidently stated - it would reset the haemorrhaging balance of payments and, by wiping the financial slate clean, put the country back on its feet again. Whilst there are numerous technical differences it is tempting to see Butler's bold proposal as a precursor to the economic firestorm of Margaret Thatcher's monetarist policies of the 1980s. In the steady, conventional 1950s, however, the status quo - and more importantly the voters' fury come election time - was prized above financial radicalism and ROBOT never saw the light of day. The future of the nation could have been dramatically different if it had.

By the time that Churchill - who had survived a stroke in 1953 - finally stepped aside his successor, the debonair but potty-mouthed baronet Anthony Eden, had been waiting for his chance at the top job for years. Eden had effectively been bred as the next Conservative leader for over a decade and when Churchill resigned he had stood for the leadership unopposed. By calling a snap general election which the Conservatives won handsomely he appeared to have proved his mettle early on. But - much as Gordon Brown would discover over 50 years later - finally securing the long cherished dream of national leadership is not the same thing as making a success of it. Eden's political career is forever associated with one word - Suez. It was the biggest political scandal till Profumo although in both scale and immorality it ranks far higher. Its legacy destroyed not only the fledgling Prime Minister but also the notion of Britain as an effective, benevolent world power.

Suez was in essence the tale of a dam and a canal. Colonel Gamel Abdel Nasser, Egyptian leader since an audacious coup in 1954, had dreams of bringing a new era of prosperity to his people by constructing a colossal dam at Aswan which would bring unprecedented amounts of electrical power. Anticipating a loan from the United States Nasser was furious when John Foster Dulles, the US Secretary of State, reneged on the deal leaving Nasser unable to fund his glorious project. In retaliation he announced, on the 26th July 1956, that the Suez Canal was now nationalized and subsequently closed it to all shipping.

Since Disraeli's fortuitous acquisition of the majority share in the canal it had become a crucial route for British trade, allowing products and resources – among them vast quantities of oil - to be transported from her imperial possessions on the other side of the world. Much like India Egypt had been granted a measure of self-government but was still very much under British control, at least until the close of the Second World War when resurgent Egyptian nationalism forced a diplomatic rethink in Whitehall. By the early 1950s voices within Parliament were wondering whether a tactical withdrawal might be the wisest course of action. Retreat from the Suez Canal, however, would be inconceivable.

Yet if Nasser's intention had been to provoke Washington his gambit singularly failed. As we have seen, the United States was virulently anti-colonial in its outlook and so, whether or not Britain was a nominal ally, they were not particularly disposed to come to her aid. But such was the canal's status and vital importance to Britain's economy that it was unthinkable that Eden and the Conservative government could sit back and do nothing.

Months of negotiations took place and got nowhere, primarily because Nasser knew that American involvement was highly unlikely and Britain was too weak to act alone. But the Egyptian leader also had a lot of international enemies. His hatred of Israel was well known and France had serious concerns about Egyptian interference in their troubled Algerian colony – not to mention their own stake in the canal. And so between them Britain, Israel and France began tentatively hatching a plot to provoke conflict in the region and reclaim the canal. The pretext for sending in an Anglo-French force as 'peacekeepers' would be a contrived Israeli attack on Egypt, an operation not only risky but wholly illegal. It was dreamt up without the knowledge of Parliament, the security services or the US President. Unsurprisingly Eden insisted that no details of the plot were written down.

It was put into action on the 5th November with a drop of British and French paratroopers joining a British convoy that had arrived from Malta. The Egyptians were caught off-guard and suffered huge losses, but at the very moment that invading troops reached the outskirts of Cairo they were given an enormous diplomatic slap on the wrist from the United Nations. The Americans - who Eden thought would be broadly sympathetic to a British attack - were incensed when they discovered the machinations going on behind their backs whilst the Russians were preparing to pour men into the region to repel the Anglo-French advance. Meanwhile Nasser simply sunk 47 ships laden with concrete and blocked the canal. Britain, along with their co-conspirators, had attracted the opprobrium of the world.

Even with no written record of the devising of the plot it was pretty clear that Britain had acted shamefully. A nebulous feeling of goodwill towards nations emerging from colonial control had taken hold of British society and there were many who thought that Nasser's seizure of the Suez Canal was perfectly justified. What was more the abrupt cancelling of the operation when the United Nations - and especially America - issued their reproof was further humiliating evidence that Britain was no longer a great power capable of independent action but a wayward child in hock to a domineering parent.

When that parent put the squeeze on its offspring's pocket money Eden recognised that the whole farrago would have to come to a premature end. A necessary further loan from the US was rejected until the British had withdrawn from Suez and so, despite the unrepentant French calling for continued fighting even though the Israelis had given up, Britain humiliatingly climbed down three days after their 'interventionist' invasion. To compound the ignominy Eden then lied to the Commons about the existence of a fabricated plot. It was not enough to save him and he resigned in January the following year, forever to be associated with an act of gross diplomatic folly and national shame. But who would take his place?

The obvious choice was Rab Butler. An intellectual with a keen grasp of political history he had been Chancellor of the Exchequer and now led the Commons, whilst his wartime Education Act - which introduced the tripartite system of grammar, secondary technical and secondary modern schools - was seen as one of the most progressive policies of the era. He had briefly taken over the running of the country when Churchill suffered his stroke in 1953 but when called upon to do the same whilst Eden was abroad during the Suez crisis he appeared indecisive and unstatesmanlike.

If any politician of the time was going to exploit such a weakness it was the current Chancellor and Butler's rival Harold Macmillan. Like Stanley Baldwin before him Macmillan had a gift for both self-presentation and self-preservation and by the time the Queen came to appoint a new Prime Minister he had secured the backing of a large number of MPs. So the better qualified but less canny Butler lost out, harbouring a grudge against his nemesis that would last until his retirement from political life in 1964.

For the first time in the modern political era ordinary British men and women had taken to the streets to demonstrate against the actions of their government. Suez was the first sign that the old deference accorded to the nation's ruling elite was beginning to crumble. Eden had made not only Parliament but the whole governing class look corrupt, foolish and - in its insistence on a perceived parity with America - deluded. His successor had a considerable job on his hands to persuade the British people that public school and Oxbridge educated gentlemen like himself had the right to run the nation. Across the country so-called Angry Young

Men - primarily working class novelists and playwrights - were beginning to pop up and question the status quo. Soon the anger would turn to something even more damning - ridicule.

Under these circumstances Harold Macmillan probably was the right man for the job. Audaciously, rather than cultivate a down-to-earth man of the people persona a la Baldwin he played up his patrician, aristocratic manner revelling in the image of a venerable old duffer with a ready wit and unflappable bonhomie. In reality, of course, he was as steely and ruthless as they came and possessed an extraordinary ability to cling on to power in the face of the most damaging setbacks.

Yet Macmillan had been a vociferous rebel in the 1930s - very much a badge of honour in the aftermath of the Second World War – and had seen working class deprivation first-hand during his 19 years as member of Parliament for Stockton-on-Tees. He had been one of a band of younger ministers who had recognised that the Conservative party desperately needed to modernise if it was to survive in an ever-changing post-war world.

In light of this it is perhaps no surprise that Macmillan's tenure as Prime Minister was characterised by a curious mixture of radical modernisation and reactionary stubbornness. On the issue of empire, for example, he oversaw a rapid shedding of colonial possessions that staggered the political establishment. The lightning withdrawal was most pronounced in Africa where, over the course of Macmillan's seven years at Number 10, Britain granted independence to Sudan, Malaya, Nigeria, Cyprus, Uganda and Kenya. The newly independent Gold Coast was renamed Ghana whilst Tanganyika and Zanzibar combined to form Tanzania. In addition, Northern and Southern Rhodesia were lumped together with Nyasaland to form the unwieldy and ultimately unworkable Central African Republic.

And yet Macmillan continued to act every inch the imperial statesman, jetting off around the globe to shake hands and exchange witticisms with important national leaders. Naturally the most important of these was the United States who Britain was desperately trying to woo again after the debacle of Suez. Macmillan's easy charm made considerable headway and, in 1960, he secured the promise of American Skybolt missiles from Eisenhower. But once again the Skybolt issue highlighted the gulf between the ambitions of the UK and the US. By the time that the charismatic John F. Kennedy had been President for a little over a year Skybolt was being superseded by yet more sophisticated weaponry and the deal with Britain was cancelled. Macmillan was devastated. Outdated or not Skybolt was a nuclear deterrent that the country had been promised to enhance her world prestige. What was more the Prime Minister had already made substantive cuts to defence, slashing the numbers in the armed forces by nearly half and abolishing conscription. Without Skybolt Britain's military capability looked desperately weak. Eventually a compromise was reached whereby Britain took possession of American built Polaris submarine missiles, albeit with a number of caveats and restrictions. Macmillan had just about managed to save face but the omens were not good for the future of the 'special relationship.'

This was all the more relevant because of the growing status of the European Coal and Steel Community, the membership of which Herbert Morrison had so blithely dismissed in the dog days of the Labour government. Following the 1957 Treaty of Rome it had morphed into the inchoate European Economic Community and was clearly developing into a significant European power bloc with serious consequences for the rest of the continent. Britain now faced a stark choice of whom to ally herself with - the United States or Europe, new world or old.

Typically Macmillan thought he could do both. Whilst still clinging desperately on to American coat-tails he also acknowledged that Britain could not afford to stand apart from any major Western European institution. His hubris was in assuming that the British would, should and could be the dominant force within such an institution. Yet again Britain's vastly inflated sense of her own importance would be her undoing.

Rather than merely seek to join the EEC Macmillan proposed a series of entirely new bodies which Britain would naturally be at the heart of. His first idea was the European Free Trade Area whose goal was fairly self-explanatory but offered nothing to the six existing members of the Economic Community – Belgium, France, Italy, Luxembourg, the Netherlands and West Germany. When that concept unsurprisingly failed to appeal he bloody-mindedly established a rival organisation in 1959 known, somewhat preposterously, as the 'Outer Seven.' The inherent weakness of that community was that the other nations involved – Sweden, Norway, Denmark, Austria, Switzerland and Portugal – were no match for the major players of the EEC. If Macmillan wanted to be involved in Europe he would have to swallow his pride and ask to join the Big Six.

By 1961 he was finally prepared to do so but he went about the process with such arrogance and bad grace that any possibility of acceptance was torpedoed from the start. His language was either dismissive or confrontational and, in the imposing figure of Charles de Gaulle, he was up against an Anglophobe French statesman who needed no excuse to bark a resounding 'non!' at a fusty Edwardian throwback. Macmillan's Polaris deal with Kennedy confirmed de Gaulle's worst suspicions of Britain's American preference and he vetoed British membership in January 1963. The popular accusations of the Macmillan government being tweedy, outdated dinosaurs were never more apposite than over their handling of the European issue.

The Conservatives' management of the economy benefitted from an incredible slice of good fortune. A number of factors such as the end of the Korean War, growing liberalization of free trade and increased European production contributed to an age of affluence which had very little to do with governmental legislation. As ever-cheaper cars, holidays and white goods rolled off the production lines the fully employed British nation possessed disposable income for the first time in living memory. Macmillan was characteristically quick to claim the credit, famously declaring in 1957 that 'most Britons have never had it so good.' The trouble was that too many of the busy production lines were located in other European countries. Italy led the continent in the manufacture of white goods and electrical appliances whilst a resurgent West Germany produced vastly more motor vehicles than Britain. Indeed, the West German economy as a whole was poised - alongside the French - to overtake Britain's. Macmillan may have been complacently basking in the glow of conspicuous consumerism but other government ministers were only too aware that the good times could not last indefinitely.

In 1958 - in an echo of the doomed ROBOT scheme of a few years previously - the Treasury devised a grand resetting of the economy with short term hardship as the price for long term gain. Once again the prospect of haemorrhaging votes in the forthcoming election persuaded Macmillan to kill the project but not before his Chancellor Peter Thorneycroft and two junior ministers – one of whom was a certain Enoch Powell of whom much more later – resigned in protest. However, things could not carry on as they were and so - in one of those delicious ironies that British politics abounds in - Macmillan became a cheerleader for economic planning.

Whilst this was not quite the directive centralised planning of Attlee and his colleagues it was still a significant departure for a Conservative government. Official bodies and commissions sprang up to formulate and oversee relations between employers and unions but predictably it all came to nought. Union fury at the establishment of the National Incomes Commission - or Nicky, as it became known -, a regulatory body to monitor wage increases and intervene accordingly when such pay rises ran counter to productivity, effectively scuppered any attempt at industrial harmony and the economy continued to veer wildly between boom and bust.

The overwhelming criticism of this government - and indeed many that had gone before - was one of amateurism. If you could become a senior cabinet figure simply by attending the appropriate public school then it followed that you must have very little expertise or specialism in your appointed field. It also implied that you knew very little about the plight of the common man. As previously noted such criticisms were hard on Macmillan, who was deeply affected by the poverty he witnessed as an MP in the North East. But the insularity of his government laid him open to accusations of furthering the interests of a privileged minority who had no real idea what they were doing.

And the voices of the younger generation were becoming ever more voluble. Whether it was the excoriating drama of John Osborne, the class warrior ire of novelist Alan Sillitoe or the intellectual irreverence of the Beyond the Fringe revue everywhere in British popular culture there was rage, mockery and contempt directed at Macmillan and his cronies. In 1961 the journalist Michael Shanks published 'The Stagnant Society,' a brief but vicious attack on class privilege and a call for a more meritocratic society. It chimed perfectly with the times.

The Profumo Affair was almost too perfect a scandal for the disrespectful modernisers. It neatly summed up everything that was rotten in the court of Westminster and the fallout – which included the suicide of Stephen Ward, homosexual society masseur and Keeler's 'manager' – made a change in the political order inevitable. Macmillan resigned on grounds of ill-health on the 10th October 1963 and everybody assumed that Rab Butler's time had finally come. But, thanks to the departing Prime Minister's meddling, the nod went instead to Alec Douglas-Home. The fact that Douglas-Home had to relinquish his peerage to accept the position demonstrates that the Conservatives had learnt nothing from recent history.

The affable but lightweight Douglas-Home led the party into the following year's election against a Labour Party who were only just recovering from their own identity crisis. The Labour leader and grammar school boy Harold Wilson played the meritocracy card effectively enough to win by four seats. It was hardly a resounding vote of confidence but Labour were back and the whole tone of the nation was about to change once again.

18

WHITE HEAT, RED MIST

Prior to 1963 hardly anybody would have imagined that Harold Wilson would lead Labour into the forthcoming general election let alone become the next Prime Minister. The man currently in charge of the party, Hugh Gaitskell, had succeeded in remodelling Labour to appeal not just to the grassroots working class voters but also to significant sections of the lower middle class. He had done this by moving the emphasis away from unconditional state control and the primacy of communality and embracing the new twin gods of consumerism and fun. The Attlee government may have been altruistic and industrious but it had also felt humourless, austere and puritan - although given the severity of the conditions it could hardly have felt otherwise. Gaitskell wanted to show the voters that the Labour party was not against aspiration, individualism or having a good time. In his eyes the world had moved on and Socialism needed to adapt. Personal freedom mattered more to him than a stubborn insistence on public ownership – so much so that he attempted to remove the sainted clause four concerning nationalisation from the party rulebook. Over thirty years later another Labour leader with strikingly similar views would try to do the same.

Gaitskell's doctrinal flexibility outraged the hard-left old guard who saw him as a Judas to their great Socialist project. Chief among this influential band was Nye Bevan, the man who had founded the NHS and then resigned - with Wilson - when Chancellor Gaitskell imposed fees for spectacles and dentistry to fund rearmament. Narcissistic, wild and magnetic Bevan was totemic to many in the party, a courageous colossus who had delivered the finest institution in the welfare state. When Gaitskell won the 1955 leadership contest with ease the Bevanites considered breaking away to form their own political party but, although his loathing of the Labour leader remained undimmed, Bevan was eventually coaxed back to the shadow cabinet before his death in 1960.

Without their talisman the left cast about for someone to fight their cause. They alighted, albeit reluctantly, on Harold Wilson. Wilson's principled resignation in the early 50s counted for something but since then he had proved slippery, untrustworthy and fond of intrigue. Yet he was undoubtedly accomplished and intelligent and - in the absence of anybody better - would have to do. Then in 1963 - and to everyone's shock - Gaitskell suddenly died at the age of 56, thrusting Wilson into the limelight. Even then it seemed unlikely that he would rise to party leader. The mercurial and frequently pissed George Brown was the more popular choice, but his bid was scotched by James Callaghan's decision to run as well - thereby splitting the anti-Wilson vote - and 'Nye's Little Dog' stole in.

If you believe the claims of the KGB defector Anatoliy Golitsyn, however, Wilson's rise to power was preordained by Moscow. For the new Labour leader was, in fact, a Soviet agent and – even more sensationally – the luckless Gaitskell had been assassinated to clear his path. These assertions were taken seriously enough by MI5 to prompt exhaustive investigation of Wilson, no doubt contributing to his already rampant paranoia. That they could produce no evidence whatsoever of a Soviet plot never completely scotched the rumours of Wilson's supposed double life.

But upon becoming Labour leader Wilson never looked back, swiftly managing the impossible and uniting the Gaitskellites and the Bevanites behind his new vision of a modern, scientific technocracy with skilled people in the right positions acting with dynamism and purpose. At the 1963 Labour party conference, in one of the keynote speeches of the era, Wilson enthused about the 'white heat of technology' that would shape the lean, efficient new Britain. It was a vision that also intoxicated an electorate jaded by the public school amateurism of the Conservative years. Wilson was a grammar school boy who milked his faux-working class Northern roots shamelessly. Here was a textbook example of the new, driving meritocracy that Labour promised to instil throughout the land.

Squeaking into Downing Street by four seats the new Prime Minister was keen to show that his ministry would be a clean break with the past. However, before the task of transforming the nation into a thrusting, professional machine could begin he would need to address an alarming issue bequeathed by his Conservative predecessor.

Superficially Britain appeared to be on its uppers by 1964 with low unemployment and higher productivity resulting in a corresponding rise in living standards. But when James Callaghan took up his post as Chancellor of the Exchequer he made a horrifying discovery. The previous government had thrown caution to the wind in the interests of courting public opinion and overspent spectacularly. Consequently the nation was in debt to the tune of £800million. Suddenly all Labour's carefully researched economic plans were thrown into jeopardy and it looked almost inevitable that Wilson would have to take action that would blow a hole in his credibility.

The only two realistic options were deflation and devaluation - with concomitant deflation - and both ran counter to every claim and promise made in Labour's election manifesto. Wilson's victory had been down to his insistence that he would bring a new professionalism and technical skill to managing the economy and that the days of 'stop-go' would be banished forever. Deflation would mean that the dreaded cycle of boom and bust would begin all over again within a few months of Labour retaking office. Wilson's pre-election confidence in his party's fiscal rectitude would be fatally undermined and, with a Parliamentary majority of just four, it was conceivable that it could finish them off completely.

If deflation went against everything that Wilson's government stood for then devaluation went against everything the Labour party as a whole stood for. Stafford Cripps' 1949 devaluation had been a crushing blow to

Socialist pride and was still fresh in the minds of many party members. Then, as now, it had felt like an admission of failure on the part of a planned economy and a tacit acceptance that the vagaries of the market would always win out. But in the late 40s it could be explained away as an aberration brought about by the lingering aftermath of the Second World War and tiresome American belligerence. Both those factors were harder to sell to the public in the mid-1960s.

And so, faced with an economic Hobson's Choice, Wilson decided to do neither. The measured financial planning would continue to be implemented under the aegis of the new and exciting Department of Economic Affairs, under the exuberant leadership of the Deputy Prime Minister George Brown. To say that the Treasury were put out by the arrival of this new departmental kid on the block would be putting it mildly. The DEA's remit was infuriatingly vague and the more sober Callaghan - literally as well as figuratively - was determined that a liability such as Brown would not attempt to intrude on his patch. Cue some richly farcical moments as important papers were smuggled between departments and key staff members found themselves mysteriously reallocated to their rivals' offices.

None of this prevented a heroic frenzy of activity on Brown's part. He penned an exhaustive national plan and set up the National Board for Prices and Incomes to assess the merits of proposed wage and price increases. The Deputy Prime Minister also drafted a 'Statement of Intent,' which bound employers and unions together in co-operating with the government on productivity and wage and price hikes - albeit on a voluntary basis. Whilst these were all sound enough measures in principle the economy was hurtling out of control so quickly that Brown's proposals became unworkable within weeks of their implementation. When Brown was shunted off to the Foreign Office in 1966 the DEA was effectively mothballed. The failure of the department was as clear a sign as any that old school planning was useless at a time of immediate economic crisis and that only deflation or devaluation had a chance of working.

The agonising economic decision hung like a black cloud over the government's collective head. It affected almost every piece of legislation it argued over, whether directly or indirectly. Months dragged on with no sign of financial salvation and still Wilson hedged his bets and chose to hold sterling's parity. For many less ideologically minded MPs devaluation held little fear. After all, if you took the humiliation on the chin it was – almost - like wiping the slate clean. There were also those who felt a dent in Britain's enormous self-regard might be exactly the wake-up call that she needed. The increasingly stark choice between being America's junior partner or a humbled part of the European Common Market was ineluctably dependent on whether or not sterling was devalued.

Chief amongst the wily Wilson's schemes for rescuing the nation's finances was to borrow from the United States. President Johnson was prepared to fulfil such a request but - as should by now be apparent - any loan would come steeped in conditions that would have far-reaching political consequences. As the US was currently fighting an arduous and highly controversial war in Vietnam, the caveats in this instance were a continued – and costly - British military presence 'East of Suez' and 'support' for America's dubious anti-Communist entanglement. Johnson would have preferred the support to have been physical but was prepared to accept the moral variety via a public endorsement from Wilson.

Public reaction to the latter of the two demands was deeply divided. Radical, idealistic activists were disgusted at their Prime Minister acquiescing to the wholesale slaughter being perpetrated by the US, whilst more conservative minded folk considered that Wilson had done well to keep Britain out of the fighting. Either way there was no papering over the fact that the government had once again been forced to kowtow to the Americans for the sake of a financial bailout.

The other option – acceptance into the fold of the Common Market – was bitterly opposed by many hard-left Labour MPs but Wilson viewed it as precisely the kind of modern, technocratic body that 'white heat' Labour should be a part of. Yet it was the same old story here too, with Britain blustering around offending everybody and leaving Charles de Gaulle to gleefully veto the whole idea. It would take a passionate Conservative Europhile to finally secure the nation's entry to the EEC.

And yet for all this twisting and dithering and plain incompetence Labour managed to win a second term in late 1966 with an increased majority of 97. Always highly suspicious of political success the result only made the already paranoid Wilson twitchier about potential coups against him. Whilst it is true that several senior Labour figures were deeply unhappy with his manipulative style of leadership Wilson never came especially close to being deposed, even when in the summer of 1967 his hand was finally forced on the issue of devaluation.

The Six Day War between Israel and Egypt erupted in June and led to the closure of the ever contentious Suez Canal. This meant that vital oil supplies from Iraq and Kuwait were prevented from reaching Britain with the result that prices soared and the reserves started to drain away. A national dock strike was then badly handled by the government leading to an appalling loss of productivity. One by one the Treasury supremo Sir Alec Cairncross, the Chancellor James Callaghan and finally the Prime Minister Harold Wilson all accepted the necessity of devaluation. Callaghan saw it as a personal failure and had to be persuaded not to leave the front bench – he ended up at the Home Office - whilst Wilson added insult to injury by trying to make light of the whole affair to the general public. Nobody was fooled. The claim that the purchase power of the pound had not been devalued domestically may have been accurate enough but everybody knew that they would take the hit in cuts and higher interest rates as well as seeing Britain's overseas trading power compromised. It was the most high profile failure of the 1960s Labour government and, considering that Wilson had been elected on a ticket of strong economic management, called into question the government's competence in all other areas of policy as well. Fortunately for the Prime Minister there were a couple of areas of domestic policy where Labour was doing exactly what its manifesto said it would.

Our prevailing image of the 1960s is of a decade of liberation, youthful dynamism, boundless creativity and passionate political activism – the permissive society writ large. However distorted these halcyon days may have become in the public consciousness there is no doubt that politically personal freedom was high on the agenda at the Home Office. Up until the mid-60s Britain was still a nation that made homosexuality and abortion illegal, hung convicted criminals as a matter of course and operated highly prescriptive and intolerant divorce laws. By the close of the decade all of these injustices had been addressed and - at least in some measure - resolved. The spate of ethical activity in these areas was testament not only to the tenacity and firmly held beliefs of a clutch of cross-party backbenchers but also to the urbane, cultured Home Secretary Roy Jenkins who steered the legislation through in the teeth of public opposition.

The death penalty was the first of these reactionary practices to go and actually predated Jenkins' tenure at the Home Office. Like all of the above issues capital punishment was challenged by a private members' bill, in this case from the Jewish pacifist Labour MP Sydney Silverman. The call to abolish hanging had been gathering steam for a while, helped on its way by some controversial convictions such as that of the mentally retarded Derek Bentley in 1952 and the young mother Ruth Ellis three years later. In 1957 amidst growing disquiet in Parliament - although not with the general public who were still broadly in favour - the Conservative Home Secretary Sir David Maxwell-Fyfe significantly reduced the number of offences that would result in the death penalty. As soon as the door was opened a crack Silverman and his fellow campaigners rushed through. After eight more years of lobbying and numerous miscarriages of justice capital punishment was halted for a trial period of five years. It never returned.

In addition to Maxwell-Fyfe's limiting of hanging offences 1957 also saw the publication of the Wolfenden Report which advocated the legalisation of homosexual activity in private between consenting adults. Whilst Macmillan's government quickly swept the report under the carpet the idea gained momentum - particularly in literary and academic circles - leading to the foundation of the Homosexual Law Society the following year. The early 1950s had seen a witch-hunt carried out against homosexuals, bizarrely justified by the accusation that men who led double lives were more likely to be blackmailed into spying for the Russians. The notion that decriminalising homosexuality would mean that these men would no longer need to lead double lives appears to have escaped the draconian sensibilities of Maxwell-Fyfe.

When installed at the Home Office Jenkins took a number of backbenchers under his wing, creating an atmosphere in which they could formulate their campaigns with due time and diligence. In the case of decriminalising consensual homosexuality the MP in question was Leo Abse, a flamboyant Jew with a penchant for psychoanalysis. By 1967 the Parliamentary mood had changed sufficiently for the Sexual Offences Act to be passed, legalising consensual homosexual activity in private.

Jenkins' next protégé was a young Liberal politician called David Steel with a firm conviction that the outlawing of abortion required overturning. Once again public opinion was turning in favour of a change in the law following horrific accounts of both backstreet abortions and the spate of births of deformed babies resulting from the Thalidomide scandal. Key to the success of the Abortion Act of 1967 was the redefinition of the mother's health to include her mental state as well as her physical wellbeing, an amendment that acknowledged the psychological trauma that unwanted pregnancy could inflict upon vulnerable young women.

Whilst these reforms may not have been initiated by Jenkins they all chimed with his stated intentions upon becoming Home Secretary and there is little doubt that it was down to his sympathetic treatment of the bills and his heavyweight reputation that these civilizing measures were passed so comprehensively. When he became an equally productive Chancellor in 1967 – reducing the deficit worsened by devaluation with a series of tough cuts and the painful decision to withdraw British troops stationed 'East of Suez' – the department continued his good work. The 1968 Theatres Act banned stage censorship and the Divorce Reform Act of

1969 broadened the acceptable reasons for divorce from adultery to 'irretrievable breakdown.' This sufficiently ambiguous rewording enabled many women to escape bitterly unhappy marriages. Like the abolition of slavery, Lloyd George's proto-welfare state and Bevan's National Health Service the legacy of Jenkins' tenure as Home Secretary in the 1960s is something this nation should be truly proud of.

And whilst Jenkins was enhancing people's personal freedoms the swashbuckling young Education Minister Tony Crosland was attempting to level the playing field in the nation's schools. The 1944 Butler Act - which had established the tripartite system of education - had been seen as an enlightened piece of legislation during the war but twenty years on the iniquities of the bill were clear. The promised three types of schooling had in effect been reduced to two as the secondary technical schools had never gotten off the ground. What was left was a gross inequality in the standard of teaching in grammar schools - generally venerable institutions with highly qualified teachers – as opposed to that in secondary moderns with their skeleton staff and crumbling buildings. Anybody who failed their 11-plus examination was condemned to a secondary modern and likely underachievement.

If Britain was truly to be the meritocracy that the Labour government insisted upon then equality in the standard of education had to be a cornerstone policy. Crosland's intention was single-minded and brutal – the effective abolition of grammar schools and the establishment of non-preferential comprehensives. Government funding was reserved for these new egalitarian schools thus ensuring that the majority of grammar schools changed status rapidly and by the end of the decade a third of children were being educated at comprehensives. The bandwagon rolled on throughout the 70s with Margaret Thatcher - of all people - accelerating the rate of transformation.

Crosland's achievements have proven highly controversial. The advent of holistic or 'child-centred' learning in comprehensives was deeply divisive, with the educational traditionalists feeling as though the hippy ideals of the age had permeated the classroom, replacing rigour and authority.

Crosland's other major innovation - the creation of a raft of polytechnics to teach higher education technical courses – attracted the ire of underfunded universities and purists who viewed them as a dumbed-down dilution of academia. There is no doubt, however, that his actions produced the biggest revolution in education for decades.

Alongside Labour's humiliating mismanagement of the economy and its shining achievements in social reform sit two bills – one passed, one rejected – that have proved to have profound repercussions. They concern the almighty power of the trade union movement and the uncomfortable and slightly sinister British attitude towards immigration.

In 1952 the hero of the hard-left Nye Bevan published a seminal Socialist tract entitled 'In Place of Fear.' When the pugnacious Employment Secretary Barbara Castle produced her 1969 white paper on those bastions of working class pride the trade unions she opted for the title 'In Place of Strife.' From the outset this tussle would be both provocative and combative.

There had actually been a decline in the amount of industrial action during the Wilson administration with union bosses having grudgingly agreed to wage freezes to give a Labour government a fair crack of the whip. But despite this Castle was uneasy about the increasingly informal methods of union activity, with their ad hoc rules and regulations and practices that differed from union to union. 'In Place of Strife' set out a series of measures to assert the authority of the state over that of the unions - a conciliation pause of up to 28 days for particularly damaging unofficial strikes, the imposition of settlements in inter-union disputes and the process of balloting for official strikes.

Viewed through the prism of Thatcherite union obliteration these conditions appear pretty mild but in the late 60s - when the bonds between union and party were adamantine and the unions considered themselves to be propping up a weak Labour government - 'In Place of

Strife' caused an uproar. Castle was the first great female cabinet minister as well as a reluctant icon for the burgeoning feminist movement. In 1968 she had come out on strike with female workers at the Ford car plant in Dagenham over the issue of unequal pay. She also had form for making unpopular decisions - as Minister of Transport she had introduced both the breathalyser and the 70 miles per hour speed limit. But waging war on motorists was a very different thing to waging war on the trade unions.

For one thing it completely alienated the majority of her Labour colleagues who regarded the union movement as the lifeblood of the party. Many key figures in government had come from a union background, including James Callaghan, and were utterly incensed by Castle's proposals. In March the paper was thrown out by the Labour Party National Executive with some of the most loyal Parliamentary foot-soldiers voting against it. But Castle had one ace up her sleeve, the support of the Prime Minister Harold Wilson.

The pair threw themselves into the confrontation with gusto. This was expected of Castle but Wilson's willingness to enrage his party was unexpected, especially considering his perpetual terror of imagined coups. His behaviour on this matter produced more concrete talk of his ousting than any other crisis that the government endured. He attempted to pre-empt any imminent overthrow by threatening to resign if the bill was not passed, banking on the fact that such a move would surely result in the Conservatives regaining power.

The Parliamentary Labour Party was unimpressed and stuck resolutely to its guns. The inevitable finally came to pass in June 1969 when Wilson and Castle were forced into a humiliating climb-down. The bill was withdrawn under the 'solemn and binding' understanding that the TUC would do whatever lay in its power to resolve unofficial industrial action. The compromise was laughable and, indeed, 'Solomon Binding' became the biggest joke in Westminster that summer. The unions - with the unequivocal support of the vast majority of the Labour Party - had won a resounding victory which all but convinced them of their untouchability.

*

By the late 1960s the consequences of Attlee's offhand decision to make Commonwealth subjects British citizens were only too apparent. The public outcry at the ever increasing number of migrants entering the country had scared Wilson into tightening the Commonwealth and Immigrants Act in 1965. This controversial act permitted only those migrants with official employment vouchers to settle in Britain, thus reneging dramatically on the initial promise of free entry to all. The act went hand in hand with the first anti-race discrimination legislation but it was widely accepted that this was a sop to appease more liberal critics.

If a sizeable amount of the British public was unhappy with the numbers of West Indian and Pakistani families moving into areas in London and the Midlands then the potential arrival of thousands of Asian Kenyans fleeing the atrocities of the sadistic Mau-Mau regime left them horrified. There was no dispute as to these refugees' right to settle in Britain. They had British passports secured after Kenyan independence in 1963 and the legality of their coming to Britain had been unambiguously decreed by the Conservative government at that time.

But when, in 1967, they arrived in the country at the rate of a thousand a month scaremongering stories started to appear in the press and many more reactionary voters made their displeasure known. The government was split between those who felt honour bound to fulfil their promise to the Kenyan Asians and those who - either from their own racial prejudice, fears of overcrowding or political expediency - wished to slam the door in their faces.

Unfortunately for the fleeing Asians the Home Secretary James Callaghan was in the latter camp. The Commonwealth Immigrations Act was passed later that year and made highly uncomfortable reading. The right of Commonwealth subjects to settle in Britain was effectively revoked save for a miniscule quota, leaving thousands of Kenyan Asians vulnerable and stateless. It was the inverse of Roy Jenkins' civilizing Home Office acts - a

211

grubby, sordid U-turn that exposed the prejudice still very much at the heart of British culture.

As if that were not enough the following year saw the delivery of the most racially inflammatory speech in British political history. It was made by Enoch Powell, Macmillan's Health Minister and now Shadow Defence Secretary and perennial purveyor of provocative views. Powell has become a pariah for his unwavering opinions on immigration, branded a racist and consigned to the far-right scrapheap. Yet he was not a mindless thug or aristocratic bigot but possibly the most highly educated and oratorically gifted politician of his generation. He was massively influential in pioneering the monetarist theories of Thatcherism - remember his resignation with the Chancellor Thorneycroft over the mismanagement of the economy in the 50s - as well as fomenting a fundamental scepticism of the European Union. All of which makes him a polarising figure to say the least. A haunted and frighteningly intense man his uncompromising political beliefs would veer far from the mainstream of political opinion whilst proving unerringly popular with large sections of society.

What has become commonly known as the 'Rivers of Blood' speech - in fact there was only one river referenced, the 'foaming' Roman Tiber - is difficult to defend on almost every level. Claiming to quote his fearful white constituents in Wolverhampton the imagery of the 'black man holding the whip hand over the white man' and 'piccaninnies' chanting 'racialist' at little old ladies possesses a hysteria that fits the apocalyptic ancient metaphor that gives the speech its name. Without immediate repatriation, Powell entreated, Britain would see the kind of race riots that were tearing America apart. The fact that the Fascist National Front had been formed in 1967 added an extra distasteful frisson to Powell's nasty rhetoric.

It was too much for the Conservative leader Edward Heath who summarily sacked Powell as soon as he heard his words. Once tipped as a future Prime Minister Powell was now relegated to the position of 'awkward backbencher who speaks his mind no matter what'. Yet the fact remains that an awful lot of people wholeheartedly agreed - and undoubtedly still do - with Enoch Powell's views on race and immigration, as the numerous marches and demonstrations in his support clearly showed.

As Prime Minister, Heath proved equally slippery on the thorny issue of immigration. On the one hand he put his name to a small-minded act restricting British entry to those with a parent or grandparent born in the country, yet on the other he unhesitatingly accepted thousands of Ugandan Asians fleeing the barbaric dictatorship of Idi Amin. However, neither Heath nor Wilson ever fully deigned to address the issue of integration that has led to such ill-feeling and ghettoization.

The tremendous irony was that it may have been Powell's last minute support for Heath that swung the 1970 general election in favour of the Conservatives. Immensely popular with a particular type of Conservative voter the right wing maverick was being feted as the party's true leader despite his banishment to the backbenches. The publication of poor economic figures from the Treasury just prior to voting did not help and when the result came in it stunned Wilson who had called the election confident in consolidating his mandate. But it would be Edward Heath and the Conservative party who would usher in the 1970s, little realising the tumult and trauma that the decade had in store.

19

BROKEN BRITAIN

The country that Edward Heath inherited at the turn of the 1970s was in the early stages of complete economic meltdown. The only consolation was that it was not alone. The 1967 devaluation that Harold Wilson had agonised over was repeated in France in both the same year and again two years later, at the same time as Germany were also forced into joining this worrying financial trend. The alarm bells became deafening, however, when the United States began floundering under the massive inflationary cost of the iconoclastic Vietnam War, coupled with a simultaneous rise in commodity prices. In 1971 President Nixon suspended the dollar's convertibility, allowing exchange rates to float. Whilst this momentous decision removed at a stroke the constant anxiety over the depletion of Britain's reserves it would also throw out the last remaining check on fiscal irresponsibility.

A grammar school boy of even humbler origins than his Prime Ministerial predecessor Heath was not the man best equipped to deal with such a tumultuous period in British political history. Despite having a similarly meritocratic career trajectory to Harold Wilson Heath couldn't stand the Labour leader, who he viewed – with some justification - as a cocky chancer with highly elastic political principles. In contrast the new Prime Minister regarded himself as noble, serious and concerned with the national good rather than mere Parliamentary self-preservation.

Having started out on the right wing of the Conservative party Heath had moved squarely to the centre by his time in office and would travel steadily leftwards during the course of his Prime Ministerial tenure. He believed in the old pre-war virtues of consensus politics - co-operation and inclusion. The trouble was that by the 1970s the key threat to his governing authority - the trade unions – were in no mood for compromise. To compound matters Heath's aloofness and lack of personal charm meant that, however good his intentions, any policy promoting industrial harmony was doomed to fail.

From the outset luck was not on the Prime Minister's side as one after another various unions called major strikes. Dockers, dustmen and power workers all came out within months of the Conservatives' return to office and they were all awarded considerably higher settlements than expected. Yet Heath was determined to tackle the running sore of heightening union power. The Industrial Relations Act passed in 1971 was an ultimately failed attempt to stamp his authority over the unions whilst at the same time preserving a mutually conducive working relationship between employers and employees. In essence the Act subjected traditional union custom - the 'informality' that had so concerned Barbara Castle - to the full rigour of the law with a National Industrial Relations Court set up as the government's enforcement agency. Non-compulsory registration of unions would also be introduced which would separate the conscientious, law-abiding organisations from the militant and the unpredictable. Non-registration incurred fines and sacrificed rights and government protection whilst registered unions would reap all the rewards of co-operation with the state.

In Heath's eyes it was a fair and balanced agreement which demonstrated a respect for the trade union movement. To the union bosses it was just another piece of legislation with which to shackle their workers and, having seen off Castle's white paper two years earlier, they were emboldened to fight this initiative tooth and nail also. 140,000 TUC protesters marched through London as the bill made its way through the Commons, where the pro-union Labour MPs who had been so incensed by 'In Place of Strife' unleashed the full power of their righteous indignation. In any case the Act was fatally flawed by the refusal to make acquiescence to registration compulsory. Union leaders simply commanded their members not to register and the Act died with barely a whimper later in the year.

Things got even worse the following year. An unsatisfactory public sector incomes policy led to successive drops in the amounts able to be awarded in industrial settlements. Thus when the National Union of Miners lobbied for a 47% increase in wages the best the government could offer was a derisory 7%. The resultant miners' strike was like nothing seen since 1926. A young miner called Arthur Scargill took effective control and organised his strikers with the ruthlessness and tactical precision of a military general. One of his signature manoeuvres was to send 'flying pickets' to power stations and ports in a bid to totally cripple the production and distribution of energy. Following a mass brawl between miners and police at a major coke depot in Saltley, Birmingham Heath sought independent advice on the pay dispute from the eminent judge Lord Wilberforce. He soon wished he hadn't – Wilberforce's recommendation was for a wage increase of 27%. The government capitulated, meekly acquiescing to numerous fringe demands into the bargain. The public looked on askance and questioned who exactly was running the country.

The 1972 miners' strike shattered Heath's resolve and from this point on all attempts to impose governmental authority on the trade unions evaporated. In a desperate effort to appease union bosses and avert any more damaging industrial action he lurched violently to the left with policies that echoed the previous Labour administration and even the post-war Attlee government. State intervention and planning were introduced as was the concept of 'tripartism' which gave the unions equal say with the government and the Confederation of British Industry on matters of wages and investment. But by this point the union bosses believed they were perfectly capable of bringing down the government and stubbornly refused to respect any Conservative legislation.

Whilst the unions played a huge part in Edward Heath's downfall there were other forces at work that combined to lay the Conservatives low. Labour's last Chancellor, Roy Jenkins, had done a fine job of temporarily shoring up the economy but the country was now seeing a steep rise in unemployment as a delayed result. Meanwhile growth and investment were still disappointingly low and the fateful decision to float the pound following Nixon's removal of the dollar's convertibility was leading to escalating inflation.

As a skilled yachtsman Heath would have been familiar with the maritime concept of the perfect storm. In the closing months of 1973 he experienced the political equivalent. Firstly, Israel and Egypt renewed hostilities over the vexed question of the state of Palestine. The Yom Kippur War was won with surprising ease by Israel but the humiliated Arab world was intent on revenge. The Saudi-controlled Organization of the Petroleum Exporting Countries massively reduced the oil supply to those Western nations sympathetic to the Israeli cause. This was a far greater threat than that which had forced Wilson into devaluation in 1967 and it affected the whole of the Western world. Britain was still allowed a minimal amount of oil but had to pay four times as much as it would have done normally. The United States' and the Netherlands' supply was cut off completely.

Consequently inflation soared putting an even greater strain on an already dangerously stretched economy. And then the NUM chose the same moment to lodge another wage demand that the government had no hope of meeting. Faced with a combined shortage of highly expensive oil and depleted amounts of coal the government bit the bullet and announced a series of emergency measures aimed at conserving as much precious fuel as possible. Alongside a 20mph reduction in the speed limit and the curtailing of the television schedule at 10.30pm the notorious three day working week was announced in January 1974. The ongoing Troubles in Northern Ireland should not be forgotten either. The post-war dream of an efficient, professional and productive British nation appeared well and truly quashed. Not since the days of late 1940s austerity had Britain been in such a dark place, both literally and figuratively.

Inevitably the miners voted overwhelmingly to strike and Heath had no option but to dissolve Parliament and fight another general election. Given the scale of the canker then infecting the country a modern observer might have expected the Conservatives to be routed. But in the end it was only the ever contrary actions of Enoch Powell - resigning and encouraging everybody to vote Labour - that edged Heath's beleaguered ministry out. Even then Harold Wilson - for it was still he in charge of the

Labour Party - could not form a majority government and would have been kept out had Heath contrived to do a deal with the Liberals. As it was a second election settled the matter with Labour squeaking through by three seats. The electorate may not have wanted Heath but they seemed far from convinced about Wilson as well.

*

There was, of course, another issue that dominated Edward Heath's administration and which resulted in either triumphant membership of an invaluable continental trading bloc or the shameful abdication of national sovereignty and the fabled British Constitution, depending on your point of view. For it was Heath who finally led Britain into Europe and irrevocably changed the country's position on the world stage.

Membership of the European Economic Community was a personal crusade for Heath, a dedicated Europhile with prior experience of negotiating for entry with the Macmillan government. Not only was Heath utterly convinced of the necessity of joining forces with the Big Six he was also the first post-war Prime Minister to regard doing so as infinitely more beneficial to British interests than cosying up to the Americans. He was also aided by not having to face the intransigent Charles de Gaulle who had recently died. His successor Georges Pompidou knew – and liked - Heath of old. The stars seemed to be aligning for British union with Europe.

Yet the process was hardly a walk in the park. European integration was, and remains, one of the most divisive issues in British politics with both major parties split bitterly on its benefits and deficiencies. Whilst the Conservatives recognised the need to stay united behind their leader Labour MPs gave full vent to their respective deeply held beliefs. The majority were staunchly anti-membership but the pro-European minority had a formidable champion in Roy Jenkins and were perfectly capable of causing problems for their leader. Wilson himself was in a difficult position. He had spearheaded Labour's previous mishandled bid for membership against a party that was largely hostile and now had to perform a nimble volte face in order to stymie the current Prime Minister's efforts.

Heath unconsciously let him off the hook. The Prime Minister was so desperate to secure membership at any price that he did very little haggling with Pompidou, leaving himself open to accusations of forfeiting Britain's best interests. The old rules and regulations of the Common Market had not been amended in any way to accommodate British entry, meaning that the original six members would still receive preferential treatment. Meanwhile the Community budget and Common Agricultural Policy were still very much skewed towards French interests. Heath may have learnt the lessons of high-handed entitlement that blighted the Conservative bid of the 1950s but his slavish sycophancy tilted the balance too far the other way. Therefore the Leader of the Opposition could legitimately claim that he was not anti-Europe per se, merely that he opposed the terms that Heath had negotiated.

Such mealy-mouthed semantics was not enough to ruin the Prime Minister's great dream. After Pompidou had pronounced a resounding 'Oui' to British membership the proposal was passed in the Commons thanks to 69 Labour rebels - led by Jenkins - defying the whip and voting with the government. A humiliated Wilson did the only thing he could and leapt upon Tony Benn's idea of a referendum to renegotiate the terms of entry at a later date.

The decision to embrace the diktats of the Common Market was a momentous one that few people fully understood at the time. Whilst the noble British Constitution is nowhere near the definitive document that people believe it to be - consisting essentially of piecemeal pieces of legislation tacked on as and when they became relevant - European integration really did mean the loss of Parliamentary sovereignty in crucial areas. Bodies such as the European Court of Human Rights would now take precedence over British legal judgements whilst cynics and naysayers would rail against the crushing uniformity of Brussels' pronouncements in trivial matters such as metric measurements. Set against this was the creation of jobs and trade agreements that membership of such an exclusive club conferred.

When Labour got their chance to go to the country in the 1975 referendum the nation voted to stay in the EEC by 68% to 32%. There has, however, been much subsequent griping about how ill-informed much of the public felt themselves to be on the issue and that the 'Yes' campaign kept them purposefully in the dark about the extent to which Britain was ceding constitutional control. The other fascinating aspect of the referendum was the bizarre political bedfellows it created, chief amongst them the doyen of the hard-right Enoch Powell and the darling of the ultra-left Tony Benn united by their desire to maintain British sovereignty.

The two year interregnum of Harold Wilson's second period of office need only be touched on lightly. His big idea for taming the unions was termed - with echoes of Enlightenment idealism - the Social Contract. In exchange for being reasonable about wage demands the unions got pretty much whatever they wanted, demonstrated only too well by the enormous settlement awarded to the striking miners. Having had his fingers burned in the late 60s the Prime Minister was loath to provoke industrial ire again.

In a sense the policy worked as there were markedly fewer days lost to industrial action between 1974 and 1976. But the hope that union bosses would respect a policy of voluntary wage restraint was pie in the sky and soon increases were rocketing upwards at a higher rate than inflation. Wilson's Chancellor, the ruddy faced aesthete and former Communist Dennis Healey, responded in good Socialist fashion by taxing the rich to an extreme degree and providing tax breaks for the poorest.

Healey was the brightest star in a mediocre administration, headed by a tired old man in the early stages of Alzheimer's. If Wilson's passion for plots had evaporated then so had the manipulative cunning and shrewdness of his glory days. He watched dispassionately as the empire was officially wound up before abruptly resigning in April 1976. In a final piece of Machiavellian mischief he tipped off his favoured successor James Callaghan so that he could steal a march on his leadership rivals. The ruse worked and the former Chancellor and Home Secretary duly became Labour's third post-war Prime Minister, defeating the likes of Healey, Jenkins and the leftist Michael Foot over three lethargic rounds.

Despite the right kind of collectivist noises regarding nationalisation, redistribution of the wealth and income tax the mainstream of the Labour party had effectively abandoned full-blooded Socialism after the critical devaluation of 1949. They had evolved into Social Democrats - no longer intent on overthrowing Capitalism, just keeping the worst excesses of the market under control. James Callaghan represented a further incremental step to the right - a social conservative who had been uncomfortable with many of Jenkins' reforms of the 1960s and an open admirer of the new monetarist economic philosophy. Yet he was a former union man who still retained a sentimental attachment to the principles of his old comrades, a compromised position which would ultimately culminate in disaster.

Callaghan's first concern was, as ever, the economy. The dangers of a floating currency had not been heeded and sterling was plummeting ever faster, ratcheting inflation up to untenable levels. Dennis Healey, still ensconced at the Treasury, had tried everything in his power to turn the economy around but by the spring of 1976 unemployment was still rising and he felt that there was only one remaining option open to rescue the nation's finances. With a heavy heart he applied for a conditional loan from the International Monetary Fund. British governments had pleaded with the United States for loans in the past but this was different. Whilst the US deals had come with significant strings attached any offer from the IMF - and it was by no means certain that one would be forthcoming - would entail not only swingeing cuts enforceable by international law but also the humiliating act of Britain handing final control of her economic fate to the bankers of the IMF. Combined with the signing away of British sovereignty to the Common Market a few years previously, doom-mongering commentators were having a field day busily writing the obituary for the nation's political constitution.

The negotiations were further torture with the government hopelessly split between those – like Tony Benn – who rejected any loan in favour of a radical siege economy, those - like Tony Crosland - who felt naively confident that the IMF would offer a no-strings-attached deal and those - like Healey and Callaghan - who knew they would have to fight for whatever they could get. The end result was bad but not as catastrophic as it could have been - a $3.9billion loan in return for £2.5billion in government cuts over the next two years.

In real terms the medicine was not nearly as unpalatable as first feared, chiefly because the novelty of floating exchange rates meant that the Treasury's calculations were rough estimates that proved wildly pessimistic. Combined with the shrewdness of Healey's pre-application cuts and the arrival of North Sea Oil the balance of payments was swiftly back into a surplus and public spending and the rate of inflation also came down dramatically. But in a sense that just made the loan even more embarrassing. The British government could not even do its sums accurately enough to avoid trudging 'cap in hand' to the IMF, thus imposing needlessly stringent cuts on herself and abdicating the power of her leaders.

Yet Callaghan's government proved more resilient than expected and, with the economy seemingly healthier than it had been for years, Labour were able to enter into a Parliamentary pact with the Liberals that secured them an official majority for the first time since they had returned to power. The Liberals were just as desperate for an alliance as Labour after their colourful leader Jeremy Thorpe was sensationally accused of conspiring in the attempted murder of a male model who had allegedly been his former lover. Callaghan had demonstrated considerable staying power in the face of ever escalating crises and many within the Labour party hoped that the worst was now over. And then, over the course of a few months in 1978 and 79 the Prime Minister threw all the hard work away because of two stupid and eminently avoidable mistakes.

The first was a frankly bizarre song-and-dance - literally, as we shall see - over the date of the next general election. With the comparatively good news on the state of the economy almost everybody assumed that Callaghan would go to the country in autumn 1978 and had he done so there is every likelihood that Labour would have won and the Thatcherite revolution would never have taken place. But Callaghan thought he could do better by delaying until the following spring. However, he declined to make this in any way clear to the rest of the party, contenting himself with dropping cryptic and ambiguous clues at the Labour party conference by singing the old music hall number 'Waiting at the Church.' He kept his cabinet in the dark until the last possible moment and when they finally found out the majority considered it an ill-advised decision to say the least.

They would be proved right when Callaghan sabotaged himself further by setting an incredibly harsh workers' pay limit of 5% to add a further fillip to the economy. This was part of a broader strategy to distance the party from the unsuccessful attempts at industrial inclusion that had blighted both Heath and Wilson's governments. But union bosses had never been happy with the concept of wage restraint - voluntary or otherwise - feeling that it compromised their position as collective wage bargainers. Given the Prime Minister's former career it was understandable that the unions felt betrayed by his actions, especially when he sought Parliamentary consent to impose sanctions on employers who awarded pay rises at a higher rate. After Callaghan narrowly lost the vote in the Commons the decision of the TGWU to strike for 30% in support of the car workers at Ford should not have been unexpected. But now Callaghan's vexed relationship with his industrial past led him badly astray. Caught between his original hard-line stance and his affection for the union movement he sheepishly settled for 17% and opened the floodgates for other industries to chance their arms for higher pay.

One by one oil tanker drivers, road haulage drivers, British Leyland workers, sewerage workers, school staff, ambulance drivers and refuse collectors - to name but a few - came out on strike and aggressively so.

Steadily the country was coming to a standstill with whole cities effectively cut off from the rest of the nation. Even more distressing was the danger that ordinary people were put in as a result of the cessation of certain industries' activities. Vital medical supplies were unable to be transported to different parts of the country whilst masses of refuse built up attracting rats and potential disease. The nadir came when cemetery staff in Liverpool refused to bury fresh corpses leading to the medieval sight of dead bodies piling up in empty warehouses.

If union bosses were cast as money-grabbing militants for lobbying for - in many cases well deserved - pay increases for their members, then the Prime Minister added fuel to the fire by blithely denying that there was any sort of problem. He may not actually have uttered the words 'crisis? What crisis?' upon returning from a Caribbean holiday at the peak of 'The Winter of Discontent,' but his attitude seemed astonishingly blasé. In hindsight it was probably more fatalism than incompetence, having realised early on that the forthcoming election was already lost. Ironically, of course, if Callaghan had done what everybody else expected and called the election for the autumn of 1978 he would most likely have been safely back in Downing Street for another term just when disaster struck.

In February 1979 the government finally came to an agreement with the TUC, backtracking wildly on the 5% limit. Gradually the unions called off the strikes and the nation began to recover. But the damage was most definitely done and there were other Parliamentary concerns as well. For most of the previous four years Labour had had to rely on a series of unwieldy coalitions and alliances with other parties to govern the country. The Lib-Lab pact, however, was now in danger of splintering due to the Liberals eagerness for a quick election. The Scottish Nationalist Party was also in vengeful mood having been defeated by a piece of ingenious statistical sophistry on a referendum for devolution. When a Conservative motion of no-confidence was called in March the Liberals and the SNP - alongside the Ulster Unionists - allied with the opposition to defeat the beleaguered government by a single vote. In a final humiliation Callaghan went to the Queen to seek the dissolution of Parliament and the subsequent general election returned the Conservatives to power with a majority of 43 seats.

In Margaret Thatcher Britain would have her first, and to date only, female Prime Minister. Political commentators were not overly hopeful - the crises that had blighted the 1970s looked set to continue into the following decade with no foreseeable solution available. But there had always been an economic philosophy extant - foreshadowed in the ROBOT proposal of the 50s and Thorneycroft and Powell's resignations a few years later - that had not thus far been considered by a British Prime Minister. Monetarism was considered too extreme, too brutal, too dramatic to take seriously. But Thatcher had no such qualms and its implementation would change the nation forever.

20

THE BIG BANG

On 14th April 2013 a song, lasting under a minute, taken from the 1939 screen musical 'The Wizard of Oz' climbed to number two in the British charts. The explanation for the dramatic 21st century success of 'Ding-Dong! The Witch is Dead' lay in the passing of the former Conservative Prime Minister Margaret Thatcher the previous week. Over twenty years after her sensational departure from office the legacy of Thatcherism polarised opinion to the extent that thousands of ordinary Britons unashamedly gloried in her death. The BBC would only consent to play a few seconds, accompanied by an explanation of the track's relevance for those too young to remember the miners' strike or the Falklands War.

No other British Prime Minister has divided the nation as spectacularly as Margaret Thatcher. To her supporters she was a modern day Boudicca who dragged the country out of the seemingly irreversible economic decline of the 70s and lent Britain an aura of prestige that she had not enjoyed since the turn of the century. To her critics she was a heartless, ruthless uber-Capitalist who ripped the guts out of industrial communities and fostered a culture of greed, self-absorption and sociopathic individualism. Very few people are comfortable on the fence when it comes to the Iron Lady.

Had the situation at the close of the 1970s not been as dire as it was it is unlikely that Thatcher's abrasive brand of Conservatism would ever have been unleashed upon British society. But the IMF fiasco and the Winter of Discontent led many intelligent observers to conclude that the broad consensus of democratic Capitalism had failed and that it was time for both left and right to go back to ideological basics. A great deal of soul searching took place in both the Conservative and Labour parties about what it was they both stood for and whether or not that had been sacrificed in the previous decades. The post-war years had seen Labour governments forced to accept the whims of the market and their Conservative counterparts uneasily embrace central planning. Neither had worked and now the radicals on both sides suddenly found themselves being listened to. On the right this manifested itself in the kind of arguments raised by the architects of the abortive ROBOT project, as well as by Peter Thorneycroft and Enoch Powell. The bitterest of pills was about to be swallowed whole by an unsuspecting electorate.

Before monetarism became Thatcherism it was briefly known as Josephism. In 1974 Sir Keith Joseph, Minister for Housing and Local Government under Harold MacMillan and Secretary of State for Social Services under Edward Heath, publically apologised for his part in the failure of post-war British politics. According to Joseph, what was required to stop the rot was to pursue the interlinked goals of free market economics and the rolling back of the state as aggressively as possible. Taking his cue from theorists such as Friedrich Hayek and Milton Friedman, Joseph argued that the only way to control the bogeyman of inflation was to ruthlessly control the money supply in the economy. This would mean the old Keynesian virtues of public sector spending and borrowing would have to go out of the window and the Socialist doctrine of central planning and a command economy would become obsolete. Because the really scary thing about monetarism was its simplicity. Once you had a handle on the money supply it was just assumed that everything else – inflation, unemployment etc. – would sort itself out. The market - rather than the state - would work its magic, albeit after a considerable levelling-out period that would incur much heartache and hardship.

For the majority of Conservative politicians at the time it was still too much of a leap of faith to take in such heightened circumstances. One of the most implacable opponents of the theory was Edward Heath who, despite being dumped out of office by a whisker, was still the leader of the party. But as time went by - and Labour managed to make even more of a mess of things - a growing number of Conservative MPs became drawn to the clarity and decisiveness of Joseph's viewpoint.

The politician best placed to use the new teachings to their advantage was Heath's Shadow Environment Secretary Margaret Hilda Thatcher. A Lincolnshire grocer's daughter with a strong Christian faith and even stronger work ethic Thatcher was far from the traditional model of paternalistic Conservatism with its unshakeable belief in a privileged ruling class. She was a staunch neoliberal drawn by the streak of libertarianism in Joseph's message. For Thatcher the great tragedy of the post-war consensus was that the Victorian values of resolute authority, hard work and stringent rules had been jettisoned for emasculating collectivism and a sprawling, interfering state. As far as she was concerned the reassertion of individual responsibility and the freedom of the markets would produce a Britain of strong moral fibre and economic diligence. The fact that Thatcherism actually resulted in a loutish brand of hedonism and vulgar avarice is one of the great ironies of modern British politics.

Despite the manifest failures of Heath Thatcher was by no means a shoo-in for party leader. Her gender and provincial background counted against her but she had the characteristic good fortune to be the only vaguely credible candidate in a field where the 'big beasts' of the Conservative party had noticeably absented themselves. The faithful Heathite Willie Whitelaw – later to become an even more faithful Thatcherite – and the visionary Keith Joseph both ruled themselves out, whilst the eternally divisive yet undeniably popular Enoch Powell had stomped off to the Ulster Unionists in a self-righteous huff. She ended up winning the leadership almost by default and few party insiders gave her more than a few months. Yet her appeal both to the provincial middle class and the aspirational working class combined with the bleak farce of the Callaghan administration's closing months saw her romp into Number 10 in the 1979 general election.

The doubters, however, had not been assuaged. Even more than her personal history it was her shocking break with financial orthodoxy that

caused most consternation. The economy was simply in too parlous a
state for the gleaming sword of monetarism to slice through it. Thatcher's
deceptively docile Chancellor Geoffrey Howe slashed income tax wildly
but ratcheted VAT up to incredible levels, therefore hitting the poorest
hardest. Mass manufacturing bankruptcies followed along with a spike in
unemployment. If it hadn't been for the windfall of profits from North Sea
Oil the Thatcher government would have been on its knees within months
but the setbacks, general alarm and widespread calls for a change of
strategy just fuelled the Prime Minister's messianic faith in her chosen
course. The innocuous sounding Medium Term Financial Strategy
promised yearly drops in both growth and borrowing and prompted riots
in Brixton, Southall and Toxteth during the spring and summer of 1981.
The unrest had a distinctly racial tenor as the national figure for
unemployment for young black men reached 60%. Thatcher's response
was a characteristic show of defiance, sacking the doubters from her
cabinet and bringing in fellow monetarist disciples like Norman Tebbit and
the brilliant former financial journalist Nigel Lawson.

Salvation had still not occurred by the following year and even those
radicals who had fallen for the new hard-line economics were beginning
to feel taken in. Thatcherism, it seemed, was not the panacea that it had
been painted as and polls suggested that her government was even more
unpopular than the disastrous ministries of the 1970s. And then, when all
seemed lost for the Conservative party's great new hope, the leader of
Argentina's military junta did her the wonderful service of starting a war.

The Falklands War of 1982 was an incongruous piece of Palmerstonian
imperial jingoism in the shadowy age of the Cold War and labyrinthine
diplomatic institutions. It was a highly risky gamble for a fairly
unprepossessing prize halfway round the world, and that was precisely
why it played so well with the general public. True, some thought it an
embarrassing and costly exercise in sabre rattling against a nation that
had more right to the islands than Britain did. But many more - cowed by

the loss of empire and perennial international humiliation at the hands of the United States - revelled in the unashamedly patriotic defence of one of Britain's remaining colonies. To the masses it felt like the clock had been rolled back a century and the country actually mattered again.

The ownership of the Falklands - or Malvinas as they are known in South America – had been a bone of contention since the British asserted control in the archipelago in 1832. Geographically they are closest to Argentina but the majority of the population are of British descent and the predominant language is English. Discussions about granting sovereignty of the islands to Argentina had broken down in 1981 leaving the President General Leopoldo Galtieri incensed. When, for economic reasons, the British decided to withdraw their sole naval vessel in the region, Galtieri sensed the timing was propitious for an invasion to retake the islands.

The Argentine force that landed on the 1st April was well trained and prepared. The British marines present on the islands swiftly surrendered and Galtieri announced vaingloriously that the Malvinas were back in Argentinian hands. In Whitehall Thatcher was unequivocal. Backed by the Chief of Naval Staff, Sir John Leach, she authorised what became a huge task-force of troops, frigates, destroyers and jets to retake the islands. From the start she refused to listen to those – including the US President and her close friend, Ronald Reagan – who advised negotiation and some form of compromise, preferably self-determination for the islanders. In the Prime Minister's opinion a British territorial possession had been attacked by another country and it was her patriotic duty to do everything in her power to teach the invaders a lesson.

The consequences of victory at any cost became only too apparent when, on 2nd May, the British submarine HMS Conqueror launched three torpedoes at the General Belgrano, an Argentine light cruiser. This was despite the latter being outside of a mutually agreed exclusion zone and heading away from the British fleet. 321 sailors died. Some politicians and commentators claimed that the Belgrano had been specifically sunk to prolong the conflict and, whether or not that was the case, the act certainly upped the ante on both sides. 40 British crew members died when an Argentine missile subsequently sunk the destroyer HMS Sheffield.

The decision to land troops on the islands was taken a fortnight later and constituted the biggest gamble of the entire operation. Poor weather made successful landing difficult and the full force of the Argentine military machine lay in wait. But the full force was not good enough and - despite incurring heavy losses - British troops prevailed, largely thanks to American missiles and other crucial bits of kit provided by President Reagan. With both the United Nations and the United States keen on a diplomatic solution to the conflict time was running out for Thatcher's glorious all-out victory. Therefore, the ground offensive was brought forward with the twin locations of Darwin and Goose Green seen as vital to recapture as quickly as possible. The Battle of Goose Green took place over 28th-29th May and was a pivotal moment in the war. 50 Argentine soldiers were killed to Britain's 18 and almost a thousand Argentines were also captured. Darwin was taken soon after and by the time that the British reached the capital Port Stanley Galtieri's army, under the command of General Menendez, was fading fast. By the middle of June Menendez had capitulated and the war was over. The Falkland Islands would remain British.

In a little over two months Margaret Thatcher had been transformed from economic pariah to fearless heroine, proving that nothing bolsters the national mood better than a quick, successful war. To a country weaned on consensus politics and dispiriting compromise her resolute single-mindedness felt both excitingly fresh and comfortingly old-fashioned. Many felt that she had given the nation a reason to be proud again. Yet many more were disgusted at the waging of war for a tiny, irrelevant patch of land and the comparatively large numbers of casualties that had resulted on both sides. The Prime Minister may have been tough, provocative and controversial in her economic policy but an actual military entanglement had shown an even steelier, more aggressive side to her character. It was a side which would become more and more prevalent over the coming years as the battlegrounds became the streets and wastelands of Britain itself.

Buoyed by the Falklands effect and an imploding Labour party Margaret Thatcher's Conservatives coasted through the 1983 general election. Her new warrior queen image would forestall serious interrogation about her economic policy for a while but unless something changed soon the deleterious effect of her monetarist philosophy on ordinary people's lives would return to the forefront of the political argument. Fortunately for the Prime Minister she was about to do two things certain to endear her to her core support base - silence the unions and bring untold riches to the South of England. The miners' strike and the deregulation of the banking system took place almost simultaneously and constitute perfect shorthand for why Thatcher was loathed by the working class North and venerated by the middle class South.

In hindsight it seems self-evident that the strained relationship between the government and the unions was heading for a bloody reckoning. But at the time, given the agonised concessions and compromises that Parliament had made in the 70s, the National Union of Mineworkers had every right to believe that highly organised industrial action would continue to win the day. This time the flashpoint for the strike, which began in March 1984, was not pay. The ruthless new manager of the National Coal Board Ian MacGregor had threatened the closure of twenty pits - as a starting point - with the loss of a projected 64,000 jobs over two years. The coal industry was struggling to remain profitable but the scale of MacGregor's intended clear-out was unsurprisingly alarming to whole communities that relied on coal mining for survival.

The leader of the NUM was Arthur Scargill, formerly the young ideologue who had so effectively terrorised Edward Heath in 1972. In that instance his unbending militancy and organisational prowess had seen off a government desperate for industrial harmony and conciliation. This time, however, he was faced with an opponent every bit as belligerent and unyielding as he was. And, what was worse for him, the enemy had done their homework. The NCB had - with government collusion - been storing up coal at power stations for just such an eventuality and this, combined with the fact that the strike started in the spring, meant that the intended inconvenience to the general public was kept to a minimum.

Scargill also had a battle on his hands to persuade all his members that striking was the right thing to do. Balloting of miners prior to the strike revealed a worryingly high number in Nottingham, Leicester and other areas opposed to industrial action which threw Scargill's plans to call a national strike into turmoil. Ever the canny operator he decided instead on a series of 'rolling' strikes from region to region thus bypassing the need for nationwide approval. But from the start the miners would be hamstrung by internal division and unsatisfactory turnout, compounded by a lack of support from other industries' unions.

Not that Scargill let this bother him at the time. Once again utilising the famous flying pickets that had worked so well against Heath confrontation was openly sought and the police were only too happy to oblige. This was one area where Scargill's tactics worked perfectly, with undecided miners who saw the violence meted out to their colleagues by riot gear-clad coppers on horseback quickly joining the struggle. And as the months went on the violence became more and more extreme. A brutal running battle at a pit in Orgreave, South Yorkshire passed into 80s iconography whilst a Welsh taxi driver was killed for accepting a fare from a working miner.

At the same time as the shocking images from Orgreave were being transmitted via the nation's television sets a very different type of revolution was happening in the rarefied City of London. The patrician, bowler-hatted financial district of the 1950s had been steadily modernising for a while. So-called 'Eurodollar deals' exploiting American prohibition on the purchase of foreign stocks had been commonplace since the early 60s and the monolithic international banks had begun to take up residence. But British high finance was still straitjacketed by stringent regulations that prevented capital from travelling overseas.

All this parochialism was dramatically wiped out by Geoffrey Howe's abolition of exchange controls in 1979. This was an astonishing gamble for a brand new government to take and can be seen as further proof of Thatcher's immense self-assurance. Yet there are also parallels with her treatment of Britain's unionised industries - once more a venerable institution sown deep into the fabric of the nation was told it was outdated and unprofitable and forced to adapt or die. But the old school brokers were lazier and less worldly than the militant union bosses and put up very little resistance.

Three years later came the transformation that is most commonly associated with the banking revolution: the creation of the yuppie. The importing of the American international futures market trading in the ephemeral values of commodities and currencies saw fast-talking, abrasive and narcissistic chancers make millions both for themselves and their employers. The staid, musty environs of the Royal Exchange were flooded with these colourful, modern traders winning and blowing fortunes in minutes.

By 1984 the revolution was in full swing. Many of the small, insular banking firms simply couldn't compete with the influx of brash, corporate behemoths from Japan and America that now flocked to Britain. They were compelled to either do a deal with Mammon or accept defeat and shuffle away ignominiously. The London Stock Exchange was effectively blackmailed by Nigel Lawson, Howe's replacement as Chancellor, into a glitzy, corporate makeover and, by the time the iconic computer screens were installed in 1986, Britain was leading the world in the exporting of financial services.

There is no denying the cold hard fact that if Britain had not become the epicentre of the financial world in the early to mid-80s the economy would have continued to nosedive at a spectacular rate, thoroughly discrediting Thatcher's monetarism. Deregulation did vastly improve the nation's balance of payments and make a lot of people very wealthy. But that wealth was almost exclusively centred on London and the south of England and it brought with it a depressingly venal culture of greed which elevated ruthless ambition and avaricious irresponsibility into a divine virtue. It is a state of mind that continues to hold frightening sway in the banking sector to this day.

The miners in the provinces saw the explosion of ill-mannered riches in the south and reacted appropriately. The strike ceased to be just about closures and job losses. For many miners it was the last ditch defence of a way of life that had sustained their communities for generations and the noble sacrifices that many ordinary people made for the cause are heart-breaking. But the other side of the coin was their leader's unflinching determination that not a single miner would be forced out of work. This all-consuming zeal made negotiation impossible - although it is arguable whether Thatcher would have been prepared to negotiate either - and ended up ensuring that the maximum damage possible was inflicted on the industry.

Ultimately there was no way that Scargill could win. Even if he had had the backing of all of his members it is highly unlikely that he could have defeated a government machine geared to systematically crushing any resistance. Thatcher had been smarter, better prepared and better equipped than him, and by the beginning of 1985 the first strikers were making their way back to work. The trickle became a flood and in March an NUM vote resulted in an overwhelming demand to call off the strike.

The government's victory was total and now they moved in for the kill, not just against the miners but the trade unions in general. The Trade Union Act was passed in 1984 whilst the miners' strike was still ongoing. By legislating that a secret ballot had to be held before any decision on industrial action could be taken it privileged members' rights against those of union bosses and consequently increased the requirements necessary for a strike to be considered legal. So far, so 'In Place of Strife,' but worse was to come over the following years. Deregulation and enhanced employer rights deprived the unions of their modus operandi and membership fell by millions. Mining and heavy industry in Britain was decimated. It is arguable whether this decline would have occurred anyway, but the Thatcher government's merciless pursuit of industrial destruction felt unnecessarily brutal and vindictive to many. No attempt was made at rehabilitation or retraining for unemployed labourers, which the Prime Minister no doubt thought right and proper in a libertarian, individualistic society. But it left many millions feeling betrayed, embittered and thrown on the scrapheap of British industry.

The transformation of the City may have reaped rich financial dividends for the government but Margaret Thatcher had other ideas for raising cash as well. Key to her and her Chancellor's strategy was the selling off of assets in the public sector, creating a generation of shareholders and opening up vital services to the intense competition of the market. The term 'privatisation' was coined as a less clunky alternative to 'denationalisation' and the Conservatives attacked it with gusto.

The first significant privatisation was the British National Oil Corporation - a body set up by Labour in the 70s to oversee North Sea Oil production - which was sold off in 1982. At the time it was the largest privatisation the world had seen and was followed a few years later by British Telecom and British Gas. At £5.4biliion the British Gas deal was not only the biggest of the lot but also the most iconic owing to the established reputation of the company and an attention grabbing television ad campaign.

Possibly the most contentious piece of legislation on this theme was the 1980 Housing Act. This act initiated the Right to Buy scheme whereby tenants were offered the chance to purchase their council houses at a reduced rate. Whilst this gave many people a stake in the world of private property ownership it also created a shortage of social housing for those who could not afford to buy, thus engineering a dangerously undemocratic housing boom.

There was both an ideological and practical purpose to privatisation. On one level it was the obverse of the nationalising frenzy undertaken by the Attlee government and hence a striking repudiation of the Socialist precepts of public ownership and the big state. Once again Thatcher was distancing herself from the old consensus politics and giving vent to her neoliberal instincts. But the concept of a nation of shareholders was also crucial to Thatcherite doctrine, as it embedded the virtues of the market into ordinary people's lives and gave them a vested interest in her brand of aggressive Capitalism. Indeed in the rush to enable people to purchase shares the government accepted much lower offers than they could have done, rather hampering their other main aim of raising large amounts of cash. In any case the shareholding culture never really caught on.

The claim that market competition would result in better services for the general public is equally dubious. The right argued that monopolies bred laziness and the left asserted that privatisation meant corners would be cut for the sake of profit. On the evidence of both Attlee's and Thatcher's governments both assessments are probably true. Yet - in another of those delicious Thatcherite ironies - the newly privatised companies ended up being more susceptible to state control than when they were under official public ownership. Government affiliated regulatory boards sprang up to monitor productivity and market competition leading many to question exactly what the purpose of privatising these companies really was.

Arguably even more damaging was the Prime Minister's attitude to the areas of the public sector that she was unable to privatise. Her intense mistrust of state owned institutions led to her government exercising virtual omnipotence across a range of public services. Shortly after she had won her third term of office in 1987 megalomania really took hold with the establishment of myriad boards and quangos to micro-manage every aspect of education, health and the law. Responsibility for health budgets was reallocated to the Treasury whilst the government rewrote the school syllabus. Throughout the public sector proxy markets were created to encourage the principles of competition. Never has the hoary cliché 'privatisation by the back door' been more applicable.

But the classic example of senseless Thatcherite hubris was, of course, the poll tax. Local government had been a thorn in Thatcher's side ever since she became Prime Minister. For somebody who thrived on control the autonomy that local councils enjoyed was infuriating. Unsurprisingly a number became militant Labour strongholds, the most extreme example being the frankly criminal Liverpool County Council that we shall investigate in the next chapter. The most maddeningly irksome to Thatcher, however, was the Greater London Council run by the shamelessly provocative Ken Livingstone. The GLC gleefully exploited the lack of government control over council spending to fund a sharp reduction in London Transport fares and dispense welfare grants to vast swathes of the local population. Attempts to halt this Socialist profligacy were met with even more outrageous levels of overspending, goading the Prime Minister into showing Livingstone who was boss. Despite a spirited protest campaign the 1985 Local Government Act simply abolished the GLC. Once again Thatcher had demonstrated a facility to bulldoze her way through any opposition and must have felt utterly invulnerable.

Yet even by the Iron Lady's notoriously inflexible standards the ominous-sounding Community Charge was ludicrously prejudiced and patently unfair. A method of taxation that ensured that every adult in a community contributed towards their local government sounds eminently reasonable and survives to the present day in the form of council tax. The sting in the tail of the Community Charge was that it made no distinction between the relative incomes of those adults or the value of their homes. It was a one-size-fits-all, flat rate tax that would grossly disadvantage the poorest in society.

To compound the issue the poll tax was unleashed - on the Scots initially - almost overnight, despite countless warnings from members of the cabinet that it would be a disaster. They were spot on. There was mass rioting in Scotland's cities and many normally law abiding individuals risked custodial sentences by refusing to pay. Amendments and caveats were hastily written in before the charge went live in England but it was nowhere near enough to curb either the violent protests or a significant slump in Conservative approval ratings. Despite its toxic associations the Community Charge survived its creator, limping on until 1991 when John Major's Chancellor Norman Lamont finally did away with it.

By this point it was clear to all but the most devoted believers that Thatcherism was no longer fit for purpose. Controversial and divisive as she may have been, by her own lights the Prime Minister had achieved a remarkable amount during her first two terms. Since the election victory of 1987, however, she had grown more and more intractable, needlessly confrontational and – crucially - illogical. The vultures began circling. She obliged them almost immediately by losing her head over Europe.

Whilst she had been a broad supporter of Britain's membership of the Common Market Thatcher had been typically mistrustful of the Brussels bureaucrats with whom she had been forced to deal. Early on in her first term of office she had shouted down an assortment of diplomats and European leaders, refusing to budge until she had reclaimed almost £1billion from the EEC. Despite signing the Single European Act of 1986 she grew more and more antagonistic towards European Commission President Jacques Delors, railing against his desire for federalism and a single European community currency.

Her Chancellor strongly disagreed. For a while Nigel Lawson had been advising tying the pound to the considerably more reliable West German deutschmark within the Exchange Rate Mechanism. Thatcher, whose free market ethos prized floating currencies, thought this nonsense and forbade him from doing it. When Lawson went ahead with it behind her back, Thatcher found out and forced him to retract. This was not the healthiest relationship for a Prime Minister to have with her Chancellor.

Thatcher's treatment of Lawson was of a piece with how she related to her cabinet as a whole. To her the majority were 'wets,' with no passion,

239

no fire and no inclination for risk. She would publically rebuke them and made no effort to listen to their point of view. In the 'glory days' of the early 80s her recklessness had been generally rewarded but as the decade staggered to a close her punch-bags were feeling markedly less charitable.

After Delors outlined the specifics of his intended single currency Lawson, aided by his predecessor at the Treasury and now Foreign Secretary Geoffrey Howe, protested vehemently to the Prime Minister that membership of the ERM was essential for future economic survival. Thatcher responded with a cabinet reshuffle in July 1989 which saw Howe exchange the Foreign Office for the largely irrelevant post of Deputy Prime Minister. At the time the shambling, fogeyish figure of Howe must have appeared to pose little threat but Thatcher would have cause to rue the vindictiveness of her decision.

Frustrated by his leader's unwillingness to listen Lawson resigned in October, openly criticizing the Prime Minister's impossible behaviour. Events then took a slightly surreal turn when the unknown Conservative backbencher Sir Anthony Meyer challenged Thatcher for the party leadership. He was obviously routed but the interesting thing for the Prime Minister's opponents was that 60 MPs had either abstained or voted against her. If a more credible figure were to oppose Thatcher the result could be rather more interesting.

That more credible figure turned out to be her former Defence Secretary Michael Heseltine, who had resigned in a fit of pique four years previously over the Westland helicopter scandal. Ostensibly a wrangle over which company should get the rights to manufacture the eponymous pieces of military aviation Westland was in reality a variation on the old dilemma of whether Britain should ally herself with the United States or Europe. The Prime Minister was firmly on the American side and backed the bid from United Technologies whilst Heseltine favoured the European consortium companies. Yet there was still another layer to the dispute - a plain old power play between the domineering PM and the only member of her cabinet who dared stand up to her. Dashing and debonair Heseltine had a popularity in Parliament that Thatcher could never hope to rival and she saw Westland as a means to slap down any potential mutiny in the cabinet. Unfortunately for Thatcher her decision to seek legal advice about whether Heseltine had been behaving inappropriately was leaked, leading not only to her Defence Secretary's high profile resignation but also serious questions in the Commons about whether she had acted improperly. Thatcher always denied that she sanctioned the leak but the suspicions remained, threatening to derail her leadership at a crucial juncture of her second term. She rode out the storm and United Technologies won the contract but she had made a bitter enemy of a very dangerous man in the process.

Heseltine would duly challenge Thatcher but not before one of the most unexpectedly sensational resignation speeches Parliament had ever seen. Geoffrey Howe, the Prime Minister's placid whipping boy for much of the decade, delivered a withering attack on her policies and treatment of her colleagues that - for once - left the Iron Lady looking dazed and confused. Thatcher – at a Parisian summit and therefore unable to exert her terrifying authority at home - beat Heseltine in the first round ballot but narrowly failed to fulfil the criteria for an outright victory. Her allies, fearing that the second ballot could go to her deadly rival thus causing a Labour-style party split, finally persuaded her to step aside in favour of Douglas Hurd - Howe's replacement at the Foreign Office - and her relatively unknown new Chancellor John Major.

It transpired that whilst the bulk of the Conservative party no longer wanted Margaret Thatcher as leader, neither did they want Michael Heseltine. In John Major they thought they had found a candidate who subscribed to Thatcher's broad philosophy but was less divisive and more malleable. They would be in for something of a surprise. Thatcher, meanwhile, would remain a highly influential figure in retirement, particularly for the hard right of the party. She praised Tony Blair upon his accession to the Labour leadership and was honoured with a statue in Parliament, although in her final years she sank further and further into dementia. Margaret Thatcher's place in history is assured. She changed the nation in both practical and existential ways, whether for good or ill depends on your political persuasion. Her ministry is testament to the extraordinary tensions at the heart of British politics and the importance of ideology and political belief to the Parliamentary system. But, even after all her radical achievements, was consensus politics really dead?

21

CIVIL WAR

At roughly the same time as Keith Joseph was denouncing the Conservatives' part in all post-war politics Anthony Wedgwood Benn was doing a similar thing for Labour. He, like Joseph, felt that his party had badly lost their way, flailing cynically in the centre when they should have been looking to their Socialist roots. And, also like the Conservative economic prophet, he claimed to have the answer. Needless to say that was the point at which Joseph and Benn diverged.

Born into the upper echelons of English society and with a family tree comprised of high-minded Liberal MPs Benn had served early notice of his iconoclastic opinions by doggedly fighting for a change in the peerage law in the early 1960s. Inheriting his late father's title of Lord Stansgate at the turn of the decade prohibited him from taking his place as an MP in the House of Commons. For more than two years he relentlessly campaigned for the right to renounce his unwanted title, resulting in the Conservative government passing the Peerages Act of 1963. Now free to sit as a common-or-garden Member of Parliament he became part of Harold Wilson's victorious Labour government the following year. Imbuing the positions of Postmaster General and Minister of Technology with a schoolboy-ish enthusiasm and modernist verve, he was Wilson's White Heat made flesh.

Then, after the 1970 election defeat, he began to travel further and further to the left, recasting himself as a twentieth century equivalent of the radical seventeenth century Levellers. Benn stood not only for workers' co-operatives, wholesale nationalisation and mandatory reselection of MPs but also for a complete overhaul of the way government should operate. MPs were out of touch and ineffective, he asserted, and the voices of party members and activists should be heard in the formation of party policy. This went beyond the Socialist passion of

Keir Hardie or Aneurin Bevan - Benn was arguing for extra-Parliamentary revolt rather than intra-Parliamentary legislation.

Somewhat against Harold Wilson's better judgement a number of Benn's more provocative ideas about the state's direct intervention in private companies made their way into the 1974 election manifesto. When Labour edged back into power these plans were discreetly dropped. Yet undeterred Benn carried on beating the hard-left drum, advocating a siege economy of extreme protectionism at the same time as James Callaghan was pleading with the IMF.

Tony Benn was by no means a lone hysterical voice. Since the 1960s ultra-radical Trotskyite organisations had been steadily infiltrating the Labour party and establishing strong provincial bases. The most notorious - and most damaging to Labour's reputation - was Militant Tendency, a sinister gang of borderline criminals who were particularly active on Liverpool City Council. Throughout the 70s their influence was malign yet marginal but as soon as Margaret Thatcher comprehensively disposed of the most right-wing Labour government until the invention of New Labour their vitriolic accusations of party betrayal gained added credence.

It should be noted that Benn, whilst agreeing in principle with a lot of what Militant stood for, was never complicit in their underhand methods. But the hard-left party members had lost their faith in elected politicians and demanded a greater say in the running of the party and, ultimately, the country. The 1980 Labour party conference was so dominated by the left's radical agenda that Callaghan despaired of ever uniting the party and resigned a fortnight later. There was now the very real possibility that Dennis Healey would succeed him as party leader.

As Chancellor to both Wilson and Callaghan Healey was reviled in leftist circles as the man who had led his two former leaders astray, steering them towards a brand of right wing politics that made Edward Heath look like a Socialist. This assessment was somewhat unfair considering Healey's swingeing tax hikes for the wealthiest in the land but that made little difference to the Marxists and agitators of the Labour left. To try and ensure that Healey did not succeed a more suitable candidate had to be found. This is how the erudite, intellectual and hopelessly anachronistic Michael Foot came to secure the Labour leadership.

Foot was a thoroughly decent man with as strong a Socialist pedigree as you could get. A highly talented writer and journalist his legacy to the Labour party up until 1980 was a series of pamphlets and book-long polemics that helped to define the creed and doctrine of 20th century Socialism. He had co-authored the infamous 'Guilty Men' in 1940 - which irrevocably tarnished the reputations of Neville Chamberlain and other key appeasers - whilst his editorship of the left-wing 'Tribune' after the war ushered in a golden age of intellectual argument for the periodical.

But Foot was also a man out of time. A devotee of Aneurin Bevan and the more purist elements of the mythologised Attlee government he was a shambolic, meandering throwback in an age of slick media soundbites and superficiality. He was also, at 67, way past his prime and became leader primarily because he was the least offensive candidate to the greatest number of people. His narrow victory over Healey may have held the party together but Labour was still just as drenched in acrimony and loathing as before.

For one thing Dennis Healey was not finished yet. He may have lost out to a bumbling Socialist romantic in the contest for leader but there was still the deputy leadership to play for. The choice of candidate pitted against him could hardly have been more incendiary. Tony Benn had wisely concluded that he was far too divisive to lay claim to the party leadership but deputy leader was a different matter. This would be the real battle for the soul of the Labour party - centre-right pragmatism versus hard-left idealism. The contest was a predictably nasty slanging match which culminated in a fist fight in the gents toilets at the 1981 party conference in Brighton. One of the participants was the future leader Neil Kinnock, a former left wing mainstay whose fears over the growing extremism of Militant and Tony Benn had persuaded him to abstain from the leadership vote altogether. Within a few years he would take even more assertive action against the hard left. Healey won through by the closest possible margin - less than one percent of the votes -, frustrating the nascent Bennite Revolt and rescuing the party from total obliteration.

Needless to say that all of this unseemly public brawling had the Conservatives rubbing their hands with glee, especially as the Prime Minister was hardly at the peak of her popularity at the time. But one result of Labour's self-destruction was the formation of an entirely new political party, headed by disillusioned centrist Labour rebels. And at a point when both the two main parties appeared to be sprinting towards their respective extremist fringes many felt the timing was propitious for feel-good moderation.

The Social Democratic Party was the brainchild of that restless polymath and bon viveur Roy Jenkins, who had quit Westminster for Brussels in 1977 to become the sixth President of the European Commission. Assessing the state of British politics from a safe distance he concluded that what the country needed was a middle ground that encouraged the cut and thrust of the free market but retained a social conscience. He made some enquiries amongst former Labour colleagues and discovered that he was not alone in his thinking. Former cabinet ministers Shirley Williams, David Owen and Bill Rodgers had all been sickened by the rise of the hard-left and wanted out of the party. Accordingly the Limehouse Declaration was issued on 25th January 1981 which announced both the Gang of Four's resignations and the establishment of the SDP. But would anybody else be convinced?

The answer was a resounding yes. Although only 13 Labour politicians felt disaffected enough to take the plunge - the number rose to 28 the following year - the response from the public was overwhelming. The Conservatives and Labour appeared to be locked into a competition for least popular political party and any alternative seemed like a breath of fresh air to the British electorate. There was a rush to sign up for party membership and subsequent rallies and meetings were packed out with idealistic activists desperate to believe that there was a third way between ruthless, brutal Capitalism and joyless borderline Communism. In September an alliance was formed with the Liberals - who had been enjoying something of a renaissance in the previous couple of decades under the leadership of Jo Grimond and Jeremy Thorpe - and were now headed by Jenkins' young Abortion Act protégé David Steel. Approval ratings for the Alliance were significantly higher than for either of the main parties and when both Williams and Jenkins scored enormous bi-election wins over the Conservatives many party members began to believe they could pull off an extraordinary victory in the 1983 general election.

Alas there are few fairy-tales in British politics and, despite winning 25% of the national vote, the Alliance secured only 23 MPs due to the archaic nature of the first-past-the-post electoral system. By this stage the Conservatives were riding high on a post-Falklands wave of imperial pride and romped home with 44%. Labour was humiliated and Foot focused his ire on the Alliance for splitting the anti-Thatcher vote, although the fact that his party ran a horrendously amateurish campaign may have had something to do with their drubbing.

In addition to being defeated by the vagaries of the electoral system the Alliance was not immune to the kind of bitter infighting that was plaguing their rival parties. Roy Jenkins had assumed the leadership of the SDP upon his return to Parliament but the suave, calculating David Owen felt that the old master was past his prime and that it was time for him to take the reins. Owen was also the one member of the Gang of Four who was against allying with the Liberals, feeling that their respective ideologies were not reconcilable.

When Jenkins stepped down after the disappointment of the 1983 result the party embarked on a subtle journey to the right under Owen's leadership. The move away from the centre ground reflected itself in the Alliance's even poorer showing at the 1987 election. The majority of party members now regarded a formal merger with the Liberals as inevitable but once again Owen railed against what he saw as the dilution of the SDP's philosophy. The popular media perception was of Owen as a domineering bully controlling the naïve and henpecked David Steel. Regardless of how true this actually was, it made any potential partnership between the two leaders nigh on impossible.

In early 1988 the party membership voted for union and, predictably, Owen resigned. The new Parliamentary entity, led by the Liberal Paddy Ashdown, was briefly known as the Social and Liberal Democrats before dropping the 'social' in 1989. Owen refused to acknowledge the legitimacy of the new party and fought on with a rump SDP party. The Liberals also kept going for a while, mainly in Liverpool and the West Country.

The great dream of a moderate, centrist new party succeeding against all odds was dead. But the creation of the Liberal Democrats breathed new life into Liberalism and continued to provide many voters disillusioned by the Conservative-Labour duopoly with an alternative voice or, at the very least, a protest vote. All of this changed, of course, with the advent of the 2010 coalition and the sudden requirement for the Lib Dems to step up to the rigours of government. But the British political system is undeniably healthier for having them around.

Labour, meanwhile, were in freefall. Their dreadful performance in the 1983 election had convinced many MPs that the party badly needed reforming if it were ever to be electable again. Neil Kinnock - of party conference punch-up fame - won a landslide in the leadership contest but quickly realised that the role was a poisoned chalice. A powerful orator and committed left winger he was also pragmatic enough to know that to continue in Michael's footsteps - if you will pardon the pun - was Parliamentary suicide. So for a time he was forced to hedge his bets and sit on the fence, caught between denouncing former friends and attempting to rein in his own leftist instincts.

The scale of reform that the Labour party would have to undergo if it were ever to become electable was immense, and Kinnock was well aware that he would have to move slowly and subtly. The immediate concern was not rehabilitating Labour to defeat Thatcher's Conservatives but ensuring that the party was not overtaken by the SDP and thus become a complete irrelevance. Hence the new leader made incremental changes to party policy - such as bringing the Labour position on council house sales into line with that of the Conservatives – but shied away from attempting dramatic reversals on issues such as unilateral nuclear disarmament. He also held his tongue on the miners' strike - despite a venomous hatred of Arthur Scargill and his provocative methods - for fear of alienating the soft left.

There was one issue, however, that the 'Welsh Windbag' could not be silenced on. Militant Tendency had long been in effective control of the Labour run Liverpool City Council through a subsidiary group known as the Revolutionary Socialist League. By 1985 they were running wild, responding to a government rate-capping decree by illegally setting a 'deficit budget' which committed them to spending £30million more than the council's income. The result was devastating for the people of Liverpool, who witnessed their city brought to the brink of bankruptcy and had 31,000 members of council staff made redundant – all so that Militant could make their Trotskyite statement.

In 1985 at the Labour party conference – an event that was developing an annual reputation for compelling 'car-crash' viewing – Neil Kinnock gave a superlative oratorical display denouncing the criminal actions of the council leaders, most of whom were sitting a few feet away from him in the Bournemouth auditorium. On the verge of losing control Kinnock lambasted them for their arrogance and inhumanity and took the opportunity to make a more general point about the state of his party - that this was where extremism, however initially well-intentioned, led and it stopped now. There was an electrifying mixture of applause and heckling and a number of indignant walk-outs. But, as the polls later showed, Kinnock had won the day and his party could begin to rebuild.

Concrete action followed swiftly. The Liverpool District Labour Party was suspended and subjected to a rigorous inquiry that resulted in the expulsion of over a hundred Militant members from the party. The most high profile of these was the council's deputy leader Derek Hatton, who had been the most prominent heckler during Kinnock's incendiary conference speech. It would take until 1991 for Labour to be completely purged of Militant MPs but the decisive action of 1985-6 was a pivotal moment in the rehabilitation of the party.

Kinnock now grasped the nettle and set about reforming the party's image to make them more relevant to the media-obsessed 1980s. Aides and advisors such as Patricia Hewitt, Charles Clarke and Peter Mandelson remodelled Labour as a modern, dynamic party with broad appeal across class boundaries. For a while it seemed to be working but, when it came to the serious business of voting in the 1987 general election, the British public stuck with the devil they knew. Kinnock had made enormous strides but grim Conservative warnings of high Labour taxation and the unresolved issue of the party's stance on nuclear disarmament scared off the floating voters. One notable thing that Kinnock had achieved, however, was to effectively see off the SDP as a credible electoral threat. Against all the odds Labour had clawed back the middle ground.

Despite defeat Kinnock held on to his job and ramped up the makeover. Labour were creeping closer and closer to the wholesale political rebranding of the New Labour years. Indeed one of Kinnock's key campaigns in the late 80s was the dropping of the sacred Clause Four - which espoused total commitment to nationalisation - from the party's constitution. This aspiration would only become successful under Tony Blair. The official party line on nuclear disarmament also underwent a U-turn in 1989- switching from a unilateral to a multilateral standpoint - and a loosening of the legislation surrounding 'closed shops' also put distance between Kinnock and the unions.

This frenzy of activity may have had Conservative ministers running scared but the Prime Minister appeared oblivious to the threat, ploughing on with her authoritarian policies regardless. After the horrendous misjudgements of the poll tax and the party's attitude to the ERM key members of her cabinet realised that Margaret Thatcher was becoming Neil Kinnock's greatest asset. And so with typical Conservative ruthlessness she was ousted, in favour of the far less controversial John Major. Suddenly Kinnock was wrong-footed. Thatcherite excess had allowed Labour to appear moderate and compassionate but when her successor began dismantling her most hated policies many alarmed Conservative voters came back to the fold.

Yet had Labour pressure for an immediate general election paid off then it is perfectly possible that Kinnock would finally have installed himself in Downing Street. Even when the election rolled around in 1992 the deepening national recession ought to have ensured a great public hunger for governmental change. But, once again, lingering fears over Trotskyite extremism combined with memories of the bleak days of the late 1970s thwarted a widely predicted Labour victory.

Kinnock, exhausted after the longest stint of any opposition leader, resigned after the election to be replaced by his doughty Chancellor John Smith. More moderate reform and rebranding would continue for the next two years until, tragically, Smith died of a heart attack in 1994. The next Labour leader would have no qualms in reinventing the party so dramatically that it became almost unrecognisable.

22

SHADES OF GREY

Margaret Thatcher's downfall divided the Conservative government almost as badly as Callaghan's ousting had split the Labour opposition. By the time of her forced resignation in 1990 many of Thatcher's early adopters were disillusioned with the neoliberal furrow that the Prime Minister had ploughed relentlessly for the past decade. Yet there were still some influential diehards who thought she could do no wrong and were looking to her officially sanctioned successor for more of the same.

But the problem with John Major was that nobody really knew exactly what his politics was. His meteoric rise had taken place in the background to other more dramatic events and his unfussy, unassuming demeanour gave little away. The outgoing Prime Minister was sure that he was a true believer and a safe pair of hands in which to leave the grand Thatcherite project. But the level of Conservative disaffection with the last years of the Iron Lady's premiership made at least a modicum of differentiation crucial to Prime Ministerial survival.

It soon became apparent that Major was collegiate and consultative where Thatcher had been dictatorial and argumentative and for many observers that was a welcome change in governing style. The trouble was that by the early 1990s the well of grand ideas that had sustained the momentum of the Thatcher ministry had run dry and most senior party figures were both emotionally and intellectually exhausted. Neil Kinnock's Labour had the bit between their teeth and were clamouring for an early election that most Conservative MPs were convinced they would lose. After the 11 intensive years of the Iron Lady's iron rule there was a strong argument that the British public were hungry for a change of party in power, and consequently the levels of loyalty and support that Major could count on were pretty minimal from the off.

Yet what few people care to remember in the rush to pillory the Major government is how cleverly the new PM navigated the doctrinal squabbles and bristling egos during his first year in power. The supreme example of this diplomatic tightrope walking – or so it appeared at the time – was Major's brilliant renegotiation of the 1991 Maastricht Treaty. Maastricht - which ushered in the European Union and the right to free movement within it - was the most explicit declaration yet of Jacques Delors' cherished dream of a federal Europe. Primacy would be given to the lawmakers in Brussels at the expense of individual countries' constitutions.

But the dominant issue for the Conservatives was the distasteful prospect of monetary union. Major himself was quite phlegmatic about the Euro but, recognising that the bulk of his party were virulently against any threat to sterling, he argued his case forcefully to the President of the European Commission. Almost incredibly he managed to secure a seemingly perfect compromise - Britain signed the treaty to remain in the most lucrative trading bloc in the Western world but she was given special dispensation to opt-out of the inchoate single currency. A fledgling Prime Minister grappling with a horrendous economic recession had somehow secured everything he had asked for from the lofty Brussels bureaucrats. Upon his return to British shores he was feted by the majority of his colleagues as some sort of genius. The minority were busy sharpening their knives in the shadows.

The horrendous recession was bequeathed to Major by Nigel Lawson, a merciless bust to complement the almighty boom of the late 1980s. The housing bubble that had become emblematic of materialistic Thatcherism well and truly burst, with house prices plummeting by a quarter in the affluent South. The number of repossessions skyrocketed along with unemployment figures and inflation levels. The vulgar conspicuous wealth of the Thatcherite peak gave way to middle class anxiety and desperation.

In the midst of all this misery and uncertainty Major finally called a general election. He had been stalling for a while, brushing aside demands from a resurgent Labour to go to the country, but here again the Prime

Minister boxed clever. Had he caved in to pressure and called the election earlier he would almost certainly have lost. But the Maastricht result put a spring in his step and he was helped by a smart budget from his Chancellor Norman Lamont which benefitted those on low incomes – Labour's core voters. When Kinnock showed signs of strain the government piled on the pressure and ran out unexpected winners. Indeed, far from struggling across the line the party secured a record number of votes from the British electorate – a staggering 14,000,000 – although once again the creaking system of first-past-the-post rewarded them with a net loss of 40 seats from the 1987 election. All things considered Major had done remarkably well to entrench the Conservatives in government under remarkably sustained pressure.

And then the sky fell in. A fall in the US dollar harpooned the already beleaguered pound which led in turn to a precipitous drop in its standing in the Exchange Rate Mechanism. The ERM - cause of so much friction between Margaret Thatcher and her Chancellor Nigel Lawson - was a convoluted precursor to the advent of the Euro. In layman's terms it connected the key European currencies, keeping them bound tightly together until they were ready to be subsumed into one single currency. Britain also used the system as a means of combatting inflation by tying the pound to the Teutonically reliable German deutschmark.

But now the pound was falling fast and losing touch with the other currencies, especially the deutschmark which was pulling away from all of them. In an attempt to haul the pound back up again the Treasury raised interest rates to 10%, an extreme measure which didn't help one bit. Now the tension between Britain and Germany ratcheted up. If the Germans agreed to lower their interest rates the disparate currencies would have a much better chance of realigning. But the spiralling cost of the reunification of East and West Germany after the fall of the Berlin Wall meant that they were in no position to do so. So the pound continued to drop, with a series of interest rate hikes the only option to save it.

Major and Lamont remained bullish about keeping the pound in the ERM but ever increasing interest rates were having a savage effect on the general public and international traders were continuing to sell sterling at a rate of knots. Eventually the government succumbed to the inevitable. On Wednesday 16th September 1992, interest rates – which had risen to a terrifying 15% - were lowered and the pound dropped out of the ERM. Definitively losing any credibility over its management of the nation's finances Black Wednesday was the beginning of the very slow and torturous death of the Major government.

The perceived betrayal of the Germans and the shortcomings of the ERM provided those committed Eurosceptics in the Conservative party with precisely the ammunition they needed. Suddenly the former triumph of Maastricht became an abomination that would erase any sovereignty that Britain had left. The unabashed federalism of Jacques Delors - so said the Eurosceptics - was impossible to tame and would drag the United Kingdom down with it. The treaty still needed to be ratified and they would fight with every sinew to ensure that it died an ignominious death.

The Eurosceptic rebels had a totemic leader in the House of Lords. Lady Thatcher had grudgingly signed up to the ERM for the anti-inflationary reasons outlined above but her fears concerning Delors went back years and were well documented. Now the former Prime Minister encouraged Conservative MPs to turn on her chosen successor and vote with the opposition. To make matters worse Lamont, sacked by Major six months after Black Wednesday, became increasingly embittered and outspoken against Maastricht as well.

The progress of the bill through Parliament was accompanied by a nasty, personally vindictive and politically poisonous campaign as a pugnacious band of Conservative rebels consistently voted against the government on all aspects of the legislation. In much the same way that Labour seemed not to care how their squalid infighting looked to the electorate ten years earlier the Conservatives were blissfully unconcerned about demonstrating backstabbing and betrayal on a Shakespearean level. The usually anodyne John Major resorted to labelling three Conservative rebels 'bastards,' whilst pumped-up backbenchers fell over themselves to traduce their Prime Minister. Major was constantly fending off votes of confidence as his leadership was called into question on a daily basis. By the spring of 1993 the treaty had finally been ratified and the Prime Minister could claim that his authority still held. But in the process of getting Maastricht signed off he had attracted the fury of his hugely influential former mentor and his party had shown themselves to be no more united than Bennite-era Labour.

If John Major had been keen to show he was his own man over Europe he was not so quick to diverge from Thatcherite diktat in other areas of policy. Indeed his decision to privatise the railways went beyond what even Thatcher herself had thought advisable - quite correctly as it turned out.

Selling off such an iconic - if commonly derided - institution as British Rail was always going to be heretical in some quarters. Yet if it had been handled sensibly and sensitively it is not beyond the realms of possibility that it might just have worked. The cleanest method would have been to award one private company the contract for the entire network although - given the Conservative fetish for aggressive market competition - divvying up the railways between different geographical operators was also an option. In the end they decided against both possibilities, selling off the track and the majority of the stations to one company – Railtrack – and the rolling stock to a plethora of others.

This led to a phenomenally complicated system rife with Kafkaesque nightmare bureaucracy. Combined with the aggravating if expected hikes in ticket prices, negotiating the labyrinthine rules and regulations of multiple train operators bamboozled and infuriated commuters in equal measure. The government's answer was as effective a demonstration of the ironies of privatisation as you are ever likely to see. In attempting to iron out the problems caused by selling off the railways they deployed the full force of state apparatus so that they were more heavily under central control than they were when they were nationalised.

This was exactly what Thatcher had done of course, and Major also aped her meddling tendencies when it came to the public sector. This was the dread era of league tables for everything from schools to hospitals to the police force. Armies of auditors drilled down into data that was thoroughly meaningless when taken out of context - that is if the figures had not been significantly massaged beforehand. The Citizen's Charter was an exercise in obfuscation that attempted to graft the principles of the market onto public sector professions. It was a dismal failure.

But at least it wasn't 'Back to Basics.' A nebulous 1993 government campaign that proved catastrophically misnamed Back to Basics was Major's attempt to encourage the rediscovery of traditional values in all areas of public and private life. Although it was not centred on morality as such there was a definite assumption that the credo encompassed ethical as well as practical themes. Considering that the Prime Minister had previously indulged in an extra marital affair with his Conservative colleague Edwina Currie the pompous nature of Back to Basics was a little rich. Yet at least Major had the nouse to keep his infidelity under wraps until he was safely out of Westminster. Other libidinous MPs were not so careful. Having lost David Mellor, his Minister for National Heritage - or 'Fun' as Mellor unwisely phrased it - to a sex scandal the previous year the party now saw lurid revelations about Tim Yeo, Steven Norris and Hartley Booth amongst others.

The scandals were not just confined to the bedroom either. The flamboyant Neil Hamilton became embroiled in allegations that he and Tim Smith had asked parliamentary questions for the Egyptian tycoon Mohammed Al-Fayed in return for cash bribes, whilst Jonathan Aitken served seven months in prison after being convicted of perjury. More serious than all of these misdemeanours however was government complicity in the sale of arms to Saddam Hussein's Iraqi regime. Considering the Prime Minister's staunch support for the Americans during the First Gulf War of 1991 - which drummed Hussein's Republican

Guard out of neighbouring Kuwait - his government's connections to the arms company Matrix Churchill were highly disquieting.

It wasn't all doom and gloom. Major proved surprisingly adept on the world stage, standing shoulder to shoulder with the American president George Bush over the aforementioned Gulf War, whilst his pioneering negotiations seeking an end to the Northern Irish Troubles have been touched on elsewhere. If his vacillation over the hideous Bosnian conflict was inglorious, he was by no means alone amongst European statesmen in that regard. But the increasing unpopularity of his ministry and the general acceptance that an electoral drubbing was just around the corner – particularly when Tony Blair became Leader of the Opposition in 1994 – meant that there were few incentives for his colleagues to publically defend him. In 1995 Major bravely decided to call his opponents' collective bluff by resigning and challenging all-comers for the party leadership. The otherworldly Welsh Secretary John Redwood stood against him and was comprehensively defeated by 218 votes to 89. Yet again Major had won the battle but the constant infighting was losing the Conservatives the war. From 1992 until 1997 the Prime Minister – always highly sensitive to criticism – was firefighting desperately and there was only ever going to be one outcome.

But perhaps it was the outbreak of Mad Cow Disease, which rumbled along throughout the first half of the 90s, that typified the miserable, unappetising demise of the Major government. As herds of cattle developed bovine spongiform encephalopathy and died grisly deaths all over rural England, the government – and particularly the hapless Agriculture Minister John Selwyn Gummer – was desperately trying to persuade the public that there was no danger to humans from devouring British beef. The trouble was that the cause of BSE looked very much like it lay in the feed that cows were being forced to eat, which contained mashed up members of their own species. When a Welsh teenager died of a suspiciously similar disease known as Creutzfeld-Jakob Syndrome there was widespread panic both in the United Kingdom and abroad. To an outcry from British farmers the European Union banned all British beef

- yet sloppy practice in slaughterhouses and the refusal by some farmers to destroy infected cattle appeared to back up continental caution.

The government went as mad as their nation's cows, with the more Eurosceptic MPs claiming EU condemnation as further proof of British subjugation to Brussels. The macabre sight of piles of dead cows burning in the midday sun began to appear across the countryside as politicians, farmers and bureaucrats pointed accusing fingers at each other whilst frantically covering their own backs. Given the subsequent obliteration of the Conservative party in the 1997 general election it hardly feels like too much of a stretch to view the apocalyptic cow funeral pyres as a fitting metaphor for the death of a morally infected, hysterically babbling government.

23

THE CHURCH OF THE THIRD WAY

By any standards the 1997 general election was a seismic event in the history of British politics. After 18 years in government the Conservatives were decimated, with huge swings to Labour being recorded in the safest of true blue seats. Overall Tony Blair's radical reinvention of his party netted him a staggering 419 seats with a majority of 179, a feat unprecedented in post-war British elections. There was high drama on an individual level also, with senior Conservative figures such as Michael Portillo – tipped as a future party leader – sensationally losing their seats. And to round off the sensational electoral shenanigans there were crowd-pleasing ripostes to the culture of sleaze, best personified by Martin Bell's Independent 'Man in a White Suit' defeating the disgraced Neil Hamilton in Tatton.

But more than anything the election result was a ringing endorsement of the new Prime Minister Tony Blair and his pet project 'New Labour.' Yet even nearly twenty years on remarkably few people can actually articulate what 'New Labour' stood for. It is perhaps best defined by what it was not and that was the 'Old Labour' of central planning and commitment to public ownership. Blair was one of a tight-knit group of modernisers who first entered Parliament in 1983 and rapidly grew frustrated with what he saw as a dogmatic insistence on outdated principles. In this respect he inherited the mantle of Hugh Gaitskell - or even Harold Wilson - in developing a firm conviction that the party needed to reach out to the aspirational middle classes if they were to become a serious electoral force. Change had taken place under Neil Kinnock but when the more traditionalist John Smith took over in 1992 Blair - alongside his close friend the dour, prickly Scot Gordon Brown - despaired of Labour ever being truly relevant to the modern age.

Smith's sudden death in 1994 altered everything, including the relationship between Blair and Brown. Having previously made a pact that they would not compete against each other in any prospective leadership contest Tony Blair now asserted his determination to become Smith's successor. This was hard for Brown to accept as, up until recently, he had been regarded as the natural heir - an intellectual heavyweight with a sound grasp of political and, especially, Labour history. But now Blair's inherent charisma, uncanny feel for public opinion and eminent suitability to the all-powerful modern media machine saw him overtake his colleague in popularity both inside Parliament and out. We may never know precisely what Blair promised Brown if the latter agreed to give the former a clear path to power – did he promise to quit after seven years and appoint Brown his successor? – but one thing he definitely did guarantee was that Brown, as his Chancellor, would have unprecedented authority over all the nation's economic affairs including the social aspects of financial policy. It would be an assurance that would prove monumentally important both to the country and the two men themselves.

So Brown stepped aside and the twinkling, magnetic Tony Blair eased to victory in the party leadership race. From that point on it became inconceivable that he would not be the country's next Prime Minister. Even if the Conservatives hadn't been tearing themselves apart, Blair had a statesmanlike authority matched only by Margaret Thatcher in her pomp and his political message was brilliantly bland enough to be unarguable. This was a great nation, he repeatedly asserted with the actorly skill of the finest Shakesperean luvvie, but he could make it better, fairer, more harmonious for all. That really was all there was to it, but the crucial thing was that the message was honed and polished by the slickest public relations department that Westminster has ever seen.

Blair's inner circle was dominated by advisers, aides and what would become known pejoratively as 'spin doctors.' Men like the savagely rude and terrifying Alastair Campbell - the PM's Director of Communications and Strategy - or Philip Gould - the restless king of the focus group - or

Peter Mandelson, who was actually an elected MP but used to best effect as a dark manipulator of image and cunning linguistic sophist. Unsurprisingly given that 'New Labour' was itself a public relations construct Blair's party was obsessed by the media and their public image in the newspapers and television broadcasts of the day. To the horror of old school Socialist politicians the Blair machine made no bones about courting the right wing press – specifically the all-powerful tycoon Rupert Murdoch – or giving publications with opposing ideological viewpoints completely different answers to the same question. Considering Blair's passionate and sincerely held religious beliefs it is interesting how merrily he was prepared to lie and distort for personal political gain. It is perhaps even more revealing that nobody at the time batted an eyelid.

Once in power the Prime Minister continued to eloquently fudge what his party's political line was. Grand sounding and inclusive terms such as Labour's 'Big Tent' and 'The Third Way' gave little of real substance away. To a lot of early critics New Labour looked a lot like Thatcherism-lite. Both Blair and Brown were open about their admiration of Capitalism and self-consciously described Labour as a Social Democratic party rather than a Socialist one. This distinction in itself meant that seeking financial support from the unions - Labour's traditional method of fundraising - would be impossible, especially when the Prime Minister abolished Clause Four of the Labour constitution advocating public ownership. Faced with this financial dilemma the government increasingly cosied up to big business and super-rich oligarchs in pursuit of financial donations. Conflicts of interest inevitably followed as Blair became accused repeatedly of granting Labour donors excessive favours. Formula One supremo Bernie Ecclestone and steel magnate Lakshmi Mittal were just two of the big hitters said to have inordinately benefitted from governmental influence. Nye Bevan was doubtless spinning in his grave.

Another deviation from Labour ministries past was the whole style of governing favoured by the Prime Minister. Inspired by the informality of the Clinton administration across the Atlantic Blair presented himself in a much more Presidential guise than any of his predecessors, valuing the input of his cabal of press officers and spin doctors more highly than that of his ministerial colleagues. Indeed, his contempt for his cabinet was matched only by Thatcher's antipathy to hers - whilst she brutally admonished her 'wets' in public he just frequently bypassed his colleagues altogether. Key policy decisions were made in private residences between Blair and one or two other figures with the cabinet often finding out about them after the fact. Needling politicians and press alike 'Sofa Government' became a controversial hallmark of the New Labour years. Yet it was all of a piece with the Prime Minister's disdainful attitude towards the established way of doing governmental business. He had been itching to put his stamp on Parliamentary process for years. Now, having divested himself of the troublesome and tedious task of managing the economy, he was free to launch an attack on the British constitution itself.

After New Labour came to power in 1997 a raft of legislation hurtled through Westminster which fundamentally changed the loose assemblage of ad hoc rules and regulations that had served as Britain's constitution for the past 300 years. Not all of it stemmed from the crusading zeal of the Prime Minister and not all of it worked. But taken as a whole the programme of constitutional reform that New Labour pushed through was one of the most audacious gambits of any modern British government.

Alongside the reverberations of Northern Ireland's Good Friday Agreement the biggest changes came in Scotland and Wales as the clamour for devolution became impossible to ignore any longer. The architect of Scottish devolution was not Tony Blair but Donald Dewar - Labour's earnest Scottish leader and close personal friend of John Smith - who had established a constitutional convention during Thatcher's reign that gathered momentum as the Conservatives began losing their Parliamentary seats in Scotland. The connection to Smith - 'Labour's lost leader' - made the agreements concerning devolution binding for any

Labour government and hence, whilst he was no cheerleader for the legislation, Blair's hand was forced.

A referendum duly took place which cemented Scottish support for a separate Parliament, the 'yes' votes outnumbering the 'no's by three to one. The spectre of the so-called West Lothian Question, originally raised by the Labour MP Tam Dalyell in 1977, hung over the establishment of the new Parliament and provided an easy rallying point for opponents of Scottish devolution. The question was essentially whether it was fair that Scottish MPs sitting in the House of Commons would be able to vote on measures solely affecting England whilst English MPs would be prevented from voting on Scottish matters due to the devolving of powers to the Scottish Parliament. Of more practical interest was the fact that the government of Scotland was elected via proportional representation, thus ushering in a seemingly endless era of political coalitions. Dewar became the first Scottish First Minister although Labour's hold over the country's political life was steadily challenged by the dogged Scottish National Party. *Its* part in the ongoing soap opera of British party politics would reach paramount importance in the early years of the following century.

With its remit covering health, education, local government and welfare as well as the ability to raise taxes the Scottish Parliament has given Scotland a buccaneering autonomy that has reshaped its influence in both the United Kingdom and further afield. The Welsh Assembly is a rather more muted creature with less cultural impact and fewer powers. Nevertheless its existence has led to a resurgence in patriotic pride in recent years which may yet see the nationalist Plaid Cymru make significant political gains in the future.

If Blair had been backed into a corner over devolution then his other constitutional grenades were all his own invention. A committed pro-European he devised the Human Rights Act during his first year in office. In essence the act incorporated the European Convention on Human Rights into British law and was further ammunition for those Eurosceptics who felt that Britannia was casually throwing away her sovereignty. The act put pressure on the judiciary to interpret Parliamentary legislation in the light of the rights enshrined in the Convention. If such legerdemain proved impossible then they could issue a declaration of incompatibility which registered judicial misgivings without violating the ultimate sanctity of an act of Parliament. It was a neat trick which allowed the government to have their cake and eat it - they were seen to be doing all they could to adopt European law but, when it came to the crunch, British legislation would still prevail. Yet whilst it was clever it did not really serve a valid purpose and remained a cause of Parliamentary grumbling for some years.

Reform of the House of Lords was an issue that similarly exercised the Prime Minister's attention. By the time the millennium rolled around the number of peers sitting in the upper chamber was 669 – almost half the figure recorded for the previous year. What Blair had done was to abolish the hereditary right whereby peers' offspring inherited their seats as a matter of course. Cynics pointed out that such a manoeuvre wiped out the entrenched Conservative majority in the Lords at a stroke, whilst New Labour disciples merely viewed it as a necessary modernising measure for a progressive democracy. Both views are probably right, although there is no denying the change in form and tone in the upper chamber that the House of Lords Act engendered.

The legislation kept coming. The nation's capital was asked if it wanted a democratically elected mayor and the answer was a resounding 'yes.' The London mayoral election prefigured moderate reform of local government as a whole, although Tony Blair's embarrassment at the victory of the mercurial 'Red' Ken Livingstone may have convinced him to rein in his proposals for other local authorities. The Freedom of Information Act of 2000, whilst watered-down from the original bold promise in Labour's 1997 election manifesto, granted the public unparalleled access to data held by public authorities. Not everything that had been promised transpired - an inquiry into the validity of a system of proportional representation for British elections was discreetly shelved - but an impressive amount of ground-breaking legislation did make its way onto the statute books.

In all of this Labour was trying to convey the sense that they understood that the rules and regulations that governed people's lives were unfair and inherently biased. As a new, modern, altruistic political party they were determined to break down these barriers to true democracy and treat the British public with the respect with which they were entitled. Of course there was a lot of smoke and mirrors being employed here but, for a while at least, it really did feel like New Labour genuinely cared.

Meanwhile at the Treasury the conscientious new Chancellor was busy plotting a revolution of his own. Granted astonishingly wide ranging powers as his reward for standing aside in the leadership contest Gordon Brown was determined not to waste his opportunity. His first act in his new post signalled the boldness and audacity of his vision. Historically the Conservatives had always been seen as the strongest party on the economy, with Labour administrations viewed as reckless and ill-considered when it came to the national finances. Mindful of the accusations of irresponsible tampering levelled at previous Labour Chancellors over their handling of interest rates, Brown devised a perfect way to avoid similar suspicion - he simply turned the responsibility for setting interest rates over to the Bank of England.

Such decisiveness may have been admirable but his critics still scoffed at his claim that he could stick to the miniscule spending levels set by his Conservative predecessor Kenneth Clarke for the first two years of government. But prudence and frugality were in the Chancellor's blood and, somehow, he not only achieved this feat but kept an iron fist on the nation's coffers for even longer. This stubborn restraint meant an inevitable downturn in public service reform but even here Brown had a novel, if provocative, answer. We have noted that both Blair and Brown were no enemies of market forces and had little time for the stern doctrine of public ownership, and whilst they may have baulked at further privatizations they were not averse to embracing a hybrid system that blurred the boundaries between public and private. Public Finance

Initiatives sprang up all over the public sector and essentially entailed the stumping up of private capital for public works. Left-wing traditionalists may have been outraged at this marriage of convenience between Socialism and Capitalism but New Labour – devotees of the indiscriminate melding of opposing ideologies - had no qualms about the process whatsoever.

Having kept a lid on spending for so long the Chancellor was eventually able to release the pressure in the early years of the 21st century. Billions were pumped into the National Health Service at a time when Brown's rigid parsimony was beginning to affect the quality of care that patients were receiving. The huge increase in funding led to the hiring of not only tens of thousands of extra nurses and doctors but also the dreaded managers charged with improving the service and generating miles and miles of red tape. The inexorable rise of auditors and inspectors continued even more forcefully under New Labour than under Thatcher and Major's Conservatives with the NHS and the education system bearing the brunt of the onslaught.

There were pros and cons in other areas of Brownite economic policy. The Chancellor and Prime Minister shared a sincere desire to eradicate poverty not just in Britain but globally. But whereas Blair's message was primarily abstract and visionary – and in his high profile support for the Make Poverty History campaign and Live8, Bob Geldof's rehash of Live Aid as a tool with which to persuade world leaders to cancel third world debt, typically tinged with showbiz glamour – Brown's ideas were eminently more concrete and practical. The three great prongs of his social economic reform were a national minimum wage to provide a financial safety net for workers on the lowest incomes, a job creating measure for young people known as the New Deal financed by a windfall tax on privatized public utilities companies, and tax credits for both working families and those with children to further shield the worst off from the spectre of destitution – so long as they were in work.

On the debit side were the so-called 'stealth taxes' on income tax thresholds, national insurance and stamp duty that were the bleakly austere consequence of the years of frugality, and an almighty cock-up concerning the abolition of Advance Corporation Tax. This measure hit pension funds hardest as it prevented them from claiming back tax from their dividend income, precipitating the winding up of numerous pension funds and the haemorrhaging of the value of retirement pensions. This most affected the middle England voters that New Labour had so assiduously courted and became a story which even the spin doctors of Whitehall could not make go away.

Yet the single clearest example of the power and authority resident at Gordon Brown's Treasury centred on the European question. European monetary union was very definitely on the way by the time New Labour won the 1997 election and, as a keen Europhile and aspiring international statesman, Tony Blair broadly welcomed the measure despite its obvious pitfalls and controversies. His Chancellor, however, was more circumspect and felt that rushing in to join the Euro in the first wave of member nations would be impetuous folly. Thanks to John Major Britain was not committed to join as a matter of course and Brown wanted to use this breathing space for further sober assessment.

As Prime Minister Blair could, of course, have overruled him. But Brown managed to persuade Blair that European monetary union was an economic issue rather than a political one and, under the terms of their unofficial agreement, fell solely within the remit of the Treasury. As soon as the Prime Minister conceded this somewhat contentious point the chances of Britain joining the single European currency plummeted. Brown and his colleagues came up with five economic conditions that would have to be met before monetary union could even be considered. These conditions were both impressively rigorous and gloriously vague and the probability of them ever being satisfactorily achieved was pretty much nil. The time was not propitious in 1997, 2001 or 2003, at which point Blair effectively gave up trying to twist his Chancellor's arm and admitted defeat. Given the subsequent catastrophes that the Eurozone has experienced it was arguably a sensible decision to leave well alone, but at the time it was simply the most transparent power play between the two New Labour chiefs yet seen.

For all of the Prime Minister's studied empathy, brilliant communication skills and magnetic charm it was his Chancellor who kept New Labour in power for 13 years. Under his direction employment, incomes and house prices all boomed making the average Briton wealthier and more secure. It is Brown's great tragedy that he is now remembered for being a disastrous Prime Minister rather than the finest Chancellor of the Exchequer since the Second World War. Leading the nation requires a different set of attributes to keeping control of its purse strings and - infuriatingly for Gordon Brown - his emollient rival possessed those skills in abundance. Yet when Tony Blair came unstuck the consequences were colossal. A series of events that started in New York City and led inexorably to the blood-soaked Middle East would destroy his reputation and smother the glorious legacy that he had been so desperate to attain. Nemesis was close at hand.

At a quarter to nine on the morning of Tuesday September 11th 2001 American Airlines Flight 11 crashed into the North Tower of the World Trade Center in New York City. Just over 15 minutes later another aeroplane – Flight 175 – flew straight into the South Tower. Less than two hours after that both towers had completely collapsed leaving 2,763 people dead. At 9.37am a third American Airlines plane was flown into the side of the Pentagon in Virginia whilst a fourth – the now iconic Flight 93 – was brought down in a field in Pennsylvania after a heroic attempt by passengers to regain control of the aircraft from the four hijackers. It was believed to have been headed for the White House. In total just shy of 3,000 people were killed. The attacks – by far the most horrific terrorist atrocities the United States has ever seen – were claimed by al-Qaeda, a militant Islamist terrorist organisation, and their leader the elusive Osama bin Laden. The world could not - and still cannot - quite believe that it had happened.

Tony Blair had always been quick to conjure the right phrase and emotion for a major national - or international - crisis. He had had previous experience after the shocking death of Princess Diana mere months after he had taken office, uniting the nation in grief and beseeching the stand-offish monarchy to recognise the people's trauma. He responded appositely to 9/11 as well - considerably better, in fact, than the US President George W. Bush had done. 'Dubya' was part of a Republican Presidential dynasty - his father George senior had instigated the First Gulf War - lampooned as backward and bigoted. He was not at first sight a natural bedfellow for the metropolitan man-of-the-people who had drawn inspiration from Bush's smooth Democrat predecessor Bill Clinton. Yet the two leaders shared a deeply held Christian faith and a rather simplistic view of good and evil, although possibly more to the point Tony Blair was the latest in a long line of British Prime Ministers who fell for American razzle-dazzle.

It wasn't long before the White House began to make noises about waging a War on Terror, a worryingly abstract conflict that seemed to provide a de facto justification to invade any country that may have any connection to the training or funding of al-Qaeda terrorists. And so it proved when, a month after the attacks, the United States – aided by Britain - invaded Afghanistan, home to the savagely repressive Taliban regime. The US bombing was unimaginably brutal but it accomplished its aims swiftly - in just five weeks the Taliban had fled Kabul forcing bin Laden into hiding. Now the Bush administration turned its eyes towards Iraq.

Retribution for Afghanistan may have been bloody but there were at least clear links between the Taliban and al-Qaeda. In the case of Iraq involvement with bin Laden's murderous band was much less obvious. Yet for a whole host of potential reasons - requisition of oil, unfinished Bush family business, the religiously motivated purging of an 'evil' force from the Middle East – the President was determined to find a trigger to

270

provoke the sinister sounding 'regime change.' Blair, who had spent much of the Afghan conflict schmoozing potential allies in the region, understood Bush's intentions but recognised the considerable risks.

The biggest obstacle to overcome was the United Nations, without whose permission any invasion would be illegal. America didn't much care for UN decrees - as the great Western superpower they would do whatever they wanted regardless. But for Britain and for Blair official sanctioning was vital. Caught between trying to pacify Bush and respect international law the Prime Minister searched around desperately for a convincing case to put forward to the United Nations. He found it in the bombastic concept of Weapons of Mass Destruction. There was widespread concern in the international community that Saddam Hussein may possess WMDs but there was also precious little proof. Hussein had been notoriously unwilling to allow weapons inspectors into Iraq which set Blair's mind racing. A year on from 9/11 the British government produced a dossier claiming to prove that Saddam Hussein possessed WMDs that could be activated within 45 minutes and hit key British interests abroad. This alarming document was backed up by another circulated in February the following year which, rather embarrassingly, turned out to have been lifted wholesale from an internet PhD thesis.

The UN were intrigued enough to grant a resolution calling for further weapons searches – which Hussein characteristically ducked – but stopped short of giving the official go ahead for invasion. Bush was getting impatient and irritated with his British counterpart for stalling whilst a significant portion of the British people were very visibly protesting against any attempted illegal war. The Labour party too were deeply split on the issue with leading ministers such as Robin Cook resigning on political principle. Meanwhile no weapons of mass destruction had been uncovered and Blair was increasingly mocked as a Yankee lapdog. Yet with Conservative support the Prime Minister secured enough of the Commons to win the vote on invading Iraq.

A 'shock and awe' bombing campaign ripped through Baghdad in late March 2003 and by April British forces had seized Basra. Hussein went

271

into hiding but was discovered in December and put on trial the following year. The US had to wait seven more years to uncover Osama bin Laden, a Special Forces unit murdering the terrorist mastermind during a raid on his Pakistani compound. Iraq had proved almost as much of a walkover for the British and Americans as Afghanistan. But without a clear 'road map' of how to deal with the fallout euphoria would rapidly turn to paranoia, disaffection and bloody reprisals.

More immediately worrying for Blair was that military victory had not sufficiently altered public opinion. The thousands who had marched through London in protest on the eve of invasion were just as angry as ever and, even more damagingly, the media outlets that the New Labour press corps had worked tirelessly to win over were champing at the bit to bring down the Prime Minister. When a BBC journalist called Andrew Gilligan questioned the veracity of the September 2002 dossier on a May broadcast of the esteemed Radio 4 Today programme the government responded ferociously. Gilligan claimed to have inside information that threw considerable doubt on the claims that any WMDs that Hussein possessed could be readied within 45 minutes. Sensationally he accused the government - and specifically Alistair Campbell – of 'sexing up' the facts to suit its own bellicose agenda.

Campbell responded by declaring a war of his own on the BBC, wildly asserting that the corporation had an anti-war bias which compromised their supposed neutrality and demanding a full and unequivocal apology. Both the Director General of the BBC, Greg Dyke, and his chairman, Gavyn Davies, refused to back down and thus subjected Gilligan's accusations to more intense scrutiny. It was now that events shifted dramatically from an unseemly establishment spat to genuine tragedy.

In the course of a Commons Committee investigation Gilligan's source was outed as Dr. David Kelly, a shy, conscientious British weapons inspector concerned by perceived liberties being taken with the truth. Caught in the middle of this knock-down, drag-out fight between the alpha males of Whitehall and the media his nerve was ripped to shreds. In July he slit his left wrist in woodland near his Oxfordshire home and was found dead the next morning. Many felt that Blair himself was ultimately culpable. The subsequent inquiry set up under Lord Hutton absolved the government of responsibility, both in the presentation of the 'dodgy dossier' and for Kelly's tragic suicide. Dyke and Davies lost their jobs and Tony Blair survived to fight another day. But, with the inquiry commonly regarded as a whitewash, the Prime Minister's reputation was at an all-time low. The image of him as a political messiah come to deliver the nation from sleaze and incompetence was forever tarnished, although it is a mark of how deep in the doldrums the Conservatives were that Labour still contrived to win the 2005 general election.

Things went from bad to worse. On 7th July 2005 Britain suffered its own 9/11 when 52 people were killed by bombs on three tube trains and a bus in Tavistock Square. Two weeks later saw a further series of attacks on the capital but, mercifully, no casualties. However, the next day and with national paranoia at fever pitch, a Brazilian immigrant named Jean Charles de Menezes was shot dead by police who mistakenly believed him to have been involved in the plot. Britain felt as scared and vulnerable as she had in the darkest days of the Second World War or at the height of the Cold War. And a lot of people held Tony Blair directly responsible.

The situation in Iraq was even more desperate. The British and American forces had handed control over to an interim Iraqi government but the results were grimly reminiscent of the slaughter that followed in the wake of British withdrawal from India. However unpleasant Saddam Hussein's regime may have been its secularism had kept a lid on age-old religious and geographical enmities. With their dictator deposed these feuds resurfaced once more and the allied forces were completely powerless to diffuse them. Scores of civilians and soldiers died, despotic countries like Iran and - most infamously - Syria gained in strength and confidence, and international terrorism flourished in a manner undreamt of before the Iraq invasion. Iraq is commonly referred to as Tony Blair's Suez. This is wholly inaccurate - it was almost unimaginably worse.

It was not just Iraq that dominated the final years of the Blair premiership. Whatever exactly had been promised during that fateful North London pow-wow in 1994 Gordon Brown was becoming increasingly restive about the Prime Minister keeping to his side of the bargain and making way for his Chancellor to succeed him. In 2004 Blair announced – without any prior consultation with Brown – that he was intending to serve a full third term, irreparably damaging any lingering camaraderie between the two men. In the short term the move achieved its aim of reassuring the voters who kept Labour in power at the following year's election. But, as bleak news from Iraq made the headlines on an almost daily basis and allegations of ministerial irregularity made Blair's promise that his party would be 'purer than pure' look ridiculous, it became apparent that the ersatz UK President had gone on long enough.

Gordon Brown finally achieved his life's ambition and became Prime Minister – uncontested - in 2007. After a honeymoon period in which he appeared strong and competent he fell into the same trap that had scuppered Jim Callaghan by dithering over whether or not to call an early election. By sending clear signals that he would do so and then clumsily backtracking he appeared weak and indecisive where, in the past, he had been perceived as no-nonsense and assertive. As he was struggling to formulate a new plan the global credit crunch exploded in 2008 and ruined his reputation.

The worst economic recession since the 1930s was caused by a concatenation of complex events, from the selling of sub-prime mortgages in the United States to a more general irresponsibility and risk taking culture practiced by the financial sector. Whilst there had been a handful of prophets who warned that the good times could not last world leaders had brushed such concerns aside as crude point scoring gambits. Now the public began to question why Brown, as Chancellor for the past decade, had not seen such an almighty collapse coming. Suddenly his innovative behaviour at the Treasury was declaimed as blinkered recklessness.

The dire state of monolithic American financial services firms such as Lehman Brothers impacted brutally on the health of British banks. In February 2008 Northern Rock was nationalised, followed swiftly by a sweeping and hugely expensive bank rescue package designed to stabilise the industry. With the banks judged 'too big to fail' these drastic financial measures were carried out at great cost to the taxpayer and confirmed the idea in most people's minds that the unrepentant millionaires who had precipitated the crisis were getting away with it. The continued payment of eye-watering bonuses to chief executives hardly helped the perception of 'fat cat' city bosses laughing at the poverty of the masses.

The sense of inequality between the haves and have-nots was exacerbated the following year when the expenses scandal broke. Reported in the midst of the recession it transpired that numerous MPs had been exploiting lax Parliamentary rules to claim huge amounts of expenses on everything from a cup of Horlicks to the notorious floating duck house of Conservative grandee Sir Peter Viggers. Whilst most protested that they had been operating within the rules - which had, of course, been devised by politicians - a handful were convicted for fraud, resulting in a clutch of custodial sentences. The esteem in which Members of Parliament are held had never sunk lower.

The Prime Minister himself was guilty of the greatest sin imaginable in 21st century politics - he was horrendously media unfriendly. Whereas his predecessor rewrote the book on positive public image - at least before the debacle of Iraq - Brown was awkward and stilted, lacked empathy and possessed an unfortunately chilling smile. Allegations of indecisiveness continued to dog his leadership - particularly concerning his climb-down over the controversial 10 pence tax rate - whilst his turbulent relationship with his second-choice Chancellor Alistair Darling enjoyed a similarly high profile to his own stormy partnership with Tony Blair. Brown's bumbling tenure in Downing Street was conveniently encapsulated by an absolute howler during the 2010 general election campaign. A Labour constituent in Rochdale who had challenged the Prime Minister's stance on immigration was condemned as a 'bigoted woman,' Brown uttering the comment into a microphone that he assumed was switched off.

Gordon Brown had gone from being the model Chancellor to the most comically hapless Prime Minister in living memory. Meanwhile, after years in the political wilderness under a succession of out-dated, ineffective leaders, the Conservatives had their own Tony Blair seemingly on the cusp of great things. David Cameron was young, media savvy and - crucially in terms of electability - much more in the centre of his party than his recent forebears. He had been leader of the opposition since 2005, easing into the role gradually and maturing into a highly credible future Prime Minister. With Brown at his lowest ebb going into the election campaign there was surely nobody that could stop the Conservative leader's smooth ascent to the top job. But in 2010 the face of British politics decisively and dramatically changed as all of the old certainties crumbled into dust.

24

THE NEW POLITICS

During the 2010 general election campaign something rather unexpected happened. Forced to choose between Gordon Brown's beleaguered Labour government and David Cameron's aloof Conservatives a significant proportion of the electorate decided that they didn't much like the idea of either of them.

One of the main innovations of the election run-up was a series of television debates between the leaders of the three main parties - an idea condemned by many as a Presidential gimmick borrowed from the US but which now looks set to become a fixture of 21st century electioneering. Everybody could predict that the then Prime Minister would not come out of the televisual process well and there was a general assumption that the youthful, more media friendly Cameron would be able to use these head-to-heads to conclusively kill off Labour's weak challenge. But both men had reckoned without the third man standing behind the prime time podiums.

The Liberal Democrats had always been little more than an outlet for protest votes, generally liked but not recognised as a credible party of government. Yet in the media glare it was their leader Nick Clegg who came across best - natural, informal and sincere where Brown looked typically uncomfortable and Cameron appeared smug and patronising. The Conservative leader had always suffered from a perception of his being a privileged toff with no understanding of the common man, but, whilst Clegg was public school educated also, he wore his comfortable background with the same lightness that Tony Blair had in his all-conquering early years.

'Cleggmania' swept the nation with opinion polls showing sharp spikes in Lib Dem support that thoroughly alarmed both the other main parties.

Could the nearly century-old governmental duopoly of Conservative and Labour be seriously under threat? The answer was both yes and no. When the votes were counted the Liberal Democrats had performed drastically worse than they had hoped, actually conspiring to lose five seats. But of far greater significance was that the Conservatives had failed to win an outright majority, falling short by 20 seats. For the first time since 1974 Britain had a hung Parliament.

Back then the result of the undecided election was a Conservative minority government soldiering on for eight months before a second contest returned Labour with a paltry majority of three. In the midst of a 21st century global recession another election was a course of last resort and frantic negotiations took place in a desperate effort to avoid such an undesirable situation. It rapidly became clear that the underperforming Liberal Democrats held the balance of power and that their leader was a political kingmaker. A coalition between the Lib Dems and either of the other parties would be enough to form a government. Ideologically Clegg's party were more suited to a union with Labour - although it was made clear that any such coalition would require the departure of Gordon Brown - but a marriage of convenience between the second and third placed parties in a general election would suffer from an insurmountable credibility problem.

Ultimately Clegg opted for the only realistic option - forming a coalition with the Conservatives which made him Deputy Prime Minister to David Cameron's premier. This presented its own set of problems. The two parties had diametrically opposed positions on a number of key issues and it was obvious that a certain amount of compromise would be required on both sides to make the arrangement work. However, it didn't take a genius to realise that it would be the Lib Dems - as the junior partners - who would have to back down on a number of their keystone manifesto promises.

Two of these pledges were the opposition to a rise in student top-up fees - introduced by Blair - from £3,000 to £9,000 and a commitment to a change in the electoral voting system from first-past-the-post to proportional representation. On the former they were comprehensively humiliated by their supposed allies with the Prime Minister flatly refusing to back down on the university fee hike. Students formed a sizeable percentage of the Liberal Democrats core support and Clegg's craven capitulation on such a fundamental point of policy provoked an enormous backlash against the party. A referendum was granted on the issue of electoral change but full-on proportional representation was taken off the table at an early stage and replaced by the watered down compromise of the 'Alternative Vote.' It was a halfway-house that the Liberal Democrats didn't really want and it showed in their lacklustre campaigning. The debate failed to excite the nation and first-past-the-post remains the template for British elections to this day. The other Lib Dem 'red line' was further reform of the House of Lords and, although a bill was formulated in 2011, it was withdrawn by the Prime Minister after it became clear that many Conservative backbenchers would defy a three line whip and vote against it.

Clegg doggedly peddled the line that Liberal common sense was tempering the wilder desires of the Conservatives but since this was almost impossible to prove either way it did neither him nor his party many favours. Having been offered a chance at wielding power - albeit in a shared government - Clegg would have been vilified for turning it down. Yet by allying his party with another so different in outlook it was inevitable that the Liberal Democrats would be made to look like spineless, unprincipled hypocrites. By the end of the coalition's first term - now fixed at five years after an act passed in 2011 - the Liberal Democrat leader and Deputy Prime Minister looked like a broken man.

But what of the senior partners in this exotic new form of government? Having attempted to paper over the glaring differences between his party and the Lib Dems in a cosy press conference in the Downing Street rose garden Cameron set about trying to tackle the economic meltdown. His Chancellor and closest friend George Osborne suffered even more from the same contemptuous posh-boy syndrome that the Prime Minister did.

Cameron could at least appear good humoured in a condescending way but Osborne looked cold and shifty and rather alarmed by the working class. His task was to reduce the enormous financial deficit and thus make inroads into the similarly vast national debt. His chosen method was, unsurprisingly, austerity.

In general terms this was fairly uncontroversial at the time and even Labour, with its history of extensive borrowing to stimulate growth, would nonetheless have instituted an austerity programme had they remained in power. Osborne, however, was taking no prisoners. His pledge to reduce the deficit to the point where national debt fell as a fraction of Gross Domestic Product within five years meant that brutal cuts would have to be made straightaway. To help the Treasury during such extreme circumstances the Chancellor established the Office for Budget Responsibility - an independent advisory body which provided economic forecasts and analysis - and also conducted a spending review to slash governmental spending by department. Having set stringent limits on how much cash his colleagues were allowed to splash Osborne then turned his attention to the rest of the country.

£6.2billion of cuts were announced with the figure of 1.3million public sector job losses also leaked. Osborne claimed that this mass unemployment would be covered by the creation of more posts in the private sector but for a number of years these stubbornly refused to materialise. When they did the context was frequently murky, with zero-hours contracts rapidly becoming a notorious political football. Attempts to demonstrate that the Conservatives were no friends to the venal bankers resulted in the finger-wagging Project Merlin, an initiative to ensure that banks continued lending to businesses and promised to put a stop to ridiculously high bonuses. Of more immediate concern was the selling off of the nationalised Northern Rock to Richard Branson's Virgin Money at a considerable loss and with taxpayers still responsible for the failing services.

Throughout the Chancellor's brutal austerity drive he repeatedly insisted that there was no other way. A long winded Labour leadership campaign gifted the government time to press home the narrative of New Labour overspending being responsible for the current financial collapse. Whilst elements of the argument may hold water the global nature of the recession made such claims seem rather reductive. Labour did themselves few favours, however, by electing the younger - and nerdier - Miliband brother Ed as their new leader. His sibling David was widely viewed as the more accessible and statesmanlike candidate but Ed's stronger Socialist views - although this is all relative - won the backing of the still powerful trade unions. One of Miliband's first actions as leader of the opposition was to change the rules for future party elections to one-member-one-vote, a move specifically designed to neuter the unions' block vote and demonstrate that he was not just a TUC puppet. It was a decision which was to have far reaching consequences a few years down the line.

A more effective opposition leader could have hauled Osborne - and by extension Cameron - over the coals because, for the first few years at least, 'Plan A' was manifestly not working. The deficit was not going down, unemployment was steadily rising and - even more damaging from a PR point of view - Osborne had done nothing to alter the perception that it was the poorest in British society that were paying the heaviest price. As the son of a baronet and heir to his family's hugely profitable wallpaper business one suspects that the Chancellor did not feel the pinch of the economic downturn as keenly as those who, after the 2012 budget, were forced to pay tax on pasties 'served at above ambient temperature.' The outcry over the measure compelled the government to retract it swiftly but the fact remained that, with a concomitant rise in the number of food banks handing out food to the escalating number who could no longer afford to buy it, the distribution of Osborne's austerity cuts felt grossly unfair to the struggling masses.

The following year the country's credit rating was downgraded from its traditional AAA status, a humiliating event on a par with Callaghan's crawling to the IMF. Yet by the middle of the year, after another savage budget, the data finally began to look more favourable, both in terms of deficit reduction and unemployment figures. How much massaging these figures underwent is a matter of opinion but the upturn was perfectly timed as regards the next general election. Nonetheless Osborne's confident assertion that he could halt the ballooning national debt has proved hubristic - despite the Chancellor's actions it is rising faster than ever.

*

As befits a man compared to Tony Blair David Cameron had an equally snappy way with a soundbite. At the start of his tenure he assured the nation that they were all 'in it [the recession] together' – a statement which would undergo a considerable level of mockery – and, like Blair's 'Big Tent,' he had a catchy term for his governing philosophy also. The 'Big Society' was a conscious rebuttal of the self-serving, individualistic ethos of Thatcherism and a return to the 'One Nation Conservatism' of Benjamin Disraeli and the subsequent periodic attempts to market 'Compassionate Conservatism.'

The frequent comparisons between Blair and Cameron were not entirely spurious. Both were ruthless party modernisers who had put their fingers on the root causes of voter disaffection - for Labour a perception that they were economically illiterate and stuck in a rut of class warfare, and for the Conservatives that they were a heartless establishment clique run by clubbable old codgers. Cameron realised that the toxic image of his party rendered even their more moderate proposals unacceptable to large numbers of the public. To regain power the Conservatives had to abandon their aggressive natural authority and embrace the touchy-feely 21st century.

Thus the 'Big Society' combined free market economics with civic pride and the small state with thriving community. Again like the New Labour 'Big Tent,' there was very little substance to the rhetoric and it suffered almost immediately from governmental actions that appeared to run counter to its ideology. For the inherent problem with Cameron's soft

Conservatism was that for all the empathetic soundbites the Prime Minister was a steely pragmatist at heart.

Take the example of the National Health Service. Eulogised in Danny Boyle's startling opening ceremony to the 2012 London Olympics as a source of immense national pride, under the Con-Dems the NHS came under sustained attack. The shambling Health Minister Andrew Lansley decided he would make his mark by subjecting the NHS to a radical overhaul which came dangerously close to privatising the whole system. In the same year as the wonderfully successful and uplifting Olympic Games he proposed the abolition of primary care trusts in favour of clinical commissioning groups run by both GPs and private sector interests. The predictable backlash provoked a disingenuously named 'listening exercise' involving the establishment of numerous panels and committees that, unsurprisingly, concluded that the Health and Social Care Act was perfectly acceptable.

If NHS reform is a political hot potato then so is the welfare system and this received similarly iconoclastic treatment from the Department of Work and Pensions Secretary Iain Duncan Smith. A former Conservative leader during the party's dark early 21st century days Duncan Smith had gained a reputation as being bland and colourless yet possessed of a curiously un-Conservative desire to eradicate poverty. But at the DWP he instigated the Welfare Reform Act - also 2012 - which contained arguably the single most contentious piece of domestic legislation passed under the coalition government - the under-occupancy penalty, or 'bedroom tax' as it became known colloquially.

The bedroom tax targeted those living in social housing where one or more rooms were unoccupied or otherwise considered 'spare.' Tenants with such spare rooms faced a reduction in housing benefit which would have to be funded from their own incomes. If any one policy summed up the perceived disconnect between the government - or, in fact, the political class as a whole - and the low earning sections of the British public it was the bedroom tax. Protesters argued convincingly that such a policy assumed that there was always alternative social housing for them to move into when there patently wasn't, as well as making the point that the penalty took no - or very little - account of tenants with disabilities. More than any other coalition policy the under occupancy penalty reinforced the traditional notion of the Conservatives as the 'nasty party' amongst many voters.

Yet to the core Conservative support the benefits system was nothing short of an obsession. Those on the right of the party vilified most benefits claimants as workshy scroungers and so hard-line legislation on the issue had a direct appeal to the party's base. The Welfare Reform Act included a new system of universal credit to replace six means-tested benefits which, due to its online emphasis, led to accusations of impersonality and a lack of nuance in addressing specific questions. Additionally the involvement of the European corporation Atos in carrying out work capability assessments resulted in untold claims of distress - and even suicides - due to the excessively stringent guidelines on who should be passed fit to work. Evidence of the caring, sharing nature of Cameron's 'Big Society' was hard to find in such proposals.

Over at the Department of Education Michael Gove antagonised teaching unions with his controversial plans to create a number of state-funded academies, operating independently of local authority control. Within this bracket also lay free schools which could be set up by almost anybody regardless of training or qualifications. Changes to school curricula prompted similar outrage with critics viewing Gove's insistence on both a heavy emphasis on British history and a form of learning by rote as outdated and overly patrician. Over the course of the Parliament Gove became so toxic amongst teachers that he was removed from the post for fear of losing the party votes at the 2015 general election.

With policies like these it was not long before the 'Big Society' was quietly side-lined by the coalition government. Try as he might the Prime Minister - an alumnus of Eton and the notorious upper crust Oxford drinking society the Bullingdon Club - was simply unable to convince the average person in the street that he had any understanding of their plight. In this he was not alone amongst the political class of the so-called Westminster Village. There had always been career politicians but since the rise of New Labour ministers appeared so identical in their backgrounds and work history that they came across as an alien species to the majority of the general public. A large number in both the cabinet and its shadow were public school educated and holders of the prestigious Philosophy, Politics and Economics degree from Oxford University. Few of them had had a job outside the political bubble and so lacked vital experience of the world that most of the electorate lived in. They also spoke a dialect all their own, crammed with jargon and stock phrases to forestall any awkward interview questions. So tedious did the public find these bland, sanitised MPs that the only way for a politician to achieve a level of popularity was to transform into an outlandish self-parody, as the London mayor Boris Johnson had done.

That such disaffection with Britain's 21st century Parliament did not turn to total apathy is down to the fact that several fringe parties scented blood in the malaise and pushed their agendas with focus and dynamism. In recent years both the Green party and the Welsh nationalists Plaid Cymru have made significant inroads by unambiguously promoting progressive policies in stark contrast to the fudges and half-measures of the main parties. But there were two parties in particular – one from north of the border and the other defiantly English – that altered the landscape of British politics far more than the novelty of a one-sided coalition. Both had specific, highly emotive issues to pontificate about and both had charismatic leaders who had perfected the art of telling their grassroots support what it wanted to hear. *This* was the new politics.

2004 saw the largest expansion of European Union member states to date when Cyprus, the Czech Republic, Estonia, Hungary, Latvia, Lithuania, Malta, Poland, Slovakia and Slovenia all joined up. Three years later Romania and Bulgaria were added to the mix. The right to freedom of movement inside the EU meant that citizens from any of these countries -

in addition to those from existing members - could potentially come to live and work in the United Kingdom. In 2003 the Home Office predicted an influx of no more than 13,000 migrants. By 2015 the estimated figure was 1.5million.

For a significant percentage of the British population the mass immigration of Eastern Europeans was a uniquely alarming event. Some simply resented what they saw as the dilution of the British way of life - whatever exactly that may be - whereas others mistrusted the migrants' motives, labelling them benefits scroungers and crooks. Still more were fearful of being undercut in the jobs market by the wave of cheap foreign labour. The fact that EU migrants historically claimed minimal benefits and that many were highly skilled professionals filling urgently needed gaps in the public sector cut little ice. Nervous of appearing racist or xenophobic the main political parties evaded the debate, leaving the floor open to the resurgent United Kingdom Independence Party under the bluff leadership of Nigel Farage.

UKIP's fundamental purpose was unyielding opposition to the European Union as a whole. In much the same way as the hard-line Eurosceptics in John Major's government they asserted that Brussels' bureaucrats had not only taken away Britain's sovereignty but they had also continually exploited her into the bargain. They felt strongly that the United Kingdom would be better off out of the European Union and spent years lobbying for a referendum to let the nation decide. Their showing in European elections had always been strong but their performance domestically was negligible. Now immigration and the passionate feelings it aroused proved the ideal platform from which to build the party's profile.

In Nigel Farage UKIP were blessed with a leader who knew how to relate both to his core supporters and disillusioned voters of the two main parties. It was always likely that UKIP would attract wavering right-wing Conservative voters but the new development was the number of white working class Labour supporters who were tempted to switch allegiance. UKIP as a party was something of a conundrum - half-cringeworthy comedy, half palpable threat. Politically incorrect gaffes - and just plain racist rants - were legion, with Farage compelled to sack party members on a regular basis. And yet this was skilfully played as an honest, warts-and-all antidote to the synthetic Westminster enclave. The more the party appeared to implode the more popular it became.

Suddenly the Prime Minister, by nature a pro-European, realised that he could sidestep the EU/immigration question no longer. With both the Conservatives and Labour fearful that increased support for UKIP could split the 2015 election vote and let either of the main parties into Number 10 Cameron and Miliband began to fulminate unconvincingly about the liberties that the EU had been taking and how they were going to bring them to heel. Cameron railed against the appointment of the federalist Jean-Claude Juncker as the new President of the European Commission and also became apoplectic about a £1.7billion surcharge that the EU demanded from Britain in late 2014. He later paid it off discreetly. Under increasing pressure from both Farage and the hard-right of his own party the Prime Minister consented to a referendum on British membership of the European Union should the Conservatives win the forthcoming general election.

Bolstered by myriad media appearances from the redoubtable Farage the UKIP juggernaut thundered on. At the 2014 European elections they beat Labour into second place by 2% of the vote with rumours abounding about mass Conservative defections to the party. In the end the tsunami of Conservative turncoats failed to materialise but Farage did succeed in getting some key figures to enter the UKIP fold. Within a month of each other Douglas Carswell and the appropriately named Mark Reckless had switched sides with both subsequently winning back their Conservative constituencies for UKIP. Farage himself had announced that he would stand in Thanet at the general election and he also made it clear that his party would be gunning for other Conservative-held seats. As immigration figures continued to rise and the Home Office appeared clueless and inept there were serious worries that Farage's English Army could cause a sensation come polling day.

The three centuries old union between Great Britain and Scotland was under threat the moment that a majority SNP government was returned after the 2011 Scottish elections. A referendum on the issue of Scottish independence had been a cornerstone of the party's manifesto for the last four years and its bullish, formidable leader Alex Salmond had no intention of shirking the debate now that his party had their hands on the reins of power.

Yet at the time the politicians both in Holyrood and Westminster thought that the result was a foregone conclusion. However much the Scots grumbled about their treatment at the hands of Westminster and Whitehall, the theory went, they were smart enough not to jeopardise their economy by breaking away from the union just to prove a point. In private this is what Salmond feared also. He would have been happy with a more comprehensive form of devolution – known as devo-max - than was granted in 1999, adding powers over economic policy and international affairs to those the Scottish Parliament already enjoyed over health, education and welfare. But Salmond was committed to pursuing full independence and he was not a man to approach any political objective half-heartedly.

To start with it looked like the smug certainty of Westminster was well-founded. Despite Salmond cannily dropping the referendum voting age from 18 to 16 and associating independence with a 'yes' vote on the ballot paper, the opening exchanges between the pro-union and independence camps highlighted the sheer unknowability of what an independent Scotland would look like. Faced with the former Chancellor Alistair Darling's assertions that Scotland would lose the pound and have to relocate their banking services to England the 'yes' campaign had no real riposte save to pig-headedly deny these undeniable statements. For all Salmond's charisma and inspirational rhetoric it was becoming apparent that he had no real idea how a complete break from the union would work in practice.

But never underestimate politicians' ability to snatch defeat from the jaws of victory. All three main political parties in Westminster may have been blithely dismissive about the chances of a win for the 'yes' camp but the trouble was they did nothing to hide that fact from the Scots. In a sense the issue was almost irrelevant to the Conservatives inasmuch as they only had one Scottish MP, although going down in history as the Prime Minister that lost the union would not have been the legacy that David Cameron had hoped for. Labour had infinitely more to lose as they dominated constituencies north of the border, a fact that made them appallingly complacent about the outcome of the referendum. The Scottish electorate looked at Westminster and saw nothing but condescension and apathy about their situation. And slowly the tide began to turn.

Suddenly the fact that there was no pre-planned 'road map' for independence mattered less and less to disaffected Scots - even if it all went belly-up at least it would be by their own hands rather than those of disinterested Whitehall mandarins. When a poll put the 'yes' campaign fractionally ahead Cameron, Clegg and Miliband all realised the potential cost of their arrogant stance. The three party leaders had failed to visit Scotland during the debate, partly because they thought the referendum didn't matter and partly because they were wary of exacerbating tensions by their mere presence. Now they could hardly stay away from the place. Carefully stage-managed press calls and misty eyed speeches begged the Scots to accept that the Britain and Scotland were 'better together.' But behind the scenes Labour's habit of weighing votes in previous elections rather than counting them meant that they had no contact details for thousands of their former supporters and were thus unable to encourage them to vote 'no.' Everyone from Gordon Brown to Eddie Izzard weighed in on the pro-union side but there was little sign that the kitchen sink approach was having any effect.

Ultimately victory was secured for the 'no' camp by the double whammy of a last minute concession to devo-max - the compromise that Salmond would have settled for at the start - and tougher scrutiny from Labour over the SNP's muddled plans for the NHS. When the votes were counted - certainly not weighed - the 'no' campaign had won with 55% of the vote. The union remained but the Scots had been promised substantial new powers.

And now Cameron had another headache, emanating from the right of his own party and that other unpredictable maverick group UKIP. In his desperate bid to salvage the union the Prime Minister had been forced to concede considerably more to Scotland than these factions thought proper. The West Lothian Question reared up its ugly head once more. It was all very well giving the Scots more power, they crowed, but what about the rights of the English?

Almost as soon as the result of the referendum was in Cameron went on the nationalist warpath again. There was no way that he could backtrack on the promise of devo-max but the Prime Minister now announced the establishment of a committee to look into English devolution as well. To the freshly politicised Scottish electorate – turnout in the referendum had been 84% - this looked like giving with one hand and taking away with the other. With a knife-edge general election a matter of months away Cameron was playing a dangerous game, trying to appease both the English right and the Scottish left. Time would tell if it was a game he had won or lost.

As the 2015 general election campaign hit its stride there was almost total unanimity amongst pollsters and commentators that Britain was heading for a second successive hung Parliament. Many people were appalled by the savage cuts and unequal austerity measures instituted by the coalition government yet they had little faith that Ed Miliband's faltering Labour party had any better ideas. The Lib Dems appeared to be a busted flush after five years of undignified policy climb-downs and the UKIP surge looked to have plateaued. Most questions directed at the party leaders from the media centred on who would be prepared to do a deal with whom. Conservatives and UKIP? Labour and SNP? Lib Dems and anyone? The fragmentation of the two party system seemed to herald an age of interminable coalitions. Gone were the days of class and geographical solidarity towards a particular party and, with vast swathes of the electorate thoroughly disillusioned with the out-of-touch political class, there were thousands more floating voters out there who would switch their political allegiance far more readily. This was the new politics and it was here to stay.

Or was it?

The pollsters and commentators ended up very red faced. Even when the exit poll for the 2015 general election suggested that the Conservatives would win an overall majority, many political grandees – most famously the former Liberal Democrat leader Paddy Ashdown who promised to eat his hat if the data proved correct – impatiently brushed it aside. But David Cameron's party did make it over the 326 seat threshold winning 330 in total, whilst Labour's tally of 232 was a loss of 26 from the previous election and a devastating rejection of their policies and leadership. The Liberal Democrats had been predicted to fare badly but they were annihilated, holding onto just 8 seats and waving goodbye to many senior party figures. Both Ed Miliband and Nick Clegg resigned as party leaders immediately. UKIP performed strongly in terms of votes cast, coming third with 12.9%, but their consistent second placings in contested constituencies resulted in them securing only a single seat with Douglas Carswell holding on to Clacton. Nigel Farage – who also resigned only to reinstate himself again - raged against the rank injustice of the first-past-the-post system and all supporters of the democratic principle were reluctantly forced to agree with him.

But the really big story of an election bursting with tall tales was the stunning performance of the SNP in Scotland. Before the election the Scottish National Party - now led by Nicola Sturgeon following Alex

Salmond's resignation after the referendum defeat - had six seats to Labour's 41. But the fervent nationalism fomented by the independence debate coupled with the Prime Minister's - and also partially Ed Miliband's - fighting talk about English rights saw the SNP snatch all but one of those formerly safe Labour seats. Labour, like the Conservatives before them, was effectively wiped out north of the border. The Scottish National Party now had 56 MPs in the House of Commons, making another independence referendum look inevitable at some point in the near future.

Cameron's Conservatives could hardly believe their luck. At the last minute thousands of voters had decided to stick with the devil they knew rather than risk a different government making things even worse. Labour supporters were crestfallen but in truth Miliband had never looked like a credible Prime Minister and his line on the economy was simply too vague and circumspect to convince the floating voters. The Lib Dems bemoaned the fact that they had paid the price for the coalition's unpopularity whilst the Conservatives had got away scot free, and warned that a solely Conservative government would lack the restraining influence that the Lib Dems had brought to bear in the coalition.

There may have been a modicum of truth in this assertion. In retrospect many of the Conservatives' most toxic policy decisions of this era feel like they were specifically crafted to be negotiated away in the event of another Con-Dem coalition. But when Cameron unexpectedly found himself at the head of a majority government he had little alternative but to force these extreme measures through – or at least make a half-hearted show of doing so.

Hence the U-turns came thick and fast. Osborne's highly controversial cuts to tax credits - estimated in some quarters to cost low income families £1000 per year - required the improbable intervention of the House of Lords to rethink, before the fortuitous discovery of a £27billion windfall allowed the Chancellor to abandon the scheme altogether. Plans to impose the conversion of all state schools into academies were also unceremoniously ditched amidst predictably vocal protests from teaching unions whilst over at the Health Department Jeremy Hunt provoked the fury of both medical professionals and a substantial percentage of the general public.

His dogged insistence on the imposition of a new contract for junior doctors – which would remove the opt-out for non-emergency work at weekends and lengthen the working week for a comparative drop in pay – attracted widespread opprobrium for overworking doctors and putting patients' lives at risk. After talks with the British Medical Association broke down repeatedly industrial action was called in early 2016 - one two day strike in late April comprising a full walkout with junior doctors refusing even to provide emergency care. Cast as the 21st century equivalent of Scargill's striking miners junior doctors risked alienating the British people with this potentially life threatening decision. But such was the contempt in which the Health Secretary was held at the time that support for the doctors' cause was still forthcoming and, after both sides had consented to negotiate once again, a deal was eventually thrashed out the following month.

What such a combative government needed was a strong opposition to counter its headier policy decisions but the Labour party were mired in chaos. Ed Miliband's pointed change in the party voting structure to one-member-one-vote was never intended to be tested in a party leadership contest. But his speedy standing-down necessitated the new model's implementation and resulted in bringing about the biggest political shock in Westminster politics for a generation.

The veteran left-winger Jeremy Corbyn, who had rebelled against the party whip more than any other Labour MP, was persuaded to stand in the leadership contest ostensibly to broaden the debate. He made it onto the ballot with two minutes remaining, having garnered the support of some of his fiercest critics. His opponents Andy Burnham, Yvette Cooper and Liz Kendall were all shadow cabinet ministers - and former cabinet ministers in the case of Burnham and Cooper - and polished members of the political class. And this was precisely the problem. Had the decision been down to their fellow MPs either Burnham or Cooper would have won but the move to OMOV gave rank and file party members infinitely more influence over who should lead their party. And a significant number of these members, fed up with a leadership they saw as Conservative-lite, craved a return to the traditional Socialist values that the Labour party was formed to promote in the first place.

The fact that a £3 registration charge was all that prevented anybody from casting a vote led to bitter accusations of entry-ism from both far-left and far-right but it rapidly became apparent that there was a genuine groundswell of opinion in Corbyn's favour. His views were hard-line Socialist – unilateral nuclear disarmament, widespread nationalisation, redistribution of wealth through high rates of income tax - but he was untainted by association with the Miliband opposition and his habit of refusing to stoop to personal criticism cemented the idea in people's minds that he was a more sincere, authentic breed of politician.

The trouble was that the passionate beliefs of grassroots Labour activists were not reflected within the wider electorate. Unless something truly staggering were to happen Labour under Corbyn - just like Labour under Michael Foot - would be unelectable. For Corbynistas this scarcely mattered - it was about principle rather than pragmatism – but to Labour MPs and grandees such as Tony Blair and Gordon Brown it was fundamental. There was a perception that Ed Miliband had failed to win the general election because his policies discouraged aspiration - in contrast Corbyn would make his predecessor look like Margaret Thatcher. Blair and Brown waded in to admonish those considering voting for Corbyn but their toxic presence just boosted his popularity further.

When the result of the contest was announced on 12th September Jeremy Corbyn had won by a landslide – 59.5% of the vote, beating Burnham into second place by 40%. Party members and grassroots activists may have been thrilled at pulling off such an astonishing coup but the difficulties inherent in a veteran left-wing rebel leading Her Majesty's Opposition soon became apparent. For one thing Corbyn, unlike Foot, had never come close to being a cabinet - or shadow cabinet - minister and so was making a stratospheric leap in status and responsibility. For another, the majority of his colleagues had not voted for him. Forced to assemble a shadow cabinet at speed it was inevitably comprised of many politicians who held diametrically opposed views to his. Whilst the new leader may have tried to smooth this division over with claims of healthy argument and vibrant democracy, it led to some seriously embarrassing contradictions and misunderstandings in party policy. With a large section of the press also massed against him - and Corbyn showing no desire to try and win them round - the future did not bode especially well for Labour's new leader. Subsequent events appeared to bear this out, with Corbyn's candour over his distaste for nuclear deterrents flat-footing his more circumspect colleagues and a worrying strain of anti-Semitism resurfacing in the party which many observers felt he had not responded to effectively enough. Yet the passionate activists who had swept him to power kept the faith, desperately clinging to his brand of supposed 'kinder politics' as a beacon of decency in a dark and sordid world.

Beyond the United Kingdom's borders terror and violence reign. The 2011 Arab Spring which promised so much for Middle Eastern democracy has morphed into a bloody legacy of civil war, further complicated by the Blair-Bush invasion of Iraq in 2003. The emergence of the barbaric Islamic State has outdone even Al-Qaeda in terms of unremitting savagery, and the effects of their ruthlessness have been felt in Paris, Brussels, Mali and on British holidaymakers in Tunisia to name but a handful of instances. The complex and protracted civil war in Syria vastly escalated an unprecedented refugee crisis that has engulfed the whole of Europe. In December 2015 Parliament voted to commit to air strikes against Syria by a margin of 174. In the United States the ultra right wing celebrity tycoon Donald Trump secured the Republican nomination in the forthcoming Presidential contest to the utter bewilderment and dismay of millions –

including other Republicans. Meanwhile Britain was limbering up for its most crucial political battle for generations.

In February 2016 David Cameron flew to Brussels to attempt a renegotiation of the terms of British membership of the European Union. Since appeasing UKIP and his own right wingers by consenting to a referendum on the issue of Britain's relationship to the EU the Prime Minister was acutely aware of the importance of claiming a great victory for Britannia against the flinty intransigence of the supranational machine. He secured changes to the conditions of both migrant in-work benefits and the amounts of child benefit sent back to the migrants' home countries, guarantees against ever closer union and safeguards for the City of London in regards to continental relocation. Obviously trumpeted as a major achievement the renegotiation nevertheless failed to impress the nation. Nigel Farage had built a career out of disaffection for the machinations of the EU and immediately began whipping up anti-Brussels sentiment with a vengeance. By the time that the date for the referendum had been set for June 23rd the gloves were well and truly off.

Despite David Cameron's support for British membership of the European Union there had been a legacy of virulent Euroscepticism within the Conservative party since the mid-80s and now an estimated 50% of their MPs were in favour of leaving the institution. Not wishing to appear overly prejudicial Cameron sanctioned his ministers to follow their beliefs with the result that a motley collection of high profile Conservative 'outers' quickly came into being. These included two of the most unpopular politicians in the country – the polite yet ruthless party moderniser Michael Gove and the charmless architect of the bedroom tax Iain Duncan Smith – and, arguably, the most popular – the wily faux-buffoon and ex-mayor of London Alexander Boris de Pfeffel Johnson.

Many commentators saw Johnson's sudden admission of Euroscepticism as naked careerism, jockeying for position in a potential post-Brexit leadership race. But whatever his motivation Johnson's endorsement gave the Leave campaign a much needed element of glamour and accessibility at a time when the Prime Minister was looking increasingly bitter and vulnerable. On the opposition benches the official line was Remain, and, indeed, up to 90% of Labour MPs were pro-EU. However, their leader Jeremy Corbyn had been a lifelong Eurosceptic as a backbencher and his endorsement never felt like more than a sop to desperately required party unity. As a result Labour would attract significant criticism for running a lacklustre campaign. Yet, at this point, it still seemed that a Remain victory was all but certain.

If voters in the original referendum back in 1975 had subsequently felt that they had been cheated of vital information then that was even more the case second time around. The economic argument was supposed to be where the intelligent debate was joined but with both sides massaging statistics to suit their own ends and so much assertion based on guesswork and estimates the public soon felt bamboozled and misled. Leave fulminated about the cost of EU membership – anything from £24million a day to £55million – and argued that it would be better spent on public services, whilst Remain preached that the economic benefits to trade more than outweighed the initial outlay. Leave confidently proclaimed that, as the world's fifth largest economy and one of the EU's most valuable consumers, member states would be crazy to block an independent Britain's access to the single market or impose tariffs on imports, whilst Remain lined up every major economic institution from the CBI to the FSA to spout dire warnings for a post-Brexit future. Leave labelled Remain's economic argument Project Fear whilst Remain accused Leave of leaping into the unknown. The public had hoped for information and had had to settle for name-calling.

It was the more emotive issues of immigration and sovereignty that transformed the debate from opaque and petty to divisive and toxic. As we have seen, the free movement of people around the European Union had profoundly altered the demographics of the United Kingdom, particularly alarming the white working classes in depressed areas who perceived these newcomers as threats both to their employment and way of life. As the debate rumbled on frequent mention was also made of the strain on public services and housing that mass immigration had allegedly caused. Whilst never an official part of the Leave campaign Nigel Farage and UKIP mined the seam of immigration relentlessly, consistently backed up by the right wing press. One especially controversial UKIP poster depicted a procession of Syrian refugees crossing into Slovenia with the slogan 'Breaking Point,' and was reported to the police for inciting racial hatred. Yet it was clear that Farage had his finger on the pulse of proletarian discontent and that his core supporters thoroughly agreed with his views. Neither was the official Leave campaign above xenophobic scaremongering, producing a pamphlet that erroneously claimed Turkey – bordered by Syria and Iraq amongst others – were on the verge of joining the EU. The clear implication was that Britain would be flooded with countless more immigrants, but that rather than stealing our jobs they would be blowing us all up in the name of Islamic State.

The lack of control that many people felt Britain possessed as regards her borders was bound up with a more fundamental frustration about the relinquishing of national sovereignty as a whole. Despite the fact that very few Brussels diktats had a significant effect on UK policy there was a palpable sense that the country was no longer in control of its own destiny. The cry of 'we want our country back' resounded ever more loudly throughout the land, as prominent Leave campaigners fuelled an image of a nostalgic, isolationist Britain that could be as great as she had been in the heyday of empire.

And then, a week before the referendum, the heightened passions and latent nationalism that such a tawdry campaign had spawned spilled over into tragedy. Jo Cox, the strongly pro-immigration Labour MP for Batley and Spen, was shot dead on the street prior to holding a constituency surgery. Her mentally disturbed assassin, Thomas Mair, was alleged to have shouted 'put Britain first' as he killed her. A referendum that had only been called to assuage the demands of the political right had led, through an atmosphere of poisonous rhetoric and inflamed tension, to the murder of a Member of Parliament.

Seven days later the nation went to the polls. The markets began the evening buoyant - seeming to signal a healthy win for Remain - but as the night wore on it became apparent that the depth of enmity towards the European Union had been underestimated. By 5am Leave had done enough and what had been almost unthinkable six months earlier had come to pass. Great Britain had voted for Brexit.

Four things happened almost immediately. Within an hour of the official result Scotland's First Minister Nicola Sturgeon strongly indicated that, with Scotland voting overwhelmingly to remain, she would seek to trigger a second independence referendum which would likely have a very different outcome to the first. Yet, whilst it would seem that support for the SNP's cornerstone belief would be bolstered by the split in opinion between Scotland and England on membership of the EU, the First Minister is playing a risky game. Attempts to secure continued Scottish membership when the country remains within the United Kingdom fall foul – ironically - of Brussels' manifold bureaucracy. Scotland may be a country but she is not - in European Union terms - a nation, and thus cannot strictly become a member state. Even if Scotland overcame that obstacle by securing independence through a second referendum, there is no guarantee that they would be welcomed with open arms. Their case would set a dangerous precedent which could be seized upon by Catalonia, the autonomous community within Spain, who have long campaigned for their own independence.

But Scotland was not the only country of the United Kingdom to vote decisively for Remain. Northern Ireland, precariously at peace since the Good Friday Agreement of 1998, voted to stay in the European Union by 56% to 44% and there were swift calls from Sinn Fein for a potentially tempestuous all-Ireland referendum on the issue. The Republic's status as an EU member state also raised the prospect of a hard border with its northern neighbour, which many feel could reignite sectarian tensions on the Emerald Isle once again.

Contemporaneously, the value of sterling began to nosedive on the stock exchange, falling to a 30 year low against the dollar a few days later. Whilst it is true that there was a partial recovery in the following weeks the markets' notorious fear of uncertainty mean that the economy is headed for a deeply anxious period until it becomes clear exactly what business investment and employment opportunities are going to quit the country.

And a short while after that David Cameron came out of 10 Downing Street to announce his resignation – by the time of the Conservative Party Conference in October there would be a new Prime Minister. Cameron's sudden departure opened up a vacuum at the centre of government, amidst widespread uncertainty over exactly when Britain should trigger Article 50 of the Lisbon Treaty which would initiate Brexit. Gove, Johnson and other leading Brexiteers were keen to downplay the necessity for immediate action - indeed they often appeared just as shell-shocked by the referendum result as the Remain side. The perception that Boris Johnson had treated such a momentous issue as an opportunistic game cemented ill-feeling towards him amongst his fellow MPs. And yet – as the public face of the victorious Vote Leave campaign - he still seemed a virtual shoo-in as the country's next Prime Minister.

But then, as befitted the mercenary atmosphere and frightening unpredictability of the times, came one of the greatest betrayals in British political history. Throughout the referendum campaign Boris Johnson and Michael Gove had been seen very much as a double act, a perfect political marriage of Gove's shrewdness and intellectual heft and Johnson's populist charisma and star quality. It had always been expected that there would be a Stop Boris candidate in the race for party leader but nobody had considered that that candidate might be Michael Gove. Yet a week after referendum day the Justice Secretary sensationally withdrew his support from his flamboyant campaign ally and announced that he would be standing for the leadership himself. Caught napping by this dramatic turn of events and fatally wounded by the aspersions cast by Gove on his unsuitability to lead Boris Johnson had no other option but to rule himself out of contention altogether. Four other candidates made it onto the ballot paper of whom the current Home Secretary – and Gove's bitter enemy – Theresa May was the most heavyweight contender. In the end the leadership election proved a 'coronation' for Mrs. May after her competitor in the final round, the previously unknown Leave advocate Andrea Leadsom, backed out after making inadvisable comments to a national newspaper regarding her rival's suitability to lead.

Labour, meanwhile, were in an even worse position after Jeremy Corbyn's dismissal of his Foreign Secretary Hilary Benn led to a spate of resignations from the shadow cabinet and angry calls for the Labour leader to step down. His woeful lack of enthusiasm for the official party position of remaining in the EU had given his many critics the perfect opportunity for an attempted coup. He duly lost a vote of no confidence by 172 to 40, effectively meaning that 80% of his parliamentary colleagues considered him unfit to lead the party. Yet Corbyn's massive mandate from party members – who showed very little sign of abandoning their chosen one – persuaded the beleaguered Labour leader that he had a moral duty to fight on. Party support for an alternative to the Corbyn malaise coalesced around the sparky, informal Angela Eagle who had resigned from her shadow cabinet position of Business Secretary and the 'soft-left' former Shadow Work and Pensions Secretary Owen Smith. The PLP selected Smith to stand against Corbyn but, ultimately, the Welshman's attempt to distance himself from the incumbent leader at the same time as taking great pains to agree with Corbyn on major policy points only strengthened the Labour leader's position. Far from punching a hole in Jeremy Corbyn's support his mandate actually increased as he won 61.8% of the vote.

The future for Britain is thus highly uncertain. Will the confident predictions of either the Leave or Remain side be vindicated? Will a recession of our own making be visited upon us or will we become a successful global power freed from the shackles of Brussels? Whichever scenario proves more accurate there is no denying that the country has irrevocably changed after the sensational result of 23rd June. We are now living in a deeply divided nation split firmly along geographic and generational lines and at a period when the world outside looks equally uncertain and frightening. The shock election of Donald Trump as President of the United States and the stealthy undermining of liberal democracy by Russia's Vladimir Putin makes it more vital than ever that Britain holds fast to her constitutional principles and pluralist political system.

SELECT BIBLIOGRAPHY

Black, Jeremy; A Brief History of Britain 1851-2010: A Nation Transformed (Constable & Robinson, 2010)

Brack, Duncan et al (ed.); British Liberal Leaders (Biteback, 2015)

Bryant, Chris; Parliament: A Biography Volume 2 – Reform (Doubleday, 2014)

Campbell, John; Pistols at Dawn: Two Hundred Years of Political Rivalry from Fox and Pitt to Blair and Brown (Vintage, 2010)

Chamier, George; The Greatest British Prime Ministers (Endeavour, 2012)

Clarke, Charles et al (ed.); British Conservative Leaders (Biteback, 2015)

Clarke, Charles et al (ed.); British Labour Leaders (Biteback, 2015)

Crace, John; I Never Promised You a Rose Garden: A Short Guide to Modern Politics, the Coalition and the General Election (Transworld, 2014)

Gibson, William; A Brief History of Britain 1660-1851: The Making of the Nation (Constable & Robinson, 2010)

Jenkins, Simon; A Short History of England (Profile, 2011)

King, Anthony; Who Governs Britain? (Pelican, 2015)

Lacey, Robert; Great Tales from English History (Abacus, 2007)

Lee, Stephen J.; Aspects of British Political History 1815-1914 (Routledge, 1995)

Lee, Stephen J.; Aspects of British Political History 1914-1995 (Routledge, 1995)

Marquand, David; Britain Since 1918: The Strange Career of British Democracy (Phoenix, 2008)

Marr, Andrew; A History of Modern Britain (Pan Macmillan, 2007)

Marr, Andrew; The Making of Modern Britain (Pan Macmillan, 2009)

Parker, Robert J.; British Prime Ministers (Amberley, 2011)

Radice, Giles; The Tortoise and the Hares (Politicos, 2008)

Sandbrook, Dominic; Never Had It So Good: A History of Britain from Suez to the Beatles 1956-1963 (Abacus, 2005)

Sandbrook, Dominic; White Heat: A History of Britain in the Swinging Sixties 1964-1970 (Abacus, 2006)

Sandbrook, Dominic; State of Emergency: The Way We Were 1970-1974 (Allen Lane, 2010)

Sandbrook, Dominic; Seasons in the Sun: The Battle for Britain 1974-1979 (Allen Lane, 2012)

Stewart, Graham; Bang!: A History of Britain in the 1980s (Atlantic, 2013)

Wright, Tony; British Politics: A Very Short Introduction (2nd ed.) (OUP, 2013)

21038466R00180

Printed in Great Britain
by Amazon